WALKING FREE

THE

NELLIE ZIMMERMAN

STORY

Rosezelle Boggs-Qualls
Dr. Daryl C. Greene

Densmore Reid Publications, Richmond, Indiana

To the best of the authors' knowledge, this is a true story. It is based on the recollections of Emily Street Hensel, Nellie Zimmerman's companion and friend. The events described herein have been confirmed by media reports and other documentary materials. Permission has been granted for the use of the photos and newspaper articles included in this book. Some names have been changed for confidentiality purposes.

Published by
Densmore Reid Publications
67 South 24th Street
Richmond, IN 47374

ISBN 0-9700827-2-X

Library of Congress Control Number: 2001091715

Walking Free:
The Nellie Zimmerman Story
Copyright © 2001
by Rosezelle Boggs-Qualls and Daryl C. Greene

Published by arrangement with Prinit Press, Richmond Indiana

Manufactured in the United States of America on acid-free paper.

Manufactured in the United States of America on acid-free paper.

For their encouragement, inspiration, and kind assistance, our deep appreciation to the following relatives and friends:

Fran Bailie, Keene Valley, New York
Danny and Jennifer Berlyoung, Akron, Ohio
Esther Berlyoung, Navarre, Ohio
Bela Bognar, Ph.D. Wright State University, Ohio
Anita Castora, Massillon, Ohio
Dr. Jim and A.J. Daggy, Richmond, Indiana
Mary Dee, Ph.D., University of Akron, Ohio
Theresa DiFrancis, Wright State University, Ohio
Anne Rose Greene, Richmond, Indiana
Curtis and Nancy Greene, Richmond, Indiana
Emmanuel Greene, Richmond, Indiana
Susan Hall Franklin, Shaker Hights, Ohio
Donna Jones, Union, Ohio
Jaci Jones, Stow, Ohio
Bobby Lou Kelley, Cleveland, Ohio
Connie Krell, Akron, Ohio
Andrew Miller, Attorney, Akron, Ohio
Mary Frances Young-Qualls, Cawood, Kentucky
Cheyenne A. Qualls, Canton, Ohio
Rebecca L. Qualls, Canton, Ohio
Thomas S. Qualls, Canton, Ohio
William A. (Buck) Qualls
Jim Schneck, Lancaster County, Pennsylvania
Mary Serapiglia, North Canton, Ohio
Larry Simpkins, Canton, Ohio
Karen Turner, Akron, Ohio
Gayle Warstler, Navarre, Ohio
Karen Wilson, Akron, Ohio

With Sincere Thanks,

Rosezelle Boggs-Qualls
Daryl C. Greene
Emily Street-Hensel

ABOUT THE AUTHORS

In November 2000, Hearing-impaired Rosezelle Boggs-Qualls approached her friend, vision-impaired Rev. Dr. Daryl C. Greene, to ask him to be a co-author in telling this amazing and inspirational biographical docu-drama. She had already spent more than four years in research, interviewing Emily Street Hensel, Nellie Zimmerman's companion and friend, and poring over the many scrapbooks, and other memorabilia that Emily had collected.

A social worker for more than 30 years, Rosezelle grew up in the mountains of southeastern Kentucky. Due to childhood diseases, she had lost most of her hearing by the time she was 9. She attended Pine Mountain Settlement High School, in Pine Mountain, Kentucky, and received a Degree in Social Work from Wright State University, Dayton, Ohio. Her Graduate work in Applied Behavioral Science was also at Wright State. In 1946, she married William (Buck) Qualls who is totally deaf. They now live in Canton, Ohio,

Daryl is an ordained minister in the United Church of Christ and has served churches in Kansas, Ohio, and Wisconsin. A graduate of Western Michigan University, and Andover-Newton Theological School, he completed his Doctoral Studies at Pittsburgh Theological Seminary. Due to a rare and progressive neurological disease, he began to lose central vision at the age of 6. By the time he graduated from Upper Arlington High School, near Columbus, Ohio, he was legally blind. He also has difficulty walking. He now lives in Richmond, Indiana, where he writes and speaks on how to cope with disabilities. He is the author of the book <u>You Can Feel Better: How To Cope With And Overcome Chronic Pain And Progressive Disabilities From A Holistic Christian Perspective</u> and has recorded a set of 12 <u>Healing Meditations,</u>

This book is dedicated to lifting up the memory and accomplishments of Nellie L. Zimmerman. May the story that follows serve as an inspiration to all those who struggle with handicaps. From the authors' perspective it proves that "With God all things are possible."

Anne Rose Greene,
Densmore Reid Publications

WALKING FREE
THE NELLIE ZIMMERMAN STORY

TABLE OF CONTENTS

St. Paul United Church of Christ in Navarre, Ohio. The site of Nellie's memorial service.

PROLOGUE

It was a crisp fall day in October 1995, and a feeling of anticipation washed over me as I stepped out the door and walked to the van where my husband, Buck, was already waiting.

I finger spelled, "I wonder what is going to happen at church today?"

He answered in the strained voice that belongs only to the deaf, "We're going to a funeral."

A funeral? It seemed strange to have a feeling of anticipation about attending a funeral, but as I drove along the country road toward the church, that feeling intensified.

Was it the beauty of the day speaking to my spirit? The clear blue cloudless sky made everything look brilliant.

I finger spelled to Buck, "What a perfect day!"

"Ideal!" he answered.

Driving with one hand, I finger spelled with the other, "On days like this, I truly believe that all things are possible."

My thoughts turned to my reason for our drive to the church. My pastor, Reverend Daryl Greene, of St. Paul United Church of

Christ, in Navarre, Ohio, had called. As soon as I recognized his voice, somehow I knew that this would be an important conversation.

Reverend Greene had said, "I have an unusual request. I want to know if you and Buck would be willing to attend a memorial service for a deaf and blind woman?"

He had explained. "This morning, a woman just came in off the street, marched past my startled secretary and right into my office."

Then he had told me the story.

Without introducing herself, the woman had blurted out, "Would you do a funeral for someone who is not a member of your church? What about doing one for a deaf and blind woman? What if she's been cremated?"

"Of course, I will," he had replied.

She had pressed on, "Will you do it even if I don't have any money to pay you?"

"Of course. That makes no difference."

"Well, what if I don't have a grave?"

"Then we will just have to find one!"

With every question she had become louder and more emotional, and by this time she was both shouting and crying, "I don't believe it! I have been all over Massillon looking for a pastor who would do a funeral for my friend, Nellie!"

In order to calm her down, Reverend Greene had invited her to take a seat and tell him about her friend.

Reverend Greene had paused in his story telling to ask me directly, "Have you ever heard of a deaf and blind lady named Nellie Zimmerman?"

"No, why?"

"Well, according to this woman, Nellie was well known throughout Northeast Ohio. She was an inmate of the Massillon State Hospital for nineteen years. When she was discovered there, a bitter battle was waged to have her released, and it was widely publicized. Finally, after her release, she continued to be featured in the media because of her remarkable achievements. However, for the past fourteen years or so she lived in the Deaf Colony in Columbus, Ohio. The reason I am calling you is because this woman doesn't think that there will be very many people attending the funeral. So I thought I would call you and Buck and a few other people to see if we can give her some moral support."

"Who is this woman?" I had asked.

"I think her name is Emily Hensel. But I don't know anything about her."

Buck and I were truly amazed by this story. We wanted to know more about Nellie. And we wanted to know more about this Emily. We also wanted to support our pastor for agreeing to do this funeral under such unusual circumstances.

As we entered the church, it was bathed in the morning sun. The sanctuary seemed full of light. I took note of the scene before me where a small group of perhaps thirty-five people were seated in the pews. Of them, about ten were members of the church, but the rest were strangers.

As I made my way down the aisle I noticed that most of the people who were gathered for this memorial service were handicapped in some way. I saw three-pronged canes, walkers, and wheel chairs everywhere. Some had "blind" canes, while others were signing to each other in American Sign Language.

Buck and I took our customary places in the third pew on the left. Right away I noticed the picture of a woman that had been placed on the wooden communion table at the front of the sanctuary. A petite, sweet-faced, white-haired woman was portrayed; a woman whose no-nonsense, straight-ahead, sightless gaze, straight spine, and perfectly squared shoulders spoke clearly of her profound dignity. I knew at once that this was a picture of Nellie Zimmerman. At that moment I regretted that I had not known her and, I was all the more curious to learn more about her.

A few minutes later, Reverend Greene opened the service from the rear of the sanctuary, and I began to finger spell the proceedings to Buck.

In a strong voice, the pastor declared, "Our help is in the name of the Lord, who made both heaven and earth!"

As always, I was personally inspired as I watched him make his way down the aisle, walking with his cane, using the handrail to ascend the stairs to the chancel, and then standing in the pulpit, reciting from memory the universal words that are used for Christian funerals and burials.

"Dearly Beloved, we are gathered together in the presence of Almighty God and this congregation to lift up the memory of Nellie Zimmerman as we prepare to lay her ashes to rest..."

I was always inspired while listening to Reverend Greene. Here was a man with a rare neurological disease. A disease that had destroyed so much of his vision that he was legally blind, and that also made walking very painful and difficult for him. Yet, he refused to be defined by his physical circumstances. He carried out his pastoral duties with passion, enthusiasm, and love, not only for the members of his congregation, but also for all people.

Reverend Greene recited the life story of Nellie Zimmerman, from memory. Without using any notes because of his blindness, he spoke of her long list of accomplishments, the many community, state, and national honors she had received. I finger spelled to my husband all that he said, including the many Psalms and scriptures he quoted, as he unhurriedly provided a wonderfully solemn, eloquent, and fitting tribute to Nellie Zimmerman.

As he spoke I noticed a tall, brown haired lady of medium build standing to the right of the communion table that held Nellie's picture. She was signing in American Sign Language. My husband had stopped watching my finger spelling to follow along with her signing.

Following the conclusion of the service, we drove to the cemetery to place Nellie's ashes in the grave that had been donated for that purpose. As we drove slowly along the streets of Navarre, I thought about many things. I am hearing impaired. Reverend Greene is vision impaired. But the woman whose ashes we were burying was both totally deaf and totally blind. I knew, only too well, the difference between my life's circumstances as a hearing impaired person, and my husband's life as a totally deaf person. What would he have faced if he had also lost his sight from the spinal meningitis that had taken his hearing? It was a disturbing thought. But here was someone who had lived without sound or sight! I became fascinated by her predicament, by her life story, and by her accomplishments which Reverend Greene had just recited.

About twenty people accompanied her ashes to the cemetery. Among them were several hearing and vision impaired friends of Nellie's. The interment was brief. I watched as the woman who had been signing assisted several people to enter their specially equipped vans for the handicapped.

When everyone else was gone, my husband and I found her talking with Reverend Greene. When we approached them, he turned to me and said, "Thanks for coming. Let me introduce you. This is Emily Hensel."

Emily shook hands and proceeded to talk as if she had always known us. I learned right away that she did not stand on ceremony, but began immediately to take charge of the conversation.

She said, "I am upset and embarrassed by the poor turn out today for Nellie's funeral. Over the years, there were many professionals from various fields, including social services, medicine, academia, and members of the area's civic and religious organizations, who were an integral part of Nellie's life. They stayed involved with her during the bitter fight for her release from the State Hospital, and afterwards, as she experienced life on the outside but none of these people attended her memorial service today. No one was here from Nellie's family, either."

Emily's eyes began to brim with tears. She was unable to hide her emotion as she continued, "You know, her greatest fear in life was that she would die and be placed in an unmarked grave. That she would be 'lost,' and no one could ever find her. Now, that is exactly what happened here today. I have buried her in an unmarked grave."

Reverend Greene turned directly to Emily and smoothly changed the subject.

"Buck and Rosezelle have an adult Sunday school class at 9:15 each Sunday morning. Perhaps you would like to attend."

"Yes," I said, relieved to talk about something else, "We have a great group. We not only study the church lessons, but we are like a support group and learn from each other."

Emily raised her eyebrows in surprise, and replied, "I will try to be there on Sunday."

This was my introduction to two remarkable women. Nellie Zimmerman and Emily Street Hensel. Emily did become a member of our Sunday school class. However, it was almost a year later, at one of Reverend Greene's classes on "Meditative Prayer for Healing" that she told the group she was looking for someone to write Nellie's story. In fact, she had been trying for almost twenty years to get a book written on Nellie's life.

I was very interested in hearing about her quest to find a writer for Nellie's life story. Later that same evening I was able to speak to her alone.

I said, "I have recently finished a project involving the technical writing of a social services practice manual for the Children Services agency in Akron. I'm a technical writer. And I don't know how good I would be at writing a biographical book."

Emily looked at me with interest mirrored on her face, but she did not say anything. I was not sure that she heard or understood what I had said. Later Reverend Greene told me that at the very next group session, the only session that Buck and I missed, Emily rudely interrupted the group during their silent prayer.

Suddenly, she had exclaimed as though in total surprise, "Rosezelle is going to do the book!"

Immediately, she got up and left.

Later she told Reverend Greene, "It just came to me while praying that Rosezelle was the only one to do Nellie's story. So I went home and called her."

Now, some four years later, this is Nellie's story.

=   =   =

Chapter One

NELLIE

Nellie Zimmerman was born on April 30, 1906 in Braddock, Pennsylvania. Her mother gave her the gift of life, then took her last breath and went home to be with God. Nellie's father was devastated by the death of his wife, and resolved to give Nellie a double portion of his love and devotion as a living memorial to her mother.

From the moment Nellie was placed in his arms, she became the light of his life. Under his nurturing care, Nellie became a cute, bright eyed, fair-haired little girl. She was vivacious, full of laughter, and curious about everything. Although his own vision was rapidly deteriorating, he noticed that Nellie's keen eyes missed nothing. She felt confident in almost any situation, fully self-assured, and bold. But she was never reckless or careless. Her father was also impressed by the fact that even when she was absorbed in play, no sound went unnoticed. It was obvious that she was highly attentive and intelligent.

Every evening, Mr. Zimmerman took the time to read to her. By the time she was five, Nellie could read the first-grade level children's books provided to her by her father. She could count to one hundred and write the alphabet. In 1912, at the age of six, Mr. Zimmerman enrolled her in public school. She was an outstanding student.

Soon after she was enrolled in elementary school, Mr. Zimmerman remarried. Again their home was full of warmth and laughter. She and her older sister Elizabeth spent hours together playing in their own room with their corn silk dolls, dressing and undressing them, and making new costumes for the dolls to wear. Nellie also loved to be outside. She loved to play hide and seek with her older sister, or just to walk by herself in the woods.

But Nellie had a weak constitution. This became apparent when she enrolled in public school and was exposed to the other children and all of their contagious illnesses. She suffered from more than her share of typical childhood diseases. Her father could hardly remember a time when she was not sick. These constant colds, sinus infections, and feverish illnesses took their toll. Gradually they caused her to lose her hearing. By the time Nellie was eight years old, she was deaf.

Her father did not notice the change in her hearing until Nellie was already in the second grade. One day he happened to come home from work early and was there when Nellie came bounding into the house. She greeted her father with her usual hug, and then proceeded to grab her favorite doll. Then, for her father's benefit, she began to recount all that had happened at school that day. She finished talking about school, and was chattering away to her doll when, suddenly her sister came running into the house, slamming the door behind her. He noticed that Nellie didn't even glance in her sister's direction. Obviously, she was unaware that her sister had entered the room. Nellie chattered on, talking to the doll. He watched as her sister sneaked around behind her, but only when she reached over Nellie's shoulder to grab her doll, did Nellie notice that she was there.

Her father arched his eyebrows in surprise. It was not like Nellie to be so inattentive.

Then a horrible thought crossed his mind. "What if Nellie had not noticed her sister's footsteps and the slamming of the door because she was going deaf?

Now that he was thinking about it, he realized there was other evidence of Nellie's possible hearing loss that he had overlooked. At the dinner table just the other evening, he had asked Nellie to pass the peas. Because she was looking directly at him, she understood what he said. But later, when she had been looking at her stepmother, he asked for the butter and Nellie had not responded until he reached over and touched her shoulder. There had been many more occasions when, if she was not facing him, she did not seem to hear what he was saying.

Nellie's progressive hearing loss was a traumatic circumstance for the entire family. Her stepmother could not accept Nellie's deafness. Even before Nellie was totally deaf, she left the home. Nellie had not bonded well with her stepmother and, consequently, did not really miss her very much. She thought nothing of her leaving. Likewise, Elizabeth could not accept having a deaf sister. She stopped playing with Nellie. She ignored Nellie at home, and avoided her at school. Even though they lived in the same house, Nellie's sister never attempted to communicate with her in sign language, or with finger spelling.

However, the affection between Nellie and her father grew ever stronger. He decided to hire a governess to be her personal tutor and caretaker. Nellie was particularly fond of her first governess, Anna Marie. She was an attractive young woman who had taught in a one-room schoolhouse for three years before she took the job offered by Mr. Zimmerman.

Before coming to the Zimmerman home, Anna Marie learned how to finger spell. Her first task was to teach Mr. Zimmerman. He learned quickly because he wanted to be able to communicate with his beloved daughter. At the same time she also taught Nellie how to use the deaf alphabet for finger spelling to communicate. Anna Marie was surprised to discover that Nellie was already an excellent speller by the end of the second grade. But learning how to read the finger spelling of others required both concentration and a keen mind. In order to comprehend the sentences and ideas being communicated, Nellie quickly learned how to remember the words already spelled out, even as new ones emerged.

Anna Marie was an excellent tutor. She started out spelling slowly. But as Nellie's power of comprehension improved, she gradually increased the speed of her hand signs. At first Nellie found it was a challenge to know when a word or sentence came to an end. It was not like reading, where she could easily see the spaces between each word and the period at the end of each sentence. When Anna Marie finger spelled, often there was not much of a pause that Nellie could perceive. However, within a few weeks, Anna Marie trained Nellie to read finger spelling at the speed of a normal conversation.

Mr. Zimmerman also found that the hardest part to master in finger spelling was to make the slight momentary breaks that were necessary to enable Nellie to differentiate between his words. He grew adept in communicating with her and, in a short time, he could finger spell correctly and very rapidly.

Her father made a point of spending time with Nellie when he came home from work. He talked with her at the dinner table, and he set aside time in the evenings to be with her before she went to bed. He was pleased that at the age of eight, she could spell well enough for them to communicate. Because she could still speak, he encouraged her to use her voice to talk to him, and he would finger spell to her. In the beginning, he often had to remind himself to keep his communication with her on a third grade level. Nellie had quickly learned to correctly read her father's talking fingers. As she became more proficient in spelling and in the use of the English language, their conversations with each other grew more sophisticated.

She kept up with him no matter how fast his fingers flew and seldom had to ask him to repeat anything. He became her link to the hearing world by interpreting whatever other people were saying.

Nellie's formal education ended with the completion of the second grade. In the fall of 1915, at the age of nine, it was determined that she was totally deaf and therefore was no longer allowed to attend the public school.

Although the Western Pennsylvania State School for the Deaf was an excellent institution, Nellie was never enrolled there as a student. Possibly, Mr. Zimmerman was so deeply attached to Nellie that he simply did not want her to leave home.

It was decided that Anna Marie was to be her personal tutor. She had a wonderful sense of humor and could be quite girlish with Nellie. But her first love was teaching. As soon as Anna Marie could communicate with Nellie, she set about giving her instruction in reading. While Nellie could not hear Anna Marie's spoken words, Nellie could still speak. So Anna Marie encouraged her to use her voice and had her read aloud. To improve her skill in writing, Anna Marie asked her to write book reports on what she had read. These reports were graded for spelling, grammar and sentence structure. Nellie also studied history, geography and science. Reading was her first love, but a close second was arithmetic. She received excellent instruction in math, learning to add, subtract, multiply and divide. She was fascinated by the "world of numbers."

For Nellie, a typical day consisted of a good breakfast before her morning lessons. Then she and Anna Marie would go outside and play. Sometimes it was hard to think of games to play for only two people. Hide and seek was one of the favorites. But Anna Marie had an advantage because Nellie could not hear her footsteps, or any other noises she made when hiding or trying to escape. When they grew tired of games, sometimes they would take walks in the woods, or try to catch crawdads under the rocks of a nearby stream. Anna Marie would watch her with guarded fascination because Nellie showed no fear of searching around the streambed for flat rocks, lifting them with one hand and quickly feeling around and under the rock with her other hand for the hard, little bodies of crawdads.

In the evenings Nellie enjoyed going to her father's library to pick out a book of her own choosing. And sometimes, too, they played cards. They played special card games called Rook and Old Maid. Also, they played a lot of different games using regular "Hoyle" gaming cards. The popular parlor games at the time were bidding games of Set Back, Euchre, or Bridge. Playing Gin Rummy was a lot of fun. And then there was the double deck of cards that they used to play the new card game, "Muggins."

Nellie also liked to play word games. These were primarily guessing games. Her favorites were "Culture," and "Going to Jerusalem." To play "Culture," one player thought of a famous individual, living or dead, and the other players used several specific questions to guess who the person was.

One day Anna Marie introduced a new game to Nellie. "Geography" was fun.

Anna Marie explained, "I will begin the game by giving the name of a well-known country, continent, city, or place. You, in turn, have to think of a geographic name that begins with the last letter of the previous name that I gave you. I start with America, so you need to tell me a word that starts with an 'A'."

"Arkansas!" Nellie blurted out, with a giggle.

"So my next word has to start with 'S'. Let me think... Salem!"

"Mississippi!"

"Indiana."

And so it went, until finally, Nellie was stumped. She simply could not think of any word to follow "Egypt."

"Going to Jerusalem" was a hilarious game that even Mr. Zimmerman enjoyed. Each player chose an article to take on a trip. The articles chosen could be anything. The first player then made a statement about what they would do with their article while on the trip. Something like, "When I get to Jerusalem, I'm going to <u>wear</u> my hat." The next player, having chosen a pet dog, would have to say, "When I get to Jerusalem, I'm going to <u>wear</u> my pet dog." And so on until each player thought of five different things to do with their articles. With Nellie speaking her parts aloud, and her father and Anna Marie finger spelling, each statement got even more ridiculous. All three of them would break down in gales of laughter. For Nellie, the fun times they had together never lasted long enough.

Each day, after the lessons were completed, Anna Marie wisely gave Nellie ample free time to explore wherever her curiosity led her. She was particularly interested in the Old Testament stories about God's people during Biblical times. The story of Joseph was a favorite that she read over again many times. She also liked to spend time alone in her room meditating, recalling the kinds of things she used to be able to hear. Often she would fantasize about the sounds she would be hearing, if she could hear.

Nellie could feel vibrations, but with or without a hearing device, she could hear nothing. She could not even hear herself talk. It was like being in a vacuum; there was no sound. She depended on memory alone in order to pronounce words because she had no feedback from her own voice. She relied on memory for the sounds she longed to hear again. Even though Nellie was only eight years old when she became deaf, she vividly remembered many treasured sounds, including how the rushing wind howled and the angry thunder rolled, the gurgling, splashing sounds of falling and running water, and the squeaks, squeals, chattering, brays and barks of animals. She loved to imagine how geese honked, ducks quacked, and the songbirds sang. She remembered the squeaking of doors and floors, and the smooth greasy swish of moving parts of farm machinery, the happy sound of whistling teakettles, and the clacking rhythm of the dasher used to make butter in the crock churn.

Sometimes, Nellie would even recall the music of violins, pianos, banjos, mandolins, mouth harps, singing voices, and favorite songs. She remembered the shrill sound of train and boat whistles, the jarring noises of horse-drawn wagons, and clanging fire bells. Of all the sounds she remembered though, the most treasured was the memory of her father's voice and the loving way he spoke her name.

On several occasions, during Nellie's free time, Anna Marie took her on outings. Sometimes they went to hunt for berries or mushrooms in the woods. Often they went shopping for the daily groceries, dry goods, and other everyday necessities. Whenever Mr. Zimmerman was home, he would join them for such excursions.

Nellie particularly looked forward to the weekends when her father could be home. Sometimes they would stay at home and play cards, checkers, or chess. But often he planned exciting excursions to larger cities. She looked forward to traveling with her father and Anna Marie. She enjoyed shopping in the big department stores and eating out in restaurants. These trips made her feel like a real princess in spite of her handicap.

Anna Marie lived with the Zimmerman family for almost five years. She was the first of a series of governesses and caretakers whom Mr. Zimmerman hired to teach and take care of Nellie. The time that Anna Marie spent with Nellie had a profound effect on her for the rest of her life. She had been like the mother Nellie had never known, and like a true sister as well. Not only had she instilled a love of learning in Nellie, but she had also reinforced Nellie's natural positive attitude toward life.

The gentle Mr. Zimmerman provided very well for his family. Yet he put Nellie's special needs before the needs of the rest of the family. There must have been some *old* money because there never seemed to be a shortage of funds when it came to providing for Nellie's care. He continued to hire governesses to be Nellie's teachers and caretakers. He also ensured that her life was as happy and normal as possible.

Like Anna Marie, the other caretakers lived with the family. They were given room and board, along with a salary. Each caretaker functioned like a nanny, or governess. Their responsibilities included not just providing care, but also an excellent education. They each had to either know the finger spelling method of communication with the deaf, or to agree to quickly learn this skill.

As a young teenager, Nellie was attractive, vivacious, and witty. Without exception, the caretakers her father hired took a personal interest in everything she did. Each of them, in turn, established an important and loving relationship with her. Most of the time they were with the caretaker when they went out, but oftentimes it was just Nellie and her father.

Of course, Nellie tried different hearing devices, but to no avail. It did not take her father long to realize that none of these devices were going to restore even a little bit of her hearing. Grieved by Nellie's loss of hearing, Mr. Zimmerman began to search for a cure for his daughter.

Having exhausted all medical options, he concluded that only a miracle could restore her hearing.

In the summer of her fifteenth year he took her on one particularly exciting outing. He told her they would travel a long way from home because he planned to take her on an airplane ride. At the time Nellie did not realize that her father had more than a fun adventure planned. He had arranged with the pilot to execute a special maneuver. The pilot was to take a sudden nose dive to see if the rushing air, the high-pitched whining noise of a suicide dive and the resulting sense of relief of coming out of the dive might restore part or all of her hearing. Someone had told her father that this might work.

Nellie was thrilled. She had never ridden in an airplane before. Anticipation hung over her as she waited for the day finally to arrive. After a long, anxious month, the day came. Her father had hired a man to drive them to eastern Pennsylvania where the airplane ride was scheduled to take place. As an added treat, they stayed overnight in a hotel near the airfield. After dinner that evening, her father told her of his plan to have the pilot make the sharp dive toward the ground and of his hope that it might help her hearing. Eager to please her father, she readily agreed to try the special maneuver.

The next morning, they awoke early, had breakfast, and then they were picked up by the driver who whisked them off to meet the airplane pilot. Nellie had been too excited to sleep the night before. She never dreamed she would ever ride in an airplane. The idea of going up into the sky for more than a mile and then taking a mad dive downward toward the earth made her shiver with anticipation and with fear. Most of all she was anxious to find out if the planned sudden drop through air space would accomplish the expected results. Would she really be able to hear again?

They arrived at the airfield around mid-morning and met with the pilot. He took great care to explain to her father what he was going to do and what sensations she would feel as the plane took off, made the steep dive, leveled off, and then finally landed. Her father communicated to her by finger spelling what the pilot was saying.

When they walked to the small plane, she found that it had an open cockpit with only two seats. There was no room for her father. After he gave her a big hug, and kissed her gently on the forehead, she turned to climb into the plane by herself. Her father reassured her that everything would be all right and he would stay right there to wait for her return. Then he stepped back from the plane as she took her place.

The pilot fitted her with a pair of goggles and a tight leather cap. She was shuddering with excitement, dread, and anticipation. Her thoughts were racing, and every nerve in her body was as taut as a guy wire. Her heart was beating like a trip hammer, and she could feel its pressure rising up in her throat. Nellie closed her eyes.

Silently she repeated over and over, "I have to do this! I can do this! I can do it!"

She was so busy talking to herself, repeating her resolves, and literally making herself remain fastened in her seat, that she had no time to consider changing her mind.

Suddenly they were moving. The plane was rolling along the ground. Nellie opened her eyes. At first the plane moved very slowly as the pilot taxied into position, ready for take off. Then they went faster. The ground was just a blur as if it were not even there. Shakily the plane rose into the air. Nellie was really flying. What an experience!

She felt dizzy, disoriented, and thought, "This must be what being drunk on whiskey is like."

The plane rose steadily, climbing higher into a cloudless sky. Nellie did not know anything about flying, but she could tell from the tilt of the airplane that they were doing a very steep climb.

She could not help saying aloud, "He does not have to be in such a hurry to get up there."

Then she thought, "Now that's a silly thing for me to say."

She thought they would go up in the sky about a mile, but now it felt as if they were several miles above the earth. After what seemed like an hour, the pilot stopped the steep climb. Banking the plane, he leveled off. He spent about thirty minutes flying at the same speed, making big loopy circles around the airfield. Nellie became comfortable with the motion of the plane and enjoyed herself.

All of a sudden, she gasped. It felt as if the bottom had dropped out from under them. The plane seemed to be out of control in a headlong free-fall dive toward the ground! As the plane dropped, displacing the surrounding air, it was as though the wind had gone mad. The sheer weight of the sudden rush of air that engulfed her took her breath away. She could not breathe for the longest time. She knew they were going to die. With her eyes shut tight, praying frantically, she hung onto her seat for dear life.

Meanwhile, on the ground, because her father could not see well enough to spot the airplane's location in the sky, their driver was relating to him everything the plane was doing, including when the pilot began the suicide dive.

Although her father could not follow their headlong drop toward the earth, he silently prayed for her safety and ended his supplication with a special plea.

"Lord, please heal Nellie's deafness."

As the pilot brought the plane out of the dive, leveled off, and began to climb skyward again, Nellie gasped for air, and took a deep breath.

"Lordy!" She exclaimed. "I can breathe!"

Then almost angrily, she said, "I would just as soon be killed as scared to death."

Then she thought of all the trouble her father had gone through to provide this trip for her. She was instantly ashamed of her bad temper. She was fighting to keep her teeth from chattering and her shoulders from visibly quaking. In spite of her fear, now that the plane was again traveling at the same rate of speed as before, she began to calm down, and soon she felt the same sense of pleasure from flying as she had experienced before the dive.

The pilot continued to circle around for another half hour or so. This extra time gave Nellie a chance to regain her composure. She again felt dizzy as the plane gradually dropped downward and landed. Her father hurried toward the sound of the plane. Although still dizzy and on wobbly legs, Nellie slowly walked to meet him.

When he reached her, he grabbed her in a big hug and held her a long time. She strained all of her senses, but she could not tell if he was talking. She did not respond to his exclamations of relief, as he thanked God because she was safely on the ground.

Then with a voice cracking under the strain of his emotion, he pleaded, "Can you hear? Can you hear anything? Nellie, can you hear?"

Finally, he finger spelled to her, "Are you O.K.?"

Numbly, she nodded, "Yes."

Tears ran down her father's cheeks, and brimmed in Nellie's eyes, as they slowly walked hand-in-hand back to their chauffeured car. If there ever was a question, it was clear now to them both that Nellie would have to contend with being deaf for life.

Shortly after the attempted flight therapy, the Zimmerman family moved to Canton, Ohio. Once again, Mr. Zimmerman hired governesses to tutor and care for Nellie. Because Nellie was highly intelligent and easy to teach, her caretakers had fun. They enjoyed everything they did with Nellie. Each outing they planned turned into an exciting adventure. None of the caretakers ever made a complaint about her behavior to her father, and never once did Nellie complain to him about them.

But life dealt Nellie a second blow. Up until she was about twelve, she could see perfectly, even without eyeglasses. Early in her teenage years she began to experience a gradual loss of vision. After her sixteenth birthday, her eye doctor told Mr. Zimmerman that there was no known cure for her condition, and that by the time Nellie was twenty she would undoubtedly be totally blind. Although devastated by the news, he did not waste any time. Right away he told Nellie exactly what the doctor had said. Mr. Zimmerman assured her that she would always have a personal companion who would serve as her caretaker and would also teach her how to cope with the double handicap of deafness and blindness.

Over the years her father hired many different caretakers who continued to be with her through her late teens, as a young adult, and after she was a mature woman. They provided her with companionship, education, and friendship. She continued to be an excellent student, and although she did not receive a diploma, Nellie more than succeeded in completing all the requirements of a high school education. She excelled in the sciences, knew her world geography and history, was well-read, and could write excellent essays on almost any subject.

After her sixteenth birthday, there was a frightening increase in the rate at which she lost her sight. Now her caretakers had an even more demanding responsibility toward Nellie. Not only did they serve as her companions and teachers, but they also taught Nellie many life skills. She learned how to care properly for a home, including cooking, cleaning, and sewing. They taught her how to coordinate her clothes, shop at stores, use money to make purchases, and properly care for her clothes and her other personal belongings.

As Nellie entered her twenties and her vision continued to fail, the responsibilities of her caretakers became more complex. When her vision became so poor that she could not see what their hands were saying, the finger spelling had to be done into her hands. Mr. Zimmerman contacted the Canton Society for the Blind to arrange for a home instructor to teach Nellie how to read and write in Braille. By the time Nellie's vision was completely gone, she was already able to use this new way of reading and writing. She spent no time feeling sorry for herself, but waded right in. Not only did she read and write Braille, but she also was a "speed reader" and her writing accuracy was close to one hundred percent. By the time Nellie was in her mid-twenties, she could barely tell the difference between daylight and darkness.

Sometimes she played mind games. She would work complicated math problems in her head. She also played complex word games with herself. During these mental exercises memory compensated for what she could no longer see. But it was reading that was Nellie's love. Reading opened doors to the outside world, and exposed her to a world of sight and sound, and allowed her personally to relate to different people, places and things. She was provided with Braille books, magazines, and other periodicals.

Nellie also had a treasured Braille copy of the Bible that was given to her by her father. Her Bible consisted of six volumes in all. Three volumes made up the Old Testament, two volumes contained all the books of the New Testament, and the last volume was a general concordance that included raised geographical maps of the Holy Land. Nellie's fingers were sensitive enough to trace the boundary outlines of the countries, and to follow the elevated mountain ranges and the twisting courses of rivers. Her Bible was well worn, and seldom a day passed without its being used. Over the years she memorized entire books of the Bible. As an adult her best love was the New Testament.

After years of Biblical study, Nellie had internalized a lasting love for the Son of God. She knew that God was the Father, but Jesus belonged to her. He was in her heart. She had talked to Him since she was a child and knew she would always be able to talk with Him at any time, and about any subject. Seldom were her prayers just one-sided affairs. She mentally participated in two-way conversations with "her" Jesus.

Nellie's childlike faith that Jesus would always take care of her was strong and reassuring. But even though she trusted Him explicitly, she still had one great fear. She feared that she would somehow find herself alone and not know where she was. She had terrifying nightmares. This fear was so strong that she constantly needed assurance that someone was always in her close proximity. It was when she was away from the familiar surroundings of home that the fear was strongest. She needed constantly to feel the caretaker's touch as reassurance that someone was with her who would not leave her.

As Nellie grew older, she no longer received her daily tutoring. She spent her time reading, helping with the daily household chores and socializing with her caregiver.

As he had done since she was a child, her father still made it a point to spend time talking with Nellie. In order to talk comfortably to her at mealtimes, he positioned his chair so that he was sitting beside her at the dining room table. In the evenings, he sat beside her on the divan, or he moved two straight chairs close together and they spent the time chatting beside the fire. These were always lively and special times.

Nellie had a sense of humor and a mind of her own. If she did not agree with something which was being finger spelled into her hands, or if she became angry over what someone was telling her, she would make her hands unavailable. Sometimes she would simply fold her arms across her chest, hiding her hands from view. At other times she would sit on her hands. This was her way of forcing the speaker to stop talking. She would do this, much to their chagrin, while smiling sweetly or impishly grinning broadly, depending on the person and the subject they were discussing.

Although she had lost her vision, her eyes were sensitive to bright light. Too much exposure actually caused pain. She could not see the faintest outline of objects, but she could feel the intensity of a bright light. After going outside on a bright sunny day, or being exposed to bright indoor lighting, she would often sit alone in her darkened room reading in Braille with a clean cloth tied over her eyes like a blindfold. It was not unusual for her to spend several hours sitting quietly alone with her eyes covered this way.

Her father continued to spend as much time with her as he could. Although he had to engage a driver to provide their transportation, they planned many special outings for just the two of them.

They often went shopping in Massillon or Canton. Sometimes they dressed informally and visited the many excellent small restaurants in their immediate area. Occasionally they took special trips to Akron or Cleveland. Sometimes her caretaker would accompany them and serve as their driver, but frequently they chose to take the trolley car. When they spent a day in these larger cities, Nellie was doubly excited because she loved to shop, particularly in the small specialty stores where she could take her time and savor the experience. She loved to take in the smells of the shops. She enjoyed being able to feel all the textures and to smell the merchandise. Nellie also loved to dress up when they planned to dine at fancy restaurants. She took pleasure in the taste of specialty dishes, and she enjoyed the feeling of being served.

Nellie also looked forward to visits to area parks with her father and caregiver, who described what they saw for her vision impaired father's benefit as well as hers. They spelled into Nellie's hands, and at the same time, they verbalized the same information to Mr. Zimmerman as they walked along the paths and trails. They visited historical museums where the caregiver described the displays to Nellie and Mr. Zimmerman. They even visited all the art museums and institutes in Northeast Ohio, where they made the experience interesting by describing the pictures. Nellie especially loved to touch and outline with her fingers the features of the many sculptured statues. But most of all, Nellie loved to visit the Cleveland Zoo. She spent most of her time in the children's section, where she could touch all the animals. She enjoyed digging her fingers into their fur, stroking their feathers, or feeling their skins. She loved to feed them. She would stick out her hand in their general direction and wait for them to find the food. Sometimes she got nipped by their teeth, or pecked by a beak, but she did not mind. It was fun to relate to another living being.

Mr. Zimmerman, with special insight, understood the advantages to be gained for Nellie by being exposed to new experiences. Deeply interested in learning all she could about each place they visited, she asked dozens of questions, and they kept up a lively conversation with their fingers during their excursions. They both derived genuine pleasure from being in each other's company.

Sometimes, when Mr. Zimmerman was unavailable, her caretakers took her on such excursions. They provided guidance and interpreted what was going on around them, finger spelling into her hands what they saw and felt. Each time Nellie and her caretaker went on excursions there was a lot of fun and laughter between them. Her caretakers planned all sorts of fun things for them to do, kept Nellie busy with daily activities, and filled her with anticipation of events yet to come.

Before going to sleep, Nellie would think back over the events of each day and include in her bedtime prayer her special thanks to God for the day and for keeping her safe. She would ask God to bless her caretaker, her father, and to keep them safe.

=   =   =

Chapter Two

INTO THE ABYSS

Although Nellie was shut out of the hearing and sighted world, she was still within reach of discourse, interaction, and love through her father and her caretakers. However, now that she was both blind and deaf, Nellie began to realize that no matter how well educated she was, or how correctly she could speak and write, she was totally dependent upon *them*. Without someone to communicate to her, and for her, she could not cope in a hearing and sighted world. This was frightening.

As long as Nellie could see, she managed to communicate with most hearing people by verbally talking to them and reading their writing. Because she was home schooled, she rarely met any other deaf people. Unintentionally, her father isolated her from the deaf community and people who could have provided her with a continuing social support system throughout her life. In so doing he increased by tenfold the difficulties she would encounter because of her handicaps.

As she grew older, her father continued to spend as much time with her as he could. Although he had to engage a driver to provide their transportation, they still planned many special outings. In addition to Canton and Massillon, they often visited Akron and Cleveland. Sometimes, both he and her caretaker accompanied Nellie. Oftentimes, it was just the two of them. If he did not go with her, the caretaker would be in charge.

When she reached her middle forties, Nellie knew only a few members of her extended family. After she lost her hearing, no other family member had taken responsibility for her care or even shown any interest in her. Her sister and the four nieces whom she did know, never took the trouble to learn sign language well enough to talk to her. After she became blind, they did not seem to realize that they had to touch her in order for her to know of their presence. If someone did come to visit and her father or caretaker spelled into her hand who was there, she would greet the visitor. However, when they failed to initiate any physical contact with her, Nellie did not know if they were still in the room, or where in the room they might be. Nellie did not understand this lack of contact. It bothered her that no one from the wider family ever came to visit with her, or even spelled into her hands a simple question like, "How are you?"

Nellie often speculated about the relationship, or lack of one, that she had with the rest of her family. She tried to decide if the problem was that they simply did not like her, if they felt it was too much trouble to communicate with her, or both. Not knowing, and unable to do anything about it anyway, she decided she did not really care about it all that much.

Then, when Nellie was 45 years old, life struck a third, and most horrible blow. Her father became seriously ill. Apparently, at the same time, her caretaker was summarily dismissed from her duties. Without warning, suddenly both her father and her caretaker disappeared from her life. Nellie knew, without a doubt, that something terrible must have happened to her father. Repeatedly, she felt her way though his office and his bedroom, but her search was in vain. Finally, she retreated to her own bedroom and waited for his return. She lost count of the days. Someone, who she assumed was a member of her family, came near her only to bring her meals. A tray was set down on the small bedside table. A touch on her shoulder let her know that her meal was there, and then she was alone again.

Nellie had no idea how many weeks had passed when finally, someone came into her room. She knew it was a woman because of her perfume. Without identifying herself, with a great deal of difficulty, she crudely spelled into her hands:

"Your father is dead!"

Two days later, she was led out of her home and into a car. She guessed that she was being taken to her sister's house. But no one ever told her where she was, or exactly with whom she was living. Nellie was never told exactly what had happened to her father, how he died, or even when his funeral was held. Without her caretaker there was no one to ask. There was no one who could tell her. Until now she had been spared any experience with death. All her life she had been totally dependent upon her father. Now she suddenly realized that the only person who truly loved her was gone from her life.

She was provided with her own room, a bed, dresser, table, bookcase, and chair. She was expected to sit alone in her room, read her Bible and the few other Braille materials she had brought with her and to stay out of everyone's way. As before, her meals were brought to the room. Whoever delivered them would touch her on the shoulder and leave immediately. There was little, if any communication between Nellie and the members of her family.

Sometimes, when her meals were delivered and she received her fleeting pat on her shoulder, or if someone's body brushed up against her, she would hold tight onto an arm, grab a hand, or clutch at their clothing. Most of the time she had no idea who was there, but she used her voice to ask a large battery of questions. There was not ever anyone who would or could answer. Nellie surmised that they could not understand her speech. With bitterness, she felt that if this was the case, it was because they did not stay around her long enough to learn to understand her. Never before had she felt so alone and powerless.

Unable to talk with anyone about her father, she found herself in uncontrollable tears. Remembering any small thing about him, or something they had done together, brought an overpowering rush of grief. She found that dealing with her personal needs on a daily basis had become almost impossible. She desperately needed to talk with someone.

Again, Nellie lost track of days, weeks, and months. One day she was led out of the house and into the car again. No one told her why. She felt a ray of hope as she wondered if she were going to move into a better situation. But her hopes were soon crushed. Again, she was provided with her own room, a bed, table, dresser, chair, and bookcase. Again, her meals were delivered to her room. And likewise, no one could or would talk to her. She spent at least a full year being passed around from one place to another.

As time wore on, the drastic change in her life began to take its toll. Nellie found herself getting more and more disturbed by her sedentary life. She was far too intelligent and too healthy in mind and body to be content with such a lifestyle. Nellie did not know how to deal with her growing frustration and anger. In addition, Nellie began to wonder about her father's estate. She knew nothing about what he had left to her in his will, but she wondered what had happened to the money from the sale of his house and whatever other assets he might have had. All that she knew was that she was given no money of her own. She longed to be able to hire a caretaker as before. She longed to take shopping trips again to buy new and pretty clothes and to eat in restaurants as before. Obviously such things were never even considered by those with whom she was living. Was there no money available for such things?

Once in a great while, someone brought her a wrapped present, sometimes complete with ribbon and a bow. Usually it was a nice article of clothing, a pretty scarf, or a frilly handkerchief. Nellie would gleefully open the gift and vocally express her pleasure. She hoped that the visitor would stay with her for a while, but each time she was sadly disappointed when abruptly she was left alone again.

One day Nellie simply exploded! It was a surprise even to her. She did not plan it, and she did not know it was coming until it was over. Someone came into her room, touched her on the shoulder, and made a halfhearted attempt to communicate with her. At first, not knowing who was visiting, Nellie was pleased because she was happy just to have some company. But when she asked the person a simple question and did not get any response, she could not stand it. She felt an uncontrollable surge of emotion; a heavy pressure started in her chest, and rose up to the bridge of her nose. She could not stop herself. She began to scream. Then she gave out an ear-piercing screech. While alternately screaming and screeching, she sat on her hands and bounced up and down in her chair. There was no way to communicate with her now, and no way to stop her. Finally, she wore herself out and made a decision to regain her composure.

When her temper tantrum was over, Nellie felt a tremendous release. She felt better than she had in a long, long time. However, Nellie knew that she had misbehaved and had exposed an unacceptable character weakness. With remorse, she scolded herself.

"Nice people don't misbehave like that. Nice people don't have tantrums! Why did I do that?"

In spite of her outburst, the family showed no inclination to make any positive changes in Nellie's daily care. They did nothing to alleviate her situation. All Nellie really wanted was to be included in their activities and to feel that she was a part of her family. But instead, she was still expected to sit alone in her room with nothing to do except read her old Braille books and magazines. As time went by, in spite of her sense of guilt, she felt an ever-deepening resentment toward the people who took care of her.

Months passed and nothing changed for the better. Continuing to suffer from her extreme isolation, it seemed to her as if any excitement she could generate, by whatever means possible, was better than nothing happening at all. Nellie soon discovered that she could generate attention by becoming agitated and throwing a good tantrum. After she put the guilt of her first demonstration behind her, it became easy to regress into this negative behavior again and again.

The family became frantic in their efforts to deal with the outbursts. Again she was moved to another relative's home. But the provisions of her care remained virtually the same. Therefore, as she continued to be frustrated, Nellie threw periodic tantrums.

One day, without any warning, someone came into her room and packed up her belongings. She did not know who it was, but by the scent of the perfume she knew it was a woman. She sensed the activity that was going on in the room, but did not know what the woman was doing. Nellie's clothes were folded and packed. So were her personal items, including her Braille Bible and other reading material.

With great difficulty, someone spelled into her hands, "We are taking you to a doctor."

Smiling for the first time in days, she went along. Nellie was just happy to be going anywhere.

Instead of going to a doctor's office, she was delivered to a nursing home. When she was admitted, her family signed over to the manager her Social Security benefits, and full responsibility for her care. With this move, her relatives were released from all legal and financial obligations for her care. Apparently, they believed that they were likewise released from all moral obligations to visit her as well. This was the last known contact she had with her family for almost thirty years.

The nursing home to which Nellie had been committed apparently had no one on staff who could finger spell. Neither did they employ anyone who was trained to work with the blind. She was led to her room. By feeling and touching she found her bed, and where to put her clothes. She was shown the location of the bathroom. Then she was left alone. With the exception of when she was led to the dining room for meals, she had little contact with the staff or the residents of the home. No one talked to her. When she could no longer bear the frustration of her isolation, she again resorted to throwing temper tantrums. After several such outbursts, the manager decided to turn her care over to a different nursing home. Thus evolved a pattern of moving Nellie from one inappropriate nursing facility to another.

Nellie soon discovered that if she threw a tantrum, then within the next few days she would be moved to a different facility. Over the years, Nellie lost track of exactly how many nursing homes she lived in, but thought there had been at least six or seven. Each time she was committed to another nursing home, the legal responsibility for her care was transferred.

Nellie never forgot one of those nursing homes. She never knew its name because again, there was no one there who could finger spell or write in Braille. When she arrived, a person took her by the arm and led her some distance before she reached her room. The woman placed Nellie's hands on her bed so she would know where it was. With a careful, gentle touch she showed Nellie a chest, table and chair. She stayed with her for a few minutes, allowing enough time for her to learn where each piece of furniture was located. Next, the woman took Nellie's hands and showed her where her box of clothes and other belongings had been placed. Then with two soft good-bye pats on Nellie's shoulder, she left.

"This at last seems to be a place where I can fit in and be happy!" Nellie thought.

The lady with the gentle touch left out one important piece of information. She did not show Nellie where the bathroom was located. Left all alone with her bed, table, desk and chair, Nellie was quick to understand that this was where she was now going to live. She had been disconcerted by yet another move, but she was not surprised.

Carefully, she felt, smelled, and checked the weight of each of her personal items to identify it, and then she decided where to put it. First, she put away her clothes. Underwear was put in the top drawer of the chest. Folded house dresses and two sweaters were put in the second drawer. She had not been shown a place to hang up anything, but by carefully running her hand around the wall, she located the open door to a closet. Feeling through space, she lifted her arms as high as she could and found she could reach some clothes hangers that had been left there for her. She quickly hung up her one nice dress, a duster, and a robe.

Not knowing what time it was, if and when she was going to be given something to eat, or when someone would come back, she decided she had better put the rest of her belongings away as quickly as she could. If someone did come for her, she would be ready. She had two drawers left in her chest, so she decided to put her treasured Bible in the third drawer, and the rest of her books and magazines in the bottom one. After everything was put away, she sat down on her bed, folded her hands in her lap and waited. It was a long time before anyone did come back. It was the same woman who had been with her before. She took Nellie's hand and gently placed it on her arm. Nellie went with her willingly. On the way, she felt along the walls and counted the empty spaces that were framed by door facings, and the large empty spaces that she recognized as large open rooms. She soon discovered they were going to the dining room. Smelling the wonderful aromas of many different foods, she knew it must be time for dinner. Not only had she not eaten since breakfast and was starving, but she was also parched with thirst.

The woman led Nellie on into the large dining room and positioned her in a chair in front of a full plate of food. She carefully guided Nellie's hands to touch the silverware, and helped her find her water glass. Although she was not communicating to Nellie except by bodily leading her and gently guiding her hands, they were getting along famously. Nellie again felt two soft good-bye pats on her shoulder, and then she was left alone with her food. She gingerly felt around on her plate and discovered she had meat, potatoes, green beans, and a roll. Nellie was grateful for the food and water and, after quickly saying grace, began to eat. She devoured everything on her plate, and drank all of her water. Then she sat patiently with her hands folded in her lap, waiting for someone to come back to her.

After what seemed a very long time, someone came. It was not the same person as before. Nellie knew this person was a woman, too, but she did not have a gentle touch like the other one. The woman grabbed Nellie's wrist in a tight hold, hurried her out of the dining room and down the hall toward her room. She did not give her a chance to feel along the walls, but Nellie did count the steps she was taking and knew when they had traveled far enough to have arrived back to her room and her own things. On the way back to her room, Nellie had spoken to the woman several times, using a low pitched fast mutter. She was asking about the location of the bathroom. The woman was obviously ignoring her questions.

Frantic now, and for the third or fourth time, she asked the woman, "Where is the bathroom?"

Still ignoring Nellie's question, the woman sat her down on her bed and turned loose of Nellie's wrist, and prepared to leave. Before she could make a clean break, Nellie caught hold of her arm and held on tight. At first the woman was caught by surprise. Her first instinct was to get loose from Nellie. She tried to loosen Nellie's hold on her by prying the clutching fingers away from her arm. She could not budge them.

Nellie continued to hold on as tightly as she could, and with a voice that cracked from the strain, she bawled, "Bathroom!"

There was no mistaking what Nellie had said. She felt a rippling motion as the woman's whole body shook with laughter. She reached over Nellie's clutching hand and, now with a more gentle touch, took hold of her other arm. Nellie relaxed her grip on the woman and felt herself being firmly turned to face a different direction. She was then led through a doorway, just a few steps away from her own room, to a large bathroom. Without a signal of any kind, the woman abruptly left her alone.

There was ample cabinet space in the bathroom for Nellie to put some of her personal items, but she did not know if she had to share it with others. She did not want to lose any of her toiletries, so she kept all of them in her room on top of her chest. She was not unhappy about moving again. Instead, she was vitally interested in her new surroundings. She was elated that she had been able to use her voice. Although she had ended up speaking just that one word, the woman had understood her well enough to lead her to the bathroom.

Nellie differentiated between the two women she had been in contact with so far by mentally naming the first one "Gentle Touch" and the second one "Hard Touch." The greatest difference between them was that Gentle Touch not only had a light, soft touch, but she had allowed Nellie to hold onto her arm and be led. Hard Touch was just the opposite. She had roughly grabbed Nellie's wrist and kept her off balance while she pulled her along.

Nellie knew she had been given dinner, but there was no way for her to tell when it got dark outside or what time it was. No one had come back to her after Hard Touch had shown her the bathroom. She was tired, but as was her custom before going to sleep at night, she placed one of the volumes of her precious Bible on her table. Her slender, sensitive fingers read a few passages. Carefully, she closed the Bible, replaced it in the chest, turned down her bed covers, and wearily crawled in between the cool, clean sheets. She noticed that all around her was a sickening, almost sweet, antiseptic smell. She had been in several nursing homes and was growing accustomed to this smell by now, but it still kept her awake sometimes.

Whenever Nellie was unable to sleep, she could not stop sweet thoughts of her father from crowding into her mind. Remembering the happy years she had spent with him, how much he loved her, and how much she loved him, she realized that she still missed him terribly and tears of grief overwhelmed her.

When Nellie had been so abruptly moved away from her family, she had not been too upset. Aside from her father, there had been no one in her family with whom she had become close. After her father's death, she had been left alone so much that she felt anything was better than the cruel isolation she had experienced under their care. Even if she got moved often, and did not know where she was, at least there was some activity in her life.

The next day, Gentle Touch came to take her to breakfast. Nellie remembered that once they left her room last evening, it had been a straight path to the dining room. She began counting steps and discovered that her count the night before was accurate. She quickly took her seat at the table. Happy with herself, she grinned broadly. Gentle Touch was surprised and pleased because Nellie had come with her so willingly. She had read Nellie's admission form and her medical chart. Both had indicated that she was unable to live at home because she was often violent and likely to have tantrums.

Gentle Touch smiled at the thought.

"I don't believe it. There's no way this sweet little woman could be violent."

However, not everyone was as considerate of Nellie's handicaps as Soft Touch. One major thing that the nursing home staff did not like about Nellie was that she did not abide by any rules. They did not care that she had no way of knowing what the rules were. She could be anywhere at any time. Nellie quickly learned her way around the facility by feeling her way along all the walls, counting her steps as she traveled, and mentally positioning the location of doorways and rooms with large openings like the dining and recreation rooms. Never one to respect anyone's privacy anyway, once she learned her way around the building, she would barge into the staff's private offices and interrupt their meetings. She explored the linen closets and other storage rooms, often getting in the way of the busy employees. In order to identify objects, she would proceed to touch, feel, and mentally weigh all kinds of things in her hands. The staff complained that nothing was safe from her meddling.

After several weeks of putting up with this irritating behavior, the administrator decided that what Nellie needed was something to do that would keep her occupied and out of everyone's way.

Nellie could always tell who was with her by the manner in which they touched her. From the first day, Gentle Touch never changed her way of greeting. She used a "Hello" touch on Nellie's arm and "Good bye" pats on her shoulder. Hard Touch was still rough with her sometimes, but not as bad as she was on that first day. However, one morning, after Nellie finished eating breakfast, someone whom she did not recognize touched her on her right shoulder. Later she came to recognize her as Rough Touch. This was the administrator of the nursing home. She grabbed Nellie's wrist in a viselike grip and literally pulled her to her feet. Nellie stood still, not knowing what was expected of her. Still holding tightly to Nellie's wrist, the administrator pulled her along. The woman's iron grip gave Nellie no choice but to go with her.

Nellie could not help having an uneasy feeling. They were headed toward the back of the dining room where the kitchen was located, but she did not know why. When they passed through the doorway to the kitchen, Nellie was led to the big double sinks. Nellie was so small that the sinks came up to the middle of her chest. Something was placed over her head and tied behind her back. She lowered her hands to feel the material of this new garment, and knew she was wearing an apron. Next, her hands were shoved down into hot, soapy-slick water, and then into equally hot rinse water. Rough Touch raised Nellie's right hand out of the water and placed it carefully, but firmly on a large stack of plates. After running her sensitive fingers over their surfaces, Nellie knew they were the dirty breakfast dishes, and immediately she understood Hard Touch's intentions.

"Well," Nellie thought, "They want me to wash dishes. Well, that's all right. I like to work. I don't mind this at all."

Nellie knew she was good at washing dishes. Although she had to strain on the tip of her toes to reach the dishes at the bottom of the two deep sinks, it was easy work. It took no real thought on her part, and it made the time go by quickly. That first day, as she did the breakfast dishes, she felt around inside all the cupboards, touching and identifying the different stacks of dinner china that were still in place and quickly learned where everything went. She was proud of herself. When she was finished with the dishes, she was tired but happy. Counting her steps and feeling her way, she left the kitchen and went to her room.

That same day, after she had lunch in the dining room, the administrator came to get her just as she was finishing her dessert. Nellie was led back to the kitchen and again placed in front of the sinks. This time she knew what to expect. With her apron tied in place, her deft touch located the dishes to be washed, and she began the chore. The number of dirty lunch dishes to be washed was less than there had been at breakfast. Nellie got done in record time. The exact same thing happened that evening at dinner. She did the dishes for all three meals that day. She did not get in anyone's way, and she did not bother anybody. Also, she was a really good dishwasher.

This plan worked out so well for the administrator that she gave Nellie the dishwasher job full time. Nellie did not get paid any money and received no time off.

Months passed and Nellie washed dishes after every meal. If she dallied for even a few minutes after finishing her meal, someone was immediately beside her, closing their hand on her wrist, pulling her up out of her chair, and firmly walking her to the kitchen. Nellie learned not to subject herself to the acute embarrassment she felt each time she was unceremoniously led to the sinks. To avoid this, after every meal, as soon as she finished eating, she would get up from the table, and without any visible hesitation, she would walk, all by herself, all the way into the kitchen and take her place at the sinks, ready to work.

Nellie had no way of knowing what kind of financial arrangements her family had made for her when they moved her out of their home and into the first nursing home. She did not know if she had any money of her own, but she knew she had not been given any money for a long time. Now that she was working for the nursing home she wondered if she was going to be paid. When after several weeks no pay was forthcoming, she consoled herself, knowing that she did not have an opportunity to go shopping anyway. She realized that under the circumstances, she really had no use for money. As time went on she reasoned that with the exception of having no one with whom she could communicate, she felt she had everything she needed. She enjoyed her food, she had clean clothes, comfortable shoes, and the personal items she needed. Also, she had her Braille Bible, books, magazines, and other periodicals to read.

There was not a lazy bone in Nellie's body, but after more than a year of doing every dirty dish from every single meal in the nursing home, without a single day off, she could not help feeling used. It was more than past time for some changes to be made.

Then one morning Nellie woke up with a cold. She felt she should have stayed in bed, but instead, she got dressed and went to the dining room for breakfast. While eating breakfast, her throat became even more raw and sore, making it difficult for her to swallow. Her nose began to run. Mostly because of the way she was feeling, she decided that this morning she was going to remain seated in her chair.

She was talking softly to herself, saying, "I am not going to wash any dishes today. I am sick. Let someone else do it."

All of a sudden she felt Hard Touch's hand close firmly around her wrist, but she held her arm taut and did not move out of her chair. The hand continued to pull steadily on her wrist, but she did not budge. Hard Touch went away, but it was not long before Rough Touch stood beside her. Nellie could not help flinching when she felt this hated hand firmly encircle her wrist.

Nellie's voice cracked with emotion, "I am tired of doing dishes all the time. I am sick. I don't want to do dishes today."

The administrator understood Nellie perfectly, but she acted as though she did not. She was furious because this tiny little woman was defying her and, not only that, but the administrator was being embarrassed in front of her staff and the residents! When Nellie felt the hand begin to close even tighter, she violently jerked away and quickly sat on both of her hands. Then she felt two people grab her arms. They roughly yanked her up out of her chair. Nellie did the only thing she could. She screeched with all her might. It was an ear-splitting screech. In all the time Nellie had been there, no one had heard such a sound. The administrator immediately ordered Nellie taken to her room and restrained. In order to get her there, they forced her to walk. It was either walk or lose her footing and be dragged. Nellie screeched the whole way. She was not being physically hurt, but anyone hearing her would have sworn she was being beaten unmercifully. They used bed sheets to tie her in the chair. Nellie's wrists and hands were so small they had to pull the knots very tight to make them secure enough so she could not free herself. Satisfied that she could not get loose, they left her alone. They had not gotten any farther than the door to her room when she abruptly stopped screeching. It was as if someone had thrown a switch and turned her off. Nellie could not help herself; she was grinning.

"There, now." She said aloud to no one in particular. "I guess I'm not going to wash any dishes today."

The defiance and tantrum had worked up to a point. But now she was tied to a chair. Her throat hurt, and she could not reach her runny nose to wipe it. Helplessly tied up, she was miserable.

As far as she could tell, no one came near her all that morning. She became hungry and knew she was being left there through the lunch hour. For the first time, she became concerned about what she had done and what they had, in turn, done to her. She had not known anything about restraints or the nursing home's use of them. She was in danger of soiling herself for need of the bathroom. She was battling hysteria, but knew if she moved, she would lose control of her emotions and her bodily functions. The longer she sat there, the angrier she became.

It was mid afternoon when someone came and touched her. She promptly stood up once the sheets were untied. Because her legs were cramped, she was wobbly as she hurried to the bathroom. After relieving herself, she cleaned her face and blew her nose. And then she gulped down water to quench her thirst.

No one stopped her. No one touched her. When she returned to her room, she was alone. Not knowing what else to do, she stayed where she was. When dinnertime arrived, no one came to get her. She had not eaten since breakfast. Her stomach rumbled in protest. Finally she got up and timidly ventured to the dining room and sat at her place. She sat there for a long time, but nothing happened. She had missed dinner. Unsure of herself, and unnerved from having been subjected to restraints, Nellie slowly returned to her room, sat on her bed, and mulled over in her mind what had happened to her as a result of her rebellion.

Finally, Nellie went to bed and waited until she knew it was very late. Then she very resolutely got out of bed and put on her duster and slippers. Moving as silently as a ghost, she made her way to the kitchen. Because she knew where everything was, it was short work to find sliced bread in the cupboard and butter in the large built-in refrigerator. Working quietly, she got a knife and made herself butter sandwiches. Her throat was still very sore, but it felt better as she wolfed down the bread and butter. Then a long drink of water ended her midnight meal.

She neatly put every thing away, leaving no evidence of her raid on the kitchen. She returned to her room.

Nellie was very angry. She felt that she had been treated very unjustly. The long months she had spent washing dishes for everyone in the nursing home obviously had meant nothing to them. All of her hard work had been taken for granted. She felt the pride she had taken in her work was justified because she knew she had done a good job. The more she thought about it, the more she seethed. The administrator and staff had not shown the least bit of concern or compassion for her. Instead, they had deliberately deprived her of water to drink while she was tied up and of any food to eat for over eighteen hours. The worst thing about all of this was not being able to wipe or blow her nose, and the hysteria she had felt when she could not free herself to go to the bathroom. To her, that alone was unforgivable.

She sat on the side of her bed and grew angrier. About 1:00 A.M., she stood up, stretched herself tall, and determinedly squared her shoulders. She held her chin high.

Nellie muttered through her clenched teeth, "O.K., now, I'll make sure that nobody goes to the bathroom."

With a plan firmly in mind, she did not waste any time putting it in motion. She worked quietly and methodically. For the plan to work, everything had to be done before the kitchen crew arrived to prepare breakfast. Gliding noiselessly down the hallway to the storeroom where the linens were stored, she picked up three bed sheets. Beginning with the bathrooms located just off the dining room, she carefully unfolded one of the sheets, took the bottom end of it and, feeling with one hand for the hole in the bottom of the bowl, began to feed it into one of the toilets. It was hard work. She went back to the kitchen and got a table knife. By using this, she was able to force about six inches of the sheet into the hole. Then she flushed the toilet, sending more of the cloth down into the small opening. Tugging as hard as she could, she could not pull it out. Satisfied with her work, she moved on to the next toilet bowl and repeated the process. She used the first three sheets to disable three toilets and then made a trip back to the storeroom for more sheets. Nellie disabled eight toilets before she quit. There were only three functioning bathrooms, including her own, that were left in the nursing home. She went to bed. Very pleased with her efforts, she slept soundly through what was left of the night.

The kitchen crew arrived right on time, at 6:00 A.M., and began preparing breakfast. It was not long before they discovered the first sabotaged toilet. A quick inspection of all the nursing home bathroom facilities revealed the extent of the vandalism.

They contacted the administrator, and she immediately summoned the maintenance staff and a plumber. Now that a remedy was underway to take care of the problem, the administrator turned her mind to the perpetrator of the vandalism. Her first thought was that Nellie could be the culprit.

The Administrator was furious. She was determined to move Nellie to another nursing home that same day. She went at once to her office and consulted Nellie's case file. According to the admitting paperwork, Nellie was completely in the care of the nursing home, and at "Hard Touch's" mercy. She could do whatever she liked with her. This was good. The placement she had in mind would not put up with any of her nonsense. They would deal with Nellie!

The administrator placed one phone call to the Massillon State Hospital, made the necessary arrangements to have her committed, and with this act she effectively washed her hands of further responsibility for Nellie's care.

As soon as she hung up the phone, she ordered two staff people to get Nellie ready to leave as soon as possible. Nellie was still sleeping when they came into her room. The two did not wake her right away, thinking they would allow her to sleep until they had her all packed up and ready to move. However, the administrator was right behind them. She gave Nellie a violent shake, rudely waking her.

Alarmed, Nellie immediately sat up on the side of the bed. Without a pause, her feet were quickly shoved into house slippers, and her arms were firmly placed, one at a time, into a housecoat. Nellie did not say a word. Awakened out of a sound sleep and still groggy, she allowed them to do with her whatever they pleased. The two attendants took a firm hold on both of her arms and began walking her out of her room toward the dining hall.

Nellie willingly went along, keeping pace with them and trying to count her steps. When she realized that she had been ushered too far and knew that she had passed the dining room, Nellie put her brakes on, stopping abruptly. The attendants were surprised at how strong she was. It took all their strength to force her to move down the hall and out the door. When she felt the fresh air, immediately she knew she had been taken outside.

In a panic she asked herself, "Where outside am I going, and for what reason?"

Fearing some kind of reprisal for her misdeeds of the night before, by now she was terribly frightened. She began to struggle and screech. Lifting her off the ground, the two attendants managed to move her down the walkway and to the car that was waiting to transport her. Being careful not to hurt her, they pressed her body tightly against the side of the car and released one hand so she could feel the opened car door. She knew right away that they wanted her to get into the back seat of the car.

Instantly, she realized that she was being moved, and assumed that she was being moved to another nursing home. She stopped struggling immediately, dutifully climbed into the car's back seat, and did not make another sound.

Nellie was anxious. Where was she being moved to this time? It had been over a year since she had been moved. She wondered what it would be like but again, no one communicated with her.

In spite of her fears the long trip and the pleasant motion of the car calmed her down. Maybe they had finally realized that she was sick with a cold. She comforted herself with the thought that perhaps they were taking her to see the doctor. Maybe the doctor would need a blood test. Maybe she would get a shot for her cold.

Nellie felt the car come to a stop. She felt the door open. A strong man's hand clasped her hand. He gave her time to swing herself around and get her feet planted on the ground. He helped her to her feet and led her up the stairs and into a reception room.

Her new attendant led her to a chair and placed her hands on a metal arm. Nellie seated herself. She sat there for a long time. But no doctor came to examine her. Feeling around the chair, she found it had wheels. Nellie knew what that meant. She was seated in a wheelchair.

Puzzled, she said aloud, "This must be a hospital. Why would I be in a hospital?"

When someone did finally come for her, again she felt the strong man's hands close around one of her ankles. Her feet were placed on a platform of the wheelchair near the floor. She felt wind on her face and knew she was being pushed rapidly down a long hall. It worried her not to be able to count her steps. How would she know how to get back?

The wheelchair stopped. A few minutes later she was pushed forward. She felt a lift and knew she was on an elevator. When the elevator stopped, the attendant kept pushing her forward down another corridor. Then she felt the vibration of a heavy door slamming. With a sinking feeling she realized she was right; this was not a nursing home. She was in some kind of a hospital.

As usual, no one on the staff could fingerspell. Therefore, no one told her exactly where she was, or why she was there. The attendant left her without even a pat on the shoulder.

As Nellie sat there wondering who would come and introduce her to her new surroundings, she began to think. She was not sure how she felt about the dire consequences that had resulted from her defiance of the administrator. She never wanted to risk being restrained again. As she faced these new surroundings there was a sinking feeling in the pit of her stomach, and she felt unnerved to the core. A terrifying sense of powerlessness washed over her anew.

Nellie's good sense came to her rescue. She stilled the panic she felt by remembering that Jesus was with her no matter where she was. And God would see her through this new challenge.

The days passed slowly at first as Nellie adjusted to life in this new environment. She was now living in completely new and unfamiliar surroundings and this caused her to feel disoriented. She also lost a great deal of her self-confidence. She resolved to keep to herself, and not cause any trouble. And, above all, she would not throw any more tantrums.

It took a few days in her new placement for Nellie to realize that she was sharing a limited amount of space with a great number of people. When she finally received her personal belongings, there was no place to put any of them except under her bed. She had no way of knowing that she was sharing a large warehouse-like ward that had space for enough beds to house sixty women patients.

After her frightening and infuriating experience with restraints, she was now afraid to resist rough people. She could not help flinching whenever someone's hand closed on her wrist. Her nightmares about being alone and lost now grew to include bad dreams about restraints, and of heavy hands closing tightly around her wrist, or of being forcibly led into the unknown. With no one available who could communicate with her, she was left alone with her thoughts, feelings, and nightmares.

However, as time wore on, she became accustomed to the daily routine on her ward at the state hospital. Her strong faith and dependence on God saw her through the bad times. In order to keep herself sane and mentally alert, she learned to withdraw deep into her mind. Again, she began to study her Braille Bible. She decided she would take one day at a time, do her best, and pray to God. She was comforted in the knowledge that Jesus would be with her. He would not abandon her. She left everything in His hands.

Nellie was fifty-two years old when, without any Probate Court involvement, she was admitted to the Massillon State Mental Hospital as an insane person. For more than eighteen years, no one on the hospital staff communicated with her. Perhaps the professionals responsible for her care did not even know they could communicate with Nellie by finger spelling into her hands.

And for eighteen years, Nellie had no contact with the outside world. No contact with anyone from her family. No visitors. She communicated with no one. She did not know where she was or why. As the long years of forced confinement passed, the silence that surrounded her only grew deeper.

=   =   =

Carrie Dixon, deaf volunteer at Massillon State Hospital, discovered Nellie in 1975.
Courtesy of Karen Turner, Akron

Chapter Three

THE SILENCE IS BROKEN

Spring came early in 1975, but without any outdoor privileges, or even the ability to look out the window and see the grounds below, Nellie knew nothing about the weather. She could not have known that outside the monolithic red brick walls of her confinement the flowers and trees were in full blossom. She could not have known that the song of birds filled the air.

She also could not have known that there was a kind of springtime in the social consciousness of America. The movie, <u>One Flew Over The Cuckoo's Nest</u> had just been released. It was the most recent of a good number of movies that dramatized the inhumane conditions of the nation's mental hospital system. A growing number of documentaries shown at colleges, universities, and on public television, questioned what these hospitals called their therapeutic programs. A new movement began to emerge in many communities across the nation. Largely led by social workers and community activists, it was a movement to have as many mental hospital patients as possible released from these institutions.

Among such leaders there was a growing consensus that, with proper support, many of them could live free and productive lives in the community. Those who were targeted first for release were people like Nellie, who had been committed to the mental hospital system not because they were mentally ill, but because they were physically disabled.

One sunny spring day a young nurse who had worked at the Massillon State Hospital took a job at the Apple Creek State Institute, located near Wooster, Ohio. On her first day of work she met a budding young employee named Jim Schneck. She knew nothing about Jim's background and his work with the deaf and deaf/blind. Jim was actively working for the release from Apple Creek of a deaf/blind man, named Clyde. Clyde was in his fifties and had lived in the institution most of his life. He was not mentally retarded, but was labeled as such. Jim was teaching Braille to Clyde in preparation for his release and was eager to help other institutionalized deaf or deaf/blind people win their freedom and live independently in the community.

Although she did not know Jim's background, the young nurse was fascinated as she observed his interaction with Clyde. He was finger spelling into Clyde's hands. She was amazed that he could actually carry on a lively conversation with him.

The next day during their lunch break the young nurse approached Jim. She told him that while working at Massillon State Hospital, she had been responsible for providing care for several deaf and blind adults. However, no one on the staff seemed able to communicate with them in any meaningful way.

Jim was intrigued by her story. He took it upon himself to contact the Social Services Department of the State Hospital. He asked if he could visit their blind and deaf residents or at least communicate with them in Braille through the mail. The social worker he spoke with stated that, to the knowledge of the social service staff, there were no deaf and blind residents at the institution.

Not one to be put off by the cold denial, Jim decided to pursue the matter further. He called a good friend named Carrie Dixon. Over the past few years, he and Carrie had brought about the release of several deaf inmates from other mental health institutions in Northeast Ohio. He hoped that she would be his special ally to help him identify the deaf and blind patients at Massillon State Mental Hospital.

Carrie was the perfect choice. She was deaf. Her husband was also deaf. They had one daughter who was deaf, and three daughters who were hearing.

Carrie was fluent in American Sign Language. She carried a small note pad and pencil and used that as a means of communication with hearing people. She had been active in helping deaf persons for many years and was well known within the deaf community in the Akron and Canton area. For more than ten years, she had served as a regular volunteer, working with the deaf at the Massillon State Hospital. However, in spite of her work with the institution, she was unaware of any deaf and blind residents. As Jim had anticipated, Carrie agreed to look into the matter.

An attractive woman with a fetching smile, Carrie walked with a pronounced bounce in her step; but she was also so gracious and gentle in her manner that she instantly put everyone at ease. In spite of the fact that the social services office had denied that there were any deaf-blind patients, Carrie was so well known by the rest of the hospital staff, and so pleasant in dealing with them, that she had little trouble in getting them to tell her what they knew. Her investigation indeed confirmed that at least four patients who were both deaf and blind lived in the facility.

When Carrie learned the truth, she was angry. Rather than betray her feelings, she left the building immediately.

As she drove home she grew more upset, saying to herself, "Does the hospital administration really not know that they have deaf/blind residents? Are they being uncooperative? Either way, this situation is intolerable!"

Carrie's thoughts continued to spin: "If the Social Service Department is not aware of the existence of these deaf/blind residents, then how in the world can they provide appropriate care? And, if they do know about these residents, and are not willing to tell the truth, then most likely they are being defensive! Are they being defensive because they are not providing professional services and trained staff who can communicate with these residents? Either way, it is clear that they don't want anyone looking into this..."

The next day, after her temper had cooled down, Carrie stopped by the social service office and, using the writing pad, told them what she had discovered. This time, the social worker wrote to Carrie that they were merely observing the administration's confidentiality policy. But, because they knew she would respect that confidentiality, they would bend the rules for her.

Then, they provided her with a list of four names of known deaf and blind residents. The social worker wrote to Carrie that according to their records any attempts to communicate with the patients on the list had been unsuccessful.

The social worker wrote on her note pad, "I don't believe that you will be able to get through to these people. You won't be able to have a conversation with any of them. You have helped our deaf patients. You are certainly welcome to try your hand at communicating with the deaf/blind."

Having received the necessary permission of the administration, Carrie waited until she had a free afternoon, took her list of four names, and following the directions she began her search. Walking slowly through the wards, she tried to locate and identify the persons on her list. It was difficult to spot them. She had to pick them out from the rest of the patients who were milling around inside each of the rooms. Her initial search bore bitter fruit. She found three of the four patients, approached each one and attempted to communicate with them by finger spelling into their hands. None of them gave any response.

Continuing her search for the fourth patient, Carrie was angry. She had found three individuals who the institution had claimed did not exist. Obviously, these patients had never been taught any means of communication. By refusing Jim's offer to reach out and teach communication skills to the deaf-blind, the hospital had ignored a priceless opportunity. She made a mental note of the location of each of them and promised herself that she would get back to them later.

The fourth name on her list was Nellie Zimmerman. Carrie easily located the ward in the hospital where Nellie was living. It was a large, open room that housed about sixty women. Carrie used her note pad to question the nurse at the duty station, just outside the room.

She asked, "What kind of patients do you have here?"

The nurse wrote back , "Many of the patients are senile. The rest are mentally or emotionally disturbed."

With obvious uncertainty, Carrie pulled open the heavy door and stepped inside. She entered a great hall. The center of the room was cleared except for a few tables and chairs. People were milling around everywhere. Carrie had a name. But she had no idea what Nellie looked like. Writing on her pad, she asked an aide to introduce her to Nellie.

Writing back, he said, "I'm sorry, but we are supposed to keep busy doing our work. We're not supposed to bother much with the people."

Because of the overcrowded conditions, it was difficult to maneuver among the patients. The residents in the ward were either sitting listlessly, or aimlessly moving about. Some were constantly pacing backward and forward in a slow, shuffling gait. Although Carrie couldn't hear, she could see the lips of many of the patients moving. In most cases they appeared to be talking to themselves rather than talking with each other. She realized that the room probably had a constant undercurrent of sound, a drone, due to the confused mixture of nonstop talking, chanting, laughing, giggling, or singing. The appearance of perpetual motion and meaningless noise in the room gave Carrie the impression of insane chaos.

As Carrie walked slowly through the ward and reached the center of the room, she had an inspiration. She realized that in order to find Nellie, she needed to look for someone who was being perfectly still among all the movement in the busy ward.

She stood still for several minutes and looked around. Then, she noticed a figure seated in the far corner, alone, away from everyone else. The figure was completely covered by a bed sheet. Intuitively, she knew this had to be the person she was looking for.

She thought, "I believe I have found Nellie Zimmerman."

Still, Carrie stared in disbelief. Quickly, she moved to the side of this patient, who was sitting motionless in a high backed arm chair. The bed sheet was draped over her head in a way that concealed her entire body from view. She wondered if there would be any chance of being able to communicate. Would Nellie be unresponsive like the other deaf/blind residents had been?

Slowly and carefully, so as not to startle her, Carrie removed the sheet. Instantly, she took heart. Although the woman appeared motionless, it looked as if she was fidgeting with her hands. Carrie believed that the woman was talking to herself. She believed the woman was spelling out words with her fingers. Perhaps she *could* communicate with her!

Without taking her eyes off the woman, she methodically folded the sheet, and set it aside. Nellie was sitting up straight in the wheelchair with her head tilted to one side ever so slightly. Aware that someone had removed her sheet, she was patiently waiting for that someone to do something to her. She continued to make the motion with her fingers. Looking closely, Carrie saw that the woman was not just fidgeting as she recognized the letters: h-a-l-l-o-w-e-d b-e t-h-y n-a-m-e.

Carrie gasped in awe as she recognized the familiar words of the "Lord's Prayer." Chills ran up and down her spine. She knew that she had found Nellie Zimmerman. She felt that God had sent her as an answer to Nellie's prayers. To Carrie this seemed like a sacred moment. So, she allowed Nellie to finish her prayer before she made contact with her.

Carrie used the time to privately observe this woman. Although her long snow white hair was disheveled from having been under the bed sheet, it was still beautiful. She was pale as a ghost, but she had a flawless complexion. Petite, very thin, she was dressed in a faded hospital gown and worn out house slippers. Her eyes were covered with two tattered, soiled strips of cloth that were loosely wrapped around her head. Carrie gazed in astonishment at the erect, almost regal manner of her posture. Now that she had finished her prayer, her hands were folded in her lap.

When Carrie first approached the sheet-draped figure, she guessed that this patient was totally absent minded, hiding from the world under the bed sheet. But it was obvious that she had been alert with her mind engaged, thinking, praying, or purposefully meditating.

She sensed that this woman possessed a wealth of pride and self-assurance. In sharp contrast with the behavior of the other patients in the chaotic ward, her quiet manner, physical bearing, and graceful demeanor, coupled with the quizzical, questioning tilt of her head spoke of alertness and intelligence.

Carrie thought, "If this woman was cleaned up and dressed up, she would be very attractive!"

Breathless with anticipation, she reached for the woman's hands. Carrie quickly finger spelled into her right hand just one two-letter word. "Hi."

Nellie gave a sharp gasp of surprise. The silence had been broken! She quickly responded with a deep voice, that was raspy from long disuse.

She finger spelled while speaking the words, "Oh! What's happening in the world?"

Nellie seemed visibly shaken. Carrie closely observed her struggle to maintain self-control. Although Nellie tried to present an outward appearance of calm excitement, and the tattered rags that were tied around her head completely hid her eyes, one lone tear rolled down her cheek, betraying her feelings. As more of Nellie's tears appeared, Carrie felt tears come to her own eyes.

Nellie grasped Carrie's left hand and hung on. Carrie was surprised by the strength and passion of her grip. With Nellie holding onto her one hand, Carrie looked around for another chair that she could use to sit in front of Nellie so she could comfortably reach both of her hands to talk to her.

She finger spelled into her hands, "Are you Nellie Zimmerman?" Nellie responded, signing, "Yes!"

Then Carrie began a long and remarkable conversation with a person who had been cut off from the outside world for eighteen years.

First, Nellie asked where she was.

Carrie spelled into her hands, "You are living at the Massillon State Mental Hospital. You have been here eighteen years."

Nellie's frown was visible above the tattered eye coverings. Then she gave a violent shake of her head as though in disbelief.

Carrie didn't want to upset Nellie any further but in order to help her, she did have to ask some pertinent questions.

Carrie bit her lip as she asked Nellie, "Have you had any visitors?"

Nellie responded, both verbally and by signing, "No! You are the first person who has talked or visited with me since I came here."

Carrie asked, "What about your family?"

Nellie declared, "My family is dead. I have not heard from anyone in my family for more than twenty-five years, long before I even came here."

Carrie pressed on, asking Nellie many questions about her childhood, her family, and her placement in the institution. In turn, Nellie wanted to know all about her new visitor. She asked Carrie about her family. When Carrie told Nellie she had grandchildren, she asked if they went to school, their grade levels and what they were studying.

Nellie also asked questions about what was going on in the outside world.

"What year is it? Who is president? Is there peace in the world? "

Carrie carefully answered all of Nellie's questions and made sure Nellie understood everything she spelled into her hands by questioning what she had just said to her. As Nellie talked and listened, her smile was radiant. Carrie could not help feeling sad as she learned about Nellie's life. Many times, Carrie fought back tears as she conducted this intense and lively conversation.

Time passed quickly. Carrie was startled when she felt a touch on her shoulder.

It was the nurse, pointing to her watch and silently mouthing the words, "You have to go now."

Carrie looked around and saw the staff preparing the patients to take their evening meal. She looked at her watch. Carrie could not believe it. She and Nellie had talked for more than four hours!

As Carrie reluctantly stood up to end the visit, she promised Nellie that she would come back to see her again very soon. But Nellie clung to Carrie. It was heartbreaking to see how desperate she was for human contact. Nellie anxiously questioned her. She wanted to know exactly when Carrie would be back.

Carrie spelled into her hand, "I will be back in two days. I will be back in two days. I promise!"

Nellie was still hanging onto her.

So, again, Carrie said, "Do you understand that I will keep this promise? I will be back to see you again in two days."

This time Nellie smiled and vigorously nodded her head, causing the loosely wrapped rags to drop off her eyes. For the first time, Carrie looked into Nellie's sightless eyes.

While still hanging onto Carrie with her left hand, Nellie made a fist with her right hand and bending her hand at the wrist, repeatedly moving the fist up and down, making the sign for "yes."

She continued to sign the word "Yes," repeatedly, to Carrie.

Nellie was so excited that, even though Carrie could not hear her, she also spoke in a loud, husky voice, to reinforce her signing. "Yes, yes!" "Yes, yes!"

Carrie did not cover her again with the sheet, but left it where it lay on the floor by her chair. She did not say anything to the ward staff at that time, but resolved to tell the social services staff about finding Nellie draped with a sheet. She never again wanted to find her so crudely isolated from the rest of the patients.

When Carrie left the ward, she walked quickly down the long hallway. Emotionally overcome and unnerved, she did not want to meet anyone. Finding a small, empty conference room, she stepped inside, walked to a wooden bench along a far wall, knelt down, and sobbed.

She was overwhelmed by the thought that God had sent her to find Nellie *as an answer to Nellie's prayers*. It seemed awesome that God had chosen her to be the one to break Nellie's long years of living in silence. The knowledge that this intelligent woman had been shut away for many years in a virtual prison of darkness and silence was too much to bear. She could not get over the idea that no one on the staff had ever talked with Nellie, or that no one from the outside world, not even family, had visited her since she had been admitted to the hospital.

Carrie could not stop her thoughts, "What happened to Nellie is worse than being sentenced to twenty-five years of solitary confinement! At least prisoners in solitary confinement can see and talk to their guards when they bring them food. It is as if Nellie had been thrown into "the hole" and kept in total darkness and isolation. What had she done to deserve such a cruel fate? How could she have survived such torture for so long? How could she have remained sane? How could she have survived in the midst of all that insanity in the ward?"

It took a while for Carrie to regain her composure.

She comforted herself with the thoughts, "I can't do anything more for Nellie right now. But I will keep my promise to come back and visit her again. Perhaps, some day, I can help get her out of here! Who knows? With God, all things are possible."

Carrie kept her promise to Nellie. Two days later she arrived at the State Hospital, went straight to the Social Services Department and searched through Nellie's file. She was determined to find out as much as she could about Nellie's past and present circumstances. The thin file folder indicated that her case had not demanded much attention through the years. Other than the initial reports regarding her admission, there was not much documented information about Nellie or her family. The case record revealed that Nellie had been committed to the institution at the age of fifty-two. Now she was seventy years old. There was no record of any visitation.

As Carrie made her way to Nellie's ward she wondered if perhaps Nellie's family did not know where she was. If she could only find out some information she would try to contact them. Then maybe Nellie could have another visitor.

Again, she found Nellie sitting in her chair, hiding under her bed sheet. But she noticed that Nellie had already placed another chair in front of her in obvious preparation for Carrie's visit. Carrie removed the sheet as she had done before, took her seat, and quickly finger spelled into her hand.

"Hi Nellie!"

Nellie responded by signing and saying aloud, "Yes! Yes! Yes! Hi Carrie!"

As Carrie had planned, she again asked Nellie about her family. Nellie's fingers exclaimed, "They are dead. I have no family!"

Nellie continued, rapidly finger spelling. "I don't know why I am here! I am not crazy! I don't belong in a mental hospital! I don't want to be here!"

Carrie was taken aback. How could she respond?

She patted Nellie's hand, and then spelled, "I understand what you are saying. Do you need anything right now?"

Nellie ignored Carrie's question. She was sobbing as her hand continued the frantic finger spelling.

"People hit me, steal my food, and slap my face. Please get me out of here!"

In order to calm and reassure her, Carrie gently, but firmly, held both of Nellie's hands for a few moments. She resolved in her heart that she would definitely work to have Nellie released. But Carrie knew that such an endeavor would take a long time and a lot of work. Moreover, it might not be successful. The one thing she was sure of was that she did not want to give Nellie false expectations.

Pressing her letters firmly into Nellie's palm she spelled, "I promise you I will do something about it. Right now there are other things I need to know so I can help you."

Immediately, Nellie regained her composure. She again sat quietly, giving Carrie her full attention.

Carrie spelled, "The first day I was here you were covered by a bed sheet, and you were covered again today. Why?"

Nellie responded, "I feel safer when I am covered by the sheet! When I first came here, people would come around and slap me, pull my hair, or pinch me on the arm. I could not see or hear them coming. So, I learned a long time ago to hide under my bed sheet. I guess when people can't see me they don't come around and bother me so much. It seems to work pretty well!"

Carrie then asked, "Last week you had some pieces of cloth tied round your eyes. I see that you are wearing them again today. Why?"

Nellie answered, "My eyes hurt. I don't know why."

Carrie pressed on. "Has a doctor examined your eyes?"

"I think the nurses are always around me, but, to my knowledge, I have not been seen by a doctor for a long time. When they brought me here, I thought that maybe it was to see a doctor. Did you say this was a hospital?"

In spite of themselves, they both laughed.

When Carrie recovered, she asked. "Is there anything special that you need or want?"

Nellie was quick to reply, "I read Braille! I would like some reading material, current reading material. Also, I would like to make things. It does not matter what. If I had just anything to work with, it would give me something to do."

Carrie asked Nellie about the hobbies she had enjoyed when she lived with her father. It surprised her to learn of all the things she had been able to do before her father's death. Nellie smiled as she recalled those happier times.

For the next two hours the two women talked about crafts, favorite books, and world news. Nellie was particularly interested to learn about the weather and what things looked like outside, the beauty of the spring, and the flowers around Carrie's house.

As Carrie left the ward, she again went into the conference room she had found before. She took time to make careful notes of all that Nellie had told her. This information provided her with the background she needed to form a viable action plan. First, she would take care of Nellie's immediate needs. But her long-term goal would be eventually to win Nellie's release and return her to the outside world.

Immediately, she began to implement her plan of action. Before she left the hospital, she stopped by the Social Services Department to make arrangements for a doctor to examine Nellie's eyes. The staff members were accustomed to Carrie using her writing pad to communicate with them. They quickly wrote back to her, promising to schedule the appointment with the eye doctor as soon as they could.

When Carrie came back to visit Nellie the following week, the eye doctor had already examined her. She learned that when the doctor untied her filthy blindfolds, Nellie tried to tell him something, but he could not understand what she was saying. However, when he had removed the cloths, he discovered that they masked all kinds of dust, dirt, and lint that had built up in her eyes over time. He performed a thorough cleansing. Upon further examination, he found nothing else wrong with her eyes beyond her blindness. His diagnosis was that the reason her eyes hurt and were constantly tearing was because they were trying to cleanse themselves. After his treatment, the tearing stopped immediately. He threw away her dirty blindfolds and sent her back to the ward.

When Carrie entered the ward, she noticed immediately that Nellie was not sitting under the sheet. Neither was she wearing her blindfolds. As she sat down in front of Nellie, she noticed that the tearing had stopped. Nellie had come a long way in just one week!

Carrie asked Nellie about her doctor's visit. Nellie's flying fingers told the story.

She complained, "When the doctor took off my blindfold, I tried to explain that bright light and direct sun hurts my eyes. I tried to speak to him. I tried signing. I tried making gestures and pointing to my eyes and then up toward the ceiling, but he did not put my blindfold back on. He did not respond to me at all."

Then Nellie smiled as she thought some more about the doctor's visit, and continued, "Of course, I don't think he could finger spell like you can, so I guess he could not have talked back to me, anyway. I decided that he just could not understand me. Now they have taken away all of my cloths and I need to get them back. It is so frustrating. You don't know what a blessing it is to actually be able to talk to someone after all of these years."

Carrie was surprised by Nellie's explanation for her strange looking appearance. With regard to hiding under the bed sheet, Carrie realized that Nellie had been quite inventive in learning how to cope with her situation. However, without understanding the reasons for these habits, it was easy to see how the staff would think that she was totally insane. She became even more aware that the best way she could help Nellie was to act as her communication link with the hospital staff. It was clear that if they understood her, she would get much better treatment.

An hour later, at the conclusion of her visit with Nellie, Carrie wrote notes to both the aide and the nurse who was on duty, explaining why Nellie wore her blindfold. From that time forward, the hospital staff provided Nellie with a supply of clean cloths to put over her eyes.

After Carrie's first visit with Nellie, she met with Jim and reported to him that she had found four blind/deaf residents, but had only been able to communicate with one of them. She described her visit with Nellie. Jim was excited! He wanted to meet Nellie as soon as it could be arranged. Although she had not told Nellie anything about Jim, Carrie put his name on Nellie's visitor list as a "friend" and made a notation after his name that he could visit at any time.

Before her fourth visit to Nellie, she arranged a date and time that was convenient for Jim to accompany her. She announced her arrival to Nellie by touching her on the arm and reaching for her hands.

She spelled into her palms, "Hi! I have someone with me whom I want you to meet. His name is Jim Schneck."

Nellie lifted her chin, raised her eyebrows, and in her husky voice, spoke aloud and finger spelled at the same time, "Hello."

Then with a slight turn of her head, she continued to spell, "Hello Jim. Who are you? Are you deaf?"

While Carrie found another chair for Jim, she turned Nellie over to him. He reached for Nellie's hands and began to finger spell into them.

"I am a friend of Carrie's. I wanted to meet you. No, I am not deaf, but I work with deaf children and youth. I also work with young people who are both blind and deaf."

Nellie was enthralled. She quickly spelled, "Will you come to see me, too, like Carrie does?"

Jim responded, "Yes, I will. Every chance I get."

Carrie proceeded to line up their two chairs with Nellie's. Then, with Nellie positioned in the middle, they each took hold of one of her hands. Together, they conducted a lively three-way conversation.

Nellie was in her best form. She kept up with the conversation. She had something to say about every topic they discussed. She offered her opinion with no hesitation. Jim was amazed. He knew that she was seventy years old and had been locked away from the outside world for eighteen years, but she was as lively and witty as someone half her age.

The three of them continued to talk, joke, and laugh with each other until Jim and Carrie were dismayed by the lateness of the hour. They had to leave, but promised to return.

Nellie was just as smitten with Jim as he was with her. In her prayers, she thanked Jesus for bringing both Carrie and Jim into her life. Not since she lost her father had Nellie felt such happiness.

On the way home, Carrie drove with one hand on the wheel,

while she signed to Jim with her free hand. Carrie told Jim everything she had learned about Nellie's life and the condition in which she had found her. Appalled, he vowed that he would not rest until he and Carrie had won her release. He also promised that in the meantime, he would call upon Nellie as often as he could.

Carrie continued to visit with Nellie two times a week. She kept Jim informed of her progress. At the same time she contacted agencies such as the Society for the Prevention of Blindness and asked them to supply suitable handcrafts for her. Within a few weeks Nellie received a variety of craft kits. She was overjoyed, and would sit very still for a long time just exploring their contents, feeling the textures, imagining the colors, and inhaling the crisp newness of everything she touched. Nellie proved experienced and skillful in making such items as sachet pillows, and woven potholders. Carrie also contacted the National Federation for the Blind, The American Council for the Blind and other service agencies to arrange for Nellie to receive new Braille books and magazines.

By the end of May, with all her new acquisitions, Nellie needed a special place to keep her Braille books and other reading material. She also needed a space where she could work on her crafts without being bothered or having inmates take her things. Ordinarily, the hospital did not provide any private space to any of their residents. However, mostly because of Carrie's intervention, the administration made an exception to this rule and provided her with access to a small storage room for her own use. Carrie was very pleased. With her help, Nellie had gone from a person who was completely ignored, to someone who received special consideration and privileges.

One day in early June, Carrie noticed that Nellie's old Braille Bible was much dog-eared and tattered from its continuous use. She thought that the large, heavy volumes were also quite cumbersome. She did not realize that Nellie's father had given the Bible to her many years ago, and that it was her most cherished possession. So without discussing the matter with Nellie, Carrie ordered her a new one. When it was delivered to the State Hospital, a staff member placed the new Bible in Nellie's private storage room and, without indicating what she was doing, removed Nellie's cherished old Bible.

Nellie was taken by surprise. Her old familiar Bible had disappeared. In its place was a new one. With mixed emotions, she examined it carefully. Instead of being bound in six large sections, it was formatted to make it more easily managed. Each volume consisted of only one to three books of the Bible.

When Carrie came to visit the next day, Nellie was upset with her. She was upset about losing her old Bible. But even more, she was upset that Carrie had not discussed the matter with her. But just being able to tell Carrie about her old Bible and to talk about her father made Nellie feel better. Carrie was amazed at how quickly her new friend relaxed and was ready to forgive her.

The next time Carrie visited, Nellie couldn't wait to tell her about how wonderful the new Bible was. She had explored the whole thing.

She quickly finger spelled to Carrie, "My new Bible is remarkable. It has a wonderful Concordance and even a Bible Encyclopedia! I can do real research. I can look up specific words, people, customs, and beliefs. I gave my new Bible a name! I call it my 'in pieces' Bible."

Again, Carrie was impressed by how adaptable Nellie was.

She thought to herself, "How many seventy year old women could get over losing a family Bible which they had owned for over fifty years, and in less than one week find something good to say about the new one?"

Having witnessed how well Nellie had adapted to all the recent changes, Carrie began to believe that with the proper support, Nellie could do quite well in adjusting to life in the community. That night she had a dream in which she saw Nellie walking down Main Street. Walking free!

Carrie seldom remembered her dreams, but when she awoke she remembered this one. She resolved again to work toward having Nellie released from the institution. However, Carrie kept her long-range plans for negotiating Nellie's release to herself. She did not want to risk disappointing Nellie any further than life already had.

After visiting Nellie in the ward the next day, Carrie stopped by the Social Services Department to inquire about what would be required for Nellie to be released.

The social worker on duty read Carrie's note, and immediately wrote her response to the question:

"We have no intention of ever releasing her."

"Why?"

"She is too handicapped! There is no point in even discussing your idea."

Carrie was infuriated! To hide her feelings, she left the office immediately. She decided to go to the Chapel in order to compose herself. It was quite a distance from Nellie's building to the Chapel. As she walked swiftly away, she was too engrossed in her angry thoughts to notice her surroundings. For the first time ever, the beauty of the old gothic building was lost on her.

Carrie was muttering, silently, under her breath, "Nellie is not insane! She does not belong in this insane asylum. I know exactly how you have cared for her in here. I know how you have completely ignored her. And now you want to tell me that this is the best place for Nellie to live. God forbid! When you said you did not have any deaf/blind residents here, I did not take 'No' for an answer. And now that I know the truth, I am not going to take 'No' for an answer about having her released."

By this time, Carrie had reached the Chapel. She opened the heavy door and slipped inside the cool, dark sanctuary. She slid into a pew and bowed her head.

She took a deep, quivering breath, silently praying, "Lord help me! I can't do this alone!"

Instantly, a voice in the back of her mind said, "Call Jim."

Carrie rejoiced. "Thank you, Lord."

Jim had also been calling on Nellie. But while Carrie had concentrated on doing practical things to improve Nellie's day-to-day life in the institution, Jim had focused his attention on preparing the way for Nellie's release. Now Carrie realized that if the institution was going to resist every effort they made to win her freedom, they would have to combine their forces. By working together they would win.

Jim and Carrie decided to meet regularly. They agreed that the first step was to begin to recruit others who, upon hearing Nellie's story, would also be interested in securing her release.

Carrie signed, "I feel that we should not tell Nellie about our plans until we know that they are going to work out. The administration of the Massillon State Hospital can be very stubborn. If they put all of their efforts into resisting us, we could be in for a long fight. I don't want to raise false hopes in her."

Jim signed back, "I want to tell Nellie now. I feel that she needs all the hope we can give her. She needs to know what we are doing and that, sooner or later, she will be free!"

Carrie finally agreed that some hope was better than no hope!

From that time on the two often held a planning meeting the night before their scheduled visit with Nellie. Then together, in a three-way conversation, they had a great time telling her about their plans. Nellie was vitally interested in everything they did, and relished the individual attention.

However, before Carrie could complete her plans for Nellie, a tragic accident took her life. It also took the life of her husband and one of her little granddaughters.

One evening, on her way home, she had stopped to pick up her granddaughter so the child could spend the night with her. On her arrival home, she parked her car in the attached garage and, unaware that the motor was still running, closed the garage door and went into her house. That night, all three of them went to bed and never woke up. The brief police investigation that followed the three deaths reported that carbon monoxide from the still idling motor had seeped from the garage into the house and killed them.

Their deaths were a devastating loss to their family, to their many friends, their church, the deaf community, and to Nellie.

=   =   =

Chapter Four

RESCUED

The day after Carrie's body was found, someone from the family called to tell Jim about the funeral arrangements. When he heard the news, his hand went numb. He dropped the phone. Methodically, he picked it up. He was talking and listening, but it felt as if he could not hear. Jim hung up the phone and his whole body went numb. He could not believe what he had been told; it was too horrible, too weird.

The only words that came to the lips of this man of deep faith were, "Why? Oh God! Why?"

Suddenly, he thought, "What is going to happen to Nellie?"

There was a sinking feeling in the pit of his stomach. He had depended on Carrie. Now Carrie was dead. What would he do without her?

Then a more horrible thought crossed his mind, "I am the one who will have to tell Nellie."

He flinched with dread.

Several days passed before Jim could bring himself to visit Nellie. It went against his nature to miss his regular appointment with her. He knew that he was the only one who could and would do it, but he hated to be the one to tell her the news. So he procrastinated.

When Jim finally entered the ward, he found Nellie dressed and seated in her chair as if she were expecting his visit. He approached her chair, touched her on the shoulder to let her know that he was there. Immediately her face lit up. She put her hand on his to identify her visitor.

She laughed and said, " Jim! I knew you would come today. Is Carrie here, too?"

He didn't know any way to soften the blow.

He spelled into her hands, "Carrie is dead."

Without realizing it, Jim pressed down extra hard as he spelled the words into her palms, his fingers explaining the circumstances of the tragedy. A long silence followed. It was several minutes before Nellie absorbed the full impact of this information. Jim observed her expression change from bewilderment, to denial, to sorrow. She was subdued and spoke little throughout the remainder of his visit. When he got to his feet to leave, Nellie stood up with him.

In an effort to comfort Jim, she said, "Carrie is in God's house. So why should we grieve?"

Touched by her words of faith, he finger spelled a prayer into her hands, gave her a hug and told her that he would be back in a few days.

As Jim left, he felt a heavy burden lifted from his shoulders. The unpleasant duty had been discharged. Nellie had been upset, but she had been quiet. She had been less emotional than he had feared.

But as soon as Jim left, Nellie collapsed back into her chair, dissolving into tears. She could not hold back her grief. Tears kept coming as she remembered Carrie. How Carrie had been the answer to her prayer. How Carrie had broken the silence. How she had kept her promises to visit her. How Carrie had brought her crafts and books, even her new Braille Bible.

Fresh tears rolled down her cheeks as she thought, "Carrie has been more than a helper. She was my friend. God sent her to me."

Although she had not stopped to think about it before, Nellie now realized that she loved Carrie as much as she had loved her first governess. They had talked. They had laughed. They had hoped and dreamed together. As the routine of that long day ended, a sinking feeling of finality overwhelmed Nellie.

"I will never ever again be able to look forward to Carrie's coming. My days will be long and silent. She is gone. No one will ever take her place. "

She comforted herself with thoughts about her other good friend, Jim. She spoke softly to herself.

"Just as God sent Carrie to me, so He has sent Jim."

In her mind she went over the conversations she and Jim had shared during the past few weeks, how he had spoken about her release and kept her informed about his efforts.

Whispering softly, she said, "Carrie gave me help, but Jim gave me hope!"

Never before had she completely trusted anyone except her father; but now she thought, "I have Jim!"

Her spirit began to revive as she thought about these things. She got out her Braille Bible and traced with her fingers the familiar verses of Psalm 23. When she had finished, she went back and read again, "Yea, though I walk through the valley of the shadow of death, I shall fear no evil, for Thou art with me." As she read these words, a feeling of peace washed over her from head to toe, a peace in the knowledge that though Carrie was no longer with her, God was with her still. As she wearily climbed into bed, with deep emotion, Nellie silently offered two fervent prayers, one for Carrie and one for Jim.

While she voiced her prayer of gratitude to Jesus for sending Jim to her, and for his precious friendship, Nellie's love affair with Jim began.

From the time of Carrie's death, Jim was always there for Nellie. As tragic and unexpected as Carrie's death was, it served to make Jim even more determined to set Nellie free. He realized that Carrie had carried the primary responsibility for visiting with Nellie. While she had worked to improve Nellie's situation within the State Hospital, he had been busy trying to get her out of the institution. Now he had to shoulder the full burden of both befriending Nellie and organizing for her release.

It was not in Jim's character to dilly-dally. Handsome and charismatic, with shining blonde hair neatly styled in a medium length "hippie" cut, he possessed a winning smile. His warm and pleasing personality drew people to him and to his causes.

Jim lived his life according to Mark Twain's famous admonition, "Do not look at the world with your hands in your pockets. Reach out and touch it."

Jim was a devout Christian; he had given his life to Jesus as a young teenager. He carried his strong faith forward into his early adult years, convinced that God had led him to work with multiple-handicapped people He felt that God's grace was leading him onward as he worked on Nellie's behalf. If ever there was an epitome of a knight in shining armor, dashing to the rescue, Jim Schneck was it.

He had a sense of urgency about Nellie's case. She was not a young damsel in distress; she was seventy years old. He felt that she was running out of time. It did not help that she was locked away, not only in an institution that was her prison, but also behind some eighteen years of paperwork within a die-hard bureaucratic system. Sometimes he felt that both the paperwork and the "system" had been devilishly created just to discourage him. But Jim Schneck was not about to quit!

He began to develop an action plan. He knew that prior to her release, he would have to make specific arrangements, including appropriate shelter care housing, adequate financial support, and transportation to and from medical appointments, church, and other social events. Also, he knew that she would need to have a companion who could communicate with her and for her, whenever she went outside, into the community.

Before Carrie's death, Jim had already formed a small support group to help him put together the details of his plan. The group had decided that it would be best for Nellie if she could be placed in a group home with a live-in social service staff. They had agreed that in order for Nellie to attend special events, they would have to recruit several on-call volunteers. Everyone understood that the greatest difficulty with Nellie's situation was basic communication. The companion and the volunteers would need to be able to finger spell.

Now that Carrie was gone, Jim's first step was to meet personally with the hospital's social service staff. He hoped to enlist their input and their help to further develop his plan. But his overture was immediately rejected. Just as they had said to Carrie, he was told in no uncertain terms that they had no intention of releasing Nellie.

Jim was not really upset. He half expected his proposal to be met with stiff opposition. From his point of view, this stance meant that the State Hospital, by definition, had become his enemy.

While continuing his studies at Akron University, and regularly visiting Nellie at the hospital, Jim also held regular community organizing meetings with anyone who was interested in Nellie's case. Many of them were members of the deaf community. The group became known as the "Nellie Zimmerman Volunteers."

Jim felt that the next step was to work within the system. He decided to seek the support of many different government officials, elected and appointed. He met with Ohio legislators, Federal representatives, local and regional public officials, and private organizations to win support in his fight with the hospital.

They all appeared sympathetic, but none would get personally involved or help in any way.

Jim was particularly offended by the response of one Congressman who said, "I'm sorry! But already the taxpayers' burden for maintaining patients at state mental institutions is too high. We simply don't have enough money to house, support and provide special services for all of those residents, just so that they can live in the community. There is no way that I can justify selecting any one patient for special treatment. Especially one who is seventy-one years old!"

It burned Jim's ears to hear such calloused words about the

woman he had grown to love. But what made him even angrier was the realization that, even though they were polite and ingratiating, all the politicians and state officials were giving him the same answer. None of them had agreed to get involved in Jim's fight with the hospital.

At the same time, Jim reached out to a wide variety of community groups and government agencies in order to enlist their support for Nellie's cause. His goal was to obtain for Nellie every known financial, social, medical, vocational, and educational resource that he could find. First, Jim contacted the Akron and Canton Deaf Clubs, and the Community Services for the Deaf. He discovered anew that there were very few services available for the deaf. However, he again learned that there was a wealth of services available for the blind. He lost no time in making good use of their resources.

Jim was forced to look elsewhere for support to promote her right to independent living. He approached many public and private agencies that had been created to provide educational opportunities for all blind and multi-handicapped people and asked them for help on Nellie's behalf. Most notably among them was the Bureau of Vocational Rehabilitation of Ohio that had a prestigious reputation for being advocates for handicapped people.

He was dismayed when he was told by an official, "We only take on cases in which those who are blind can be prepared and trained for employment. With Nellie's dual handicap of blindness and deafness she is neither trainable nor employable. I'm sorry, but we cannot get involved in this case."

Still hopeful, Jim approached another Bureau of Vocational Rehabilitation official who responded, "We only get involved in cases where the client has good prospects for a lifetime of gainful employment. Nellie is already seventy-one years old. Past normal retirement age! Obviously, this case is beyond our mandate. There is nothing we can do under our guidelines except to provide Braille reading materials and handcrafts for her."

It was clear to Jim that BVR would do nothing to help him in his fight with the State Hospital, or with making plans for how she would live after her release.

Contacting all of these people and waiting for their responses took a great deal of time. He did not mind investing his time in trying to "work the system," but all the negative responses were hard to tolerate.

All of the work he did on Nellie's behalf was done on his own time. All the costs involved were borne by him alone. Still studying at Akron University, and taking time to visit Nellie, there were times when he felt as if he was burning the candle at both ends.

Jim's personal level of frustration with the situation came to a head. It seemed that no matter how hard he tried, he did not get anywhere by going through the "proper" channels. Finally he decided to take a different approach. He would go public. He would spread the word about Nellie's story and the story of his struggle with the State Hospital.

The next Sunday, after church, Jim discussed his decision with the "Nellie Volunteers." The idea was eagerly embraced. They agreed that the first goal was to stir up public opinion against the State Hospital and to put enough pressure on the institution to force them to agree to Nellie's release. A second objective was to enlist more non-deaf community support for Nellie after her release. Everyone agreed that for her to live successfully outside the institution, she would need funds, resources and more volunteers. As a result of their encouragement, Jim decided to speak to as many groups and community organizations as possible.

At this time, Jim was a student at the University of Akron in Special Education. He worried that his grades would suffer, since he spent more and more time fighting for Nellie. Would he even be able to complete his education as planned?

Jim decided to turn the matter over to God. It was too late to turn back now!

Soon he reached out to a variety of local, state, and national organizations; as a result, many more groups came forward and offered to help with Jim's fight. They included:

The Akron University Law School; The Akron University Advocacy Board for the Deaf; The Akron Chapter, National Fraternal Society for the Deaf (NFSD); The Akron Lions Club; and the Akron and Canton Pilot Clubs of America. He even reached out to the International Christian Braille Mission, located in the Boulevard Church of Christ, in Charleston, West Virginia. Public interest grew.

In addition to appealing for basic volunteer services, Jim also appealed to these groups for pledges of funds to provide for Nellie's care when she was released. He was particularly grateful for the offer of free legal service by the University of Akron Law School.

The majority of the "Nellie Volunteers" were members of the Christian Fellowship Deaf Church. Jim kept them and the other Volunteers informed of all new developments.

As his community organizing efforts began to gain momentum, Jim decided to publish a regular newsletter to keep all these organizations and interested individuals informed of his progress. It was also produced in large print and Braille for his many visually impaired and blind readers.

Meanwhile, following his friend's death, Jim picked up Carrie's mantle of personal care for Nellie. He spent hours visiting with her. He acted as her friend, as her advocate with the State Hospital, and as her steadfast link to the outside world. He was convinced that hope would give her the strength she needed to endure the long journey to her freedom. Therefore, he made it a point during every visit to keep Nellie informed about what was happening in her case.

Jim discussed with Nellie all the details of his community organizing efforts, and included her in planning the contents of his newsletter. He wanted her to know the details of the plan for her independent living, about their search for adequate housing, and for financial support. Nellie was especially interested in learning the names of the people who had volunteered to help her after her release. They concluded each of their visits with a prayer and a hug.

Jim did make visits by appointment, but often they were unscheduled. Whenever her friend had some important news, much to her delight, his enthusiasm would prompt him just to "show up".

Nellie loved this warm and caring young man who had so miraculously come into her life. Like a teenager in love, she now gave a lot of thought to her personal appearance. She began hours early to get ready for a scheduled visit from Jim. The only dress she owned was the one she wore the day she was admitted. She felt she could not possibly wear that! Nellie puttered around and fretted to herself.

"Is my hospital gown clean? Are my house shoes "fitting" to wear? Is my hair combed all right? Should I wear it in a bun or loose around my shoulders?"

These were thoughts that she had not had in years! Even if no visit was scheduled, she spent the better part of her day in anxious anticipation. Jim was so unpredictable she felt she had to worry about how she looked all the time. Just as Carrie had surmised when she first met her, Jim also was aware that, cleaned up, Nellie was quite attractive.

One day Nellie asked Jim, "What time is it?"

Her fingers did not stop talking long enough for him to answer. "What day is it? What month is it? What year is it?"

Jim was amazed. These were questions she had never asked him before. But they showed that Nellie was becoming time conscious.

He realized that Nellie had no way to keep track of time. He also realized that since she was blind, no ordinary watch would be of any use to her. Her tiny wrist was too small for a large-face lady's watch. So one day Jim brought her a large Braille pocket watch. The watch had a push-button to open the lid. With her sensitive fingers, she felt the hands. She identified the hour hand and minute hand. She felt the raised marks that corresponded to the numbers. A grin spread across her face. For the first time in her life, she was able to determine what time of day it was.

Jim also brought a large stainless steel "dog collar" chain so that she could wear the watch like a pendent around her neck. The chain was long enough for her to comfortably hold the watch in her hands while seated in her wheel chair. Delighted with her new treasure, she found herself checking the time regularly.

Before she met Carrie and Jim, Nellie had resigned herself to spending the rest of her life locked away, and had seen no reason to notice the passing of time. Now that she had hope of being released, time crept by even more slowly. She was careful that no one saw just how impatient she was. Jim thought that Nellie was the most patient appearing, impatient person he had ever met..

Once Jim had become a serious advocate for Nellie at the State Hospital life became more bearable. She was checked on daily. Now that her meals were monitored, no one stole food off her plate, and she began to gain weight. Nellie was amazed at the extra attention she received. She was allowed to take a bath every day, and was given her own toiletries.

Several months passed and the State Hospital remained unmoved, adamant that Nellie would not be released. The administration stated that due to their legal liability and financial issues, Nellie could not be placed beyond their control. Jim wrote articles for church newspapers, and other organizational newsletters. The human-interest appeal that surrounded Nellie's case and the drama being played out in Massillon between Jim and the entrenched State Mental Hospital became a well-known topic. Nellie had a huge following of supporters throughout Ohio, West Virginia, eastern Pennsylvania, and western New York State. Petitions for her release were drawn up and signed by the members of several civic organizations and church groups. When the National Fraternal Society for the Deaf became involved, interest in Nellie's case by the deaf community became national in scope.

Time was passing. 1975 quickly turned into 1976, and Nellie was still living at the State Mental Hospital. Jim was always one to have more than one iron in the fire. While he was diligently working on Nellie's case, he was also busy trying to establish a group home in Massillon. It was to be a unique residential facility for young deaf and deaf/blind boys. Its purpose was to train these youth for independent living in the community. Soon this plan attracted regional attention and national recognition.

Mike Smith, a vision-impaired young man who lived in West Virginia, was interested in this new concept for providing community-based care for blind, and deaf/blind youth. He contacted Jim for more information about this comprehensive residential care program. Jim sent him the requested information about the New Life Group Home, and also placed his name on the "Nellie Zimmerman Newsletter" mailing list.

Mike became an avid supporter of Nellie's cause. It infuriated him that someone like Nellie, or even someone like himself, could be committed to a mental institution and held there against their will. The United States Supreme Court had recently ruled that a person who, according to a qualified doctor's diagnosis, was not dangerous to himself or others, could not be committed to or held at a mental institution against his or her will.

Mike presented a resolution to that effect at the 1976 State Convention of the Kanawha (River) Valley Federation for the Blind in Charleston, West Virginia. It passed unanimously. The resolution also was passed unanimously at the 1976 National Convention of the Federation for the Blind in Los Angeles, California.

The decisive action of these organizations in adopting Mike's resolution gave an invaluable boost to Nellie's case. Jim decided to take her cause to the street. His formidable group of supporters held public rallies. Some regional and national organizations held similar public demonstrations.

There was an awesome array of positive public support for Nellie, and an equal amount of negative public opinion was generated against the Massillon State Mental Hospital.

Finally, the Akron University Law School wrote a letter to the administrator of the Massillon State Hospital, threatening to sue the institution in light of the Supreme Court's ruling. Rather than face a losing battle in court, the institution backed down. The administrator wrote Jim a letter agreeing to release Nellie, if certain requirements were met. Jim would have to prove that Nellie would have suitable housing, adequate financial support, transportation, and medical care.

When Jim received the letter, he was beside himself with joy. Most of the requirements were in place already. Now that he had a green light, he made arrangements for Nellie to live at a boarding home on Roland Avenue, in Canton. The Akron and Canton Division of the National Fraternal Society for the Deaf pledged sufficient funds for living expenses, companionship, transportation, and the provision of an "on-call" interpreter. With help from the now famous "Nellie Zimmerman Volunteers," he was able to recruit more than an adequate number of people who were willing to provide transportation to appointments and take her shopping, and help her with her business affairs.

A few days later, Jim appeared at the hospital social services office and presented his plan.

In early April, the Massillon State Hospital set a date for Nellie's release. As the designated time grew imminent, an impatient Nellie could not help remembering and reliving the past. It was very hard for her not to harbor negative feelings toward her family, toward the people who had operated the nursing homes, and toward the hospital administrators who allowed her to live in silence for all those years.

One night, as she was struggling with her rising anger, Nellie remembered how she had been spelling the Lord's Prayer when Carrie found her. She got out her Bible, praying as she traced the Braille words with her fingers: "Give us this day our daily bread, and forgive us our debts, as we forgive our debtors. --- for if you do not forgive the trespasses of others, neither will your heavenly Father forgive you."

Tears flowed down her cheeks as she realized what she must do if she wanted to be right with God in her new life. She must forgive, and let her bitterness go.

More tears flowed as she thought, "After all, by the grace of God, I have survived being here in this place. And, now by the grace of God, I have been saved! Yes, Lord, I will do what you ask of me."

A feeling of inner peace washed over her as she took on a new attitude.

Then she continued to talk to Jesus, "Dear Lord, I don't think anyone was trying to be mean. They just couldn't communicate with me, and probably did the best they could. But you, dear Jesus, have answered my prayers and brought me through. That is what's important!"

The next day when Jim came to see her, Nellie had a serious talk with him. She made it clear that she wanted no negative publicity or public blame cast on her family, the nursing homes, or the State Hospital.

Jim answered that he understood. But he pressed on, finger spelling into her hands, "What will you say when people ask you how you survived? You may even be interviewed by the newspapers."

Nellie was lost in thought for a few minutes.

Then she said, "I will tell them that I survived with a lot of prayer and with the help of Jesus. There is nothing I can do about the past; but I have a whole new life to look forward to."

Moved almost to tears by Nellie's answers, Jim agreed.

He signed into her hands, "I will do as you have asked. I will say nothing negative about the care you received in the past."

As the day of her release came closer, Nellie could not help feeling anxious. Every so often she would go weak in the knees. She had lived in this ward for nineteen years. She was used to it. As wretched as it was, it had been her home. Leaving the institution meant that she would be venturing into the unknown again. How would she survive without being able to see or hear? It was exciting, and it was frightening.

When these pangs of anxiety overwhelmed her, Nellie reassured herself, "I have Jesus! I have Jim. And I have many good friends. So far I have not met them, but I know their names. I can't wait to meet them all."

Finally the day came when Jim told her that it was time to get ready to leave and that he would be back early the next morning to take her to her new home. That night, she carefully packed her Bible, books, and handcrafts. Then in preparation for leaving early the next day, she bathed, and carefully arranged her hair. With sleep impossible, she sat in her chair and waited for the long night to pass. True to his word, Jim was there early the next morning. He had worked long and hard for this moment and was almost as excited as Nellie.

Now that he was there with her, standing close by her side, all of Nellie's anxieties vanished. The staff told Jim that he could pick up her personal belongings later. He was appalled at their lack of consideration for Nellie's feelings.

Unable to mask the irritation he felt, he said, "No, I think that would worry her too much. We will take everything with us now. I don't want to have to come back here for anything."

Then he examined Nellie's packed boxes and saw nothing but her reading material and crafts. Uneasy about the possibility of their leaving something behind, he spelled into her hand.

"Where are your clothes and other things?"

"This is all I have. Everything I own is packed and ready. I am wearing all my clothes."

Jim's jaw dropped. She was wearing a faded housedress. It was the same one she wore when she was admitted nineteen years before. She had no underwear and no stockings. Jim helped her put on an old disheveled brown coat, and tied a flowered scarf over her hair. She slipped into her hospital scuffs, the only thing the State Hospital had provided for her to wear on this morning of her release

Smiling serenely, she placed her hand on his arm. Although she had few earthly possessions, Nellie was the picture of royalty in her bearing. She squared her shoulders, and held her head high with pride. A big smile was on her face as she walked out of the ward, down the long corridors and out the front door of the State Hospital.

Suddenly, Nellie stopped. "I—A-M—F_R_E_E !" she spelled with shaking, excited fingers.

It was now 1976. For the first time in twenty-five years Nellie was walking free!

=   =   =

Three is a team - Jim Schneck, Emily Street Hensel and Nellie.
The soft fur coat was Nellie's pride. Courtesy of Massillon Independent

Chapter Five

THE RUDE WOMAN

Nellie's first breath of freedom was like no other. Although she could neither see nor hear, she could certainly smell. As she stepped out the door of the Massillon State Hospital, she inhaled the scent of the spring air, the dampness of the earth, the smell of freshly mowed lawn, the aroma of the blooming bushes and trees of the hospital grounds.

She was overwhelmed as long lost memories came crowding back into her mind. She felt the fresh gentle breeze caress her face and ruffle her hair. The sunshine was warm on her back. Her heart pounded in her chest as she drank in all these sensations. Tears filled her eyes. For more than twenty-five years, she had tried to remember what it was like to be free, to be outside in the beauty of nature. But the reality of her new freedom was more exhilarating than she had ever imagined.

As Jim led her to his car, she felt the muscles in his arm. It was comforting to be in the company of a strong man, a strong friend. He was a friend who really understood her. As she slipped into her seat and felt the door slam, she felt safe, safe for the first time since her father's death.

As Jim slipped into the driver's seat, Nellie reached for his hand. She needed to feel his closeness and to be able to touch him. She needed the blessed reassurance that her sweet freedom, and their being together, driving to her new home for the first time, was not all a dream. She felt like hugging herself in delight.

Instead, she signed, while speaking aloud, "Thanks, Jim! Thank you for everything you have done for me."

More tears flowed, happy tears. When she was finally able to settle down, Nellie's senses were awakened by the vibrations of the moving car. She literally drank in the feeling of motion and freedom. She had dreamed of this moment for almost two years. It was wildly exciting.

Nellie said, "I'd forgotten how it feels to be free to go anywhere I want to go. Tell me everything you see!"

With one hand on the wheel, Jim gave his other hand to Nellie. With non-stop motion of his fingers, he tried to open her mind to all that could be seen as they drove to her new home.

Bittersweet tears were in Nellie's eyes as she thought, "This is my first car ride with someone who is a friend since Daddy died. A friend who can talk to me."

As Nellie rode along, listening to Jim's narration of the scenery outside her window, she realized that the pounding of her heart came from both exhilaration and fear.

Questions filled her mind: "What will my room be like? Will the other people in the boarding house like me? Will I like the food? Will there be anyone who can talk to me? Jim can't be with me all the time!"

Before Nellie's questions went too far in this direction, the car came to a stop. Jim helped her get to her feet, led her up the steps to the front door, and knocked.

While they waited for the housekeeper to let them in, Jim spelled into Nellie's hand, "This is it! Welcome home!"

Nellie could not help grinning as she was ushered down the hall and into her new room.

Nothing about the boarding house was fancy. Located on Roland Avenue, in Canton, the rooms were small, and sparsely furnished. Although another person might have been appalled by the lack of space, Nellie was delighted as Jim showed her the room. She paced off the space. Her room was five steps wide and six steps long. (about nine by eleven feet.) She lovingly ran her hands over her new twin bed, dresser, table, wooden chair, lamp and bookcase. Next, Jim showed her the window. Although she could not see out the window, she was pleased to find she could open it and feel the fresh breeze on her face.

She signed, and said aloud, "It has everything I need!"

Next, Jim led her down the hall, so she could count the steps to the common bathroom shared by all the residents on her floor. He also showed Nellie all of the additional space on the first floor of the boarding house that she was free to use. This included the large living room where the residents could gather to talk and watch TV, the kitchen and large dining room where everyone gathered for meals.

He knew that Nellie had never used a "blind cane" to assist her in moving around. She had explained to him that when she first lost her sight, she always had a companion to lead her wherever she wanted to go. Therefore, she had received no training in how to use a white cane. Still, Jim was astonished by Nellie's uncanny sense of direction and her ability to accurately count off steps so she knew exactly where she was at all times. After this brief tour, Jim was satisfied that Nellie would be able to easily find her way around her new quarters.

Jim carried Nellie's belongings into her room and began to put them away. She lightly grasped his arm. Surprised, he turned toward her.

"You don't need to bother with that. I can do it myself!" she said.

She reached toward him with her arms open wide. They embraced. It was a time for celebration; it was also a moment for silent reflection, remembering the long journey they had taken together to arrive at this glorious end.

He spelled into Nellie's hands, "If only Carrie could have been here with us."

She signed, "Yes."

Then Nellie smiled, "Somehow, I think Carrie knows."

Overcome with emotion, he spelled a fervent prayer of thanksgiving into Nellie's hands. He gave her a goodbye hug, with a promise to be back as soon as he could. Then he was gone.

Suddenly, Nellie was swallowed up by an overwhelming sense of loneliness. The day had been incredibly exciting. But now there was no one there to talk to, and to share her joy. The weight of all those years of silence descended upon her.

She fought back tears, telling herself, "It is better to be free in silence, than to be locked up in a silent mad house!"

With this thought in mind, she got out her Bible and traced the familiar words of Psalm 42. "God is our refuge and strength, a very present help in trouble. Therefore we will not fear though the earth should change..."

Those comforting words helped Nellie throw off her feelings of loneliness. She gave herself a good shake and got busy with getting her living quarters in order. Her room had adequate storage space for her craftwork, the "In Pieces" Bible, and her books and magazines. By suppertime, Nellie had tastefully arranged all her treasures.

She said aloud, "I'm going to be very comfortable here."

Nellie was perfectly capable of taking care of her own needs once she got her personal belongings arranged to her liking, and grew accustomed to her surroundings.

The next morning, Jim received a phone call from a reporter of the *Akron Beacon Journal.* Informed by one of the "Nellie Zimmerman Volunteers", she was eager to cover the story about Nellie's release. Jim agreed to arrange for an interview. The next day Nellie was surprised to receive a visit from Jim, the reporter and a photographer.

On Saturday morning the article concerning Nellie's release appeared. Jim arranged to have it transcribed into Braille. On Sunday morning, he presented the Braille copy to Nellie after church. As Nellie's fingers traced the raised dots, she nodded her head as she read about the events surrounding her release. The article recounted her entire life story.

Suddenly, Nellie looked up with an expression of shock.

"This article is accurate at the beginning, but then it says that my hair is white! I thought it was still brown."

The Akron Beacon Journal article went out over the wire service and was picked up by other area newspapers.

Jim was impressed by how well she had adapted to her new environment. As a very young child, Nellie had learned to take good care of her own things. It was apparent that she could still keep her person and her belongings clean and neat. But she had almost nothing to wear, not even one change of clothes.

In the process of settling in, Nellie was pleased to receive a great deal of attention, not only from Jim, but also from the Nellie Zimmerman Volunteers. Once she was free, there was an outpouring of donations. These included gifts of money, linens, toiletries, and both utility and decorative items for her room.

One of the first gifts Nellie received was from the Canton Christian Fellowship Church of the Deaf, which contributed one hundred and fifty dollars designated for new clothes. After he received their gift, Jim arrived at the boarding house with two of his Nellie Volunteers. These volunteers were also deaf.

Nellie was as excited as a teenager when they told her that they were taking her shopping. They spent the day going from store to store. At each store, they allowed her to savor the experience, patiently waiting as she explored the merchandise. Nellie immersed herself in the joy of the moment, feeling the different fabrics, smelling their newness, consulting her new friends about style and color, and mentally weighing the value of each article of clothing before she made her purchases.

At the end of the shopping spree, as they drove toward the boarding house, one of the volunteers giggled and signed to her friend, "What all did we buy?"

Jim spelled the question into Nellie's hand. Nellie grinned and signed to Jim, "Hey, I want to know the answer to that question myself."

The other volunteer began to look through the bags, laughing and signing as she explored their contents: "Well, Nellie, you bought three dresses, six pair of underwear, three bras, six pair of stockings, two pairs of good shoes, one pair of house slippers, a lightweight jacket, three sweaters, and four pretty scarves to wear on your head!"

They were all laughing, delightedly, as Jim spelled the volunteer's answer into Nellie's hand.

Suddenly, the other volunteer said out loud, "Stop the car! Jim, stop the car! Nellie needs a Sunday hat!"

Exhausted as they were, they turned around and went in search of a department store with a good selection of hats. With a lot of laughing and joking, Nellie tried on just about every hat in the store, asking her friends to describe how she looked in each one. It took some persuading to get Nellie to purchase a hat. She was giggling right along with her companions as she made her choice and bought a black one with a medium brim and a multicolored feather attached near the crown. Contrasted with Nellie's fair complexion and white hair, it was very becoming. Nellie lightly fingered the feather, tracing its spine with her fingers while one of the volunteers spelled into her hand, describing its colors. When she was a young woman, she had several hats to choose from. But that was a long time ago.

She was very satisfied with all her purchases. But she still insisted, "I would rather wear a pretty head scarf than a hat, even for church. But it sure is wonderful to have a choice. I will wear it sometimes. I promise. This has been a wonderful day for me."

After Jim and his friends said good-bye, she spent the remainder of that marvelous day carefully examining each of her new purchases and deciding where to put them. Just two days before, Nellie had been without money and clothing. Now she felt rich. The volunteers had forgotten to mention what was in her shopping bag with all the toiletries. She found embossed and perfumed soaps, lotions, cologne, mouthwash, shampoos, combs, hairbrushes, and fancy hairpins. In the privacy of her room, long after everyone else was asleep, she sat on her bed and lovingly drank in the aroma of the heady perfumes, carefully touched each of her lovely new possessions, enjoying the surfaces of the toilet articles, and the textures of her new clothing.

The last things she examined that night were the two pairs of shoes. With her fingers, she lightly traced and retraced the patterns made by the distinctive decorative stitching on the toes and heels of each pair. It would be easy to tell them apart. She was satisfied that she would not get them mixed up. She laughed softly, thinking that if she did get them mixed up, that would be embarrassing. She examined them again before finally putting them away.

Before Jim drove his volunteers to their homes, he took time to sign to each of them, "This has been a wonderful day for me, too! Nellie may not be able to see or hear, but she sure is fun to be around! I really enjoyed watching her as she chose the things she wanted to buy. Her happiness and excitement are contagious. We all had a good time, didn't we? This is what setting the deaf and deaf/blind *free* is all about!"

Two days later, a couple more of the Nellie Volunteers stopped by to visit. They were both deaf and could communicate quite well by finger spelling. Nellie was delighted when they offered to help her coordinate her clothing. They began by describing to her the different colors, styles, and textures of her dresses and, with Nellie's input, they paired them with sweaters, shawls, and scarves. Now she had several coordinated outfits. When they finished, Nellie put on a fashion show for them. She was beaming as they finger spelled their praise into her hands.

Tears came to her eyes when one of the volunteers said, "I only wish that I was as beautiful as you are!"

It seemed like an eternity since Nellie had felt pretty!

From that day on, rarely did Nellie fail to properly coordinate her outfits. She was very much aware of her personal appearance and took pride in how she presented herself.

Both the residents of the home and the Nellie Volunteers soon realized that Nellie was a well-organized and punctual woman. An early riser, she would get up quietly, have her bath, dress, and be ready for the day before anyone else knew she was out of bed. Depending on what her scheduled activities were for the day, she prepared herself very carefully. Whether she was expecting to go out for an appointment or to a social outing of some kind, she made sure she was not late. Usually, she was ready to go hours ahead of time. When her transportation volunteers came for her, they always found her ready and waiting.

Occasionally, Nellie's transportation volunteer was late. But Nellie never showed the slightest hint of impatience. She sat quietly in her chair in the room, almost motionless. Once in a while, she touched the open face of her watch, checking the time; that was the only outward sign of uneasiness. Every inch a lady, when her driver finally did arrive, no matter how late, she smiled sweetly and greeted her chauffeur graciously.

While Nellie grew accustomed to her new life, the other residents of the boarding house felt uncomfortable with her. It bothered them that she could not see them. No matter what they were doing, they always had to make way for her. They were irritated when she did not look at them when they came into the room or when they were talking at the table. Sometimes, Nellie would try to talk to them at the dinner table. But her low-pitched, raspy voice was difficult for them to understand. To make matters worse, unable to finger spell, they were not able to talk back to her, or to get to know her.

Nellie was grace in motion. She had a regal bearing, and moved silently as she counted her steps. She always used slow, careful, fluid movements whenever she reached for anything. With her slender fingers and soft, sensitive touch, she found her way around her new home. Nellie had no way of knowing that her uncanny ability to move around the residence as silently as a ghost was unnerving to the people she lived with. She would startle them by suddenly appearing in their midst.

One day a group of three residents approached the manager of the house and complained.

"We don't like this Nellie! She is always sneaking around the house. Can't you get rid of her?"

As time passed and the excitement and novelty of her new life in the boarding home began to wear off, Nellie grew even hungrier for attention. Just as some people ache for a hug from a loved one, Nellie ached for someone with whom she could talk. It bothered her that no one in the house could or would communicate with her. Sometimes Nellie had to wait two or three days for someone to stop by with whom she could communicate. This was very disturbing.

Jim tried to be sensitive to her need to just sit and talk. He called on Nellie at least once a week. Each time he visited her in the boarding home, he stayed and talked with her as long as he could. Anything that was happening in the world was likely to come up for discussion. Before the end of each visit he would explain about upcoming church and community social events and, together, they would make up her schedule for the coming week. However, with all of his other commitments Jim could not provide all the individual attention she needed. Other volunteers came to drive her to appointments, and activities, but some of them were not proficient in finger spelling.

In between these all too infrequent visits, Nellie sat in her room alone. When no visit was scheduled, she tried to busy herself by reading her Braille books and magazines, by working on her handicrafts, and by studying her Bible. But she also couldn't help recalling the happy days she had shared with her father. She remembered his voice and his words of love and admiration. These memories created a growing desire in her to feel like that again. Most of all, she wanted to feel that she was more than a charity case. She wanted to win the true acceptance of others, and to have a real friend.

Jim came the closest to being a real friend. She wanted to be with him the most. However, he couldn't be with her as much as she wanted. So she invented ways to extend his visits. To make them last longer, she would disagree with him, or surprise him with an off the wall response.

Then he would be forced to ask, "What did you say?"

She would gleefully respond at length. Whenever this happened, it led to a whole new subject of conversation between them and would expand their time together. Even though she knew she was being devious, Nellie thoroughly enjoyed her contrived extra time with Jim.

However, he soon realized that he could not expect to stop by for a quick visit. His visits then became more infrequent. This meant that Nellie spent more days alone and in silence.

It was hard on Nellie to accept this new deprivation. Her feelings of unjust treatment still ran deep. She had survived the long years at the State Hospital, but now she felt like she was in another prison.

After going along with everything for about three months, Nellie could take the silence no longer. One night at 1:30am, she decided to vent her unhappiness. She deliberately walked out of her bedroom, threaded her way through the short hallway, the dining room, and kitchen, then out the back door onto the back porch. She paused to get her bearings. Then she took two steps to the right, walked six steps forward to the vertical banister post, grasped hold of it with her left hand, keeping herself well away from the steep porch steps. Taking a firm grasp on the post, she held steady, tilted her head back as far as she could and yelled. She did not yell anything in particular; she just yelled. Her blood-curdling scream was loud enough to wake all the residents in the house and to wake all of the neighbors down the block.

As soon as the frantic housekeeper could put on her bathrobe and get downstairs she was at Nellie's side. She patted Nellie on the shoulder. Nellie stopped screaming. But since the housekeeper could not communicate with Nellie, she had no way of asking her what was wrong. She led Nellie back to her room and immediately called Jim!

Nellie went to bed quietly. She slept until dawn. To her surprise, Jim arrived almost as soon as her feet hit the floor. He had stopped by before he went to work to find out why she was so upset. Nellie had only one concern. *She was in her nightclothes.*

Nellie's thoughts were frantic, "I have to get into my into my housecoat. Jim has never seen me like this. My hair is a mess! I'm not properly dressed to receive company."

She hurriedly put on her robe and slippers, and smoothed down her hair. Then she turned on all her charm to show him how delighted she was that he was there.

She could not sense his emotions as he spelled into her hand, "Hi Nellie, what happened last night? What is wrong?"

She laughed, "Oh, I was just so lonely! It's been four days since anybody talked to me. I couldn't stand it any more! I don't know if I was yelling at you, or at the world, or at God."

Again, she laughed, "I feel better now. Now that you are here!"

Jim listened to Nellie's story with mixed emotions. He could see that she was smiling and laughing. But what she was saying was serious! And what she had done was serious!

Although he sympathized with her frustration, his flying fingers spelled into her hands, "I guess that I don't understand how lonely it must be for you sometimes. But I don't know what I can really do about it."

He paused, took a deep breath, and then scolded her, "You'll just have to live with it and keep your feelings to yourself. You simply cannot go around yelling at the neighborhood at all hours of the night!"

He saw a look of shock cross Nellie's face and relented. It was the first time he had ever shown her any disapproval of her behavior.

Lovingly, he patted her hand, saying, "I have to leave to go to work now, but I'll stop by again later tonight."

He gave her a hug, and was gone.

When he left Nellie's room, the housekeeper stopped him in the hall and asked him to come into her office. As they went into the room, she closed the door to talk privately.

First, she demanded, "I need to know what was wrong with Nellie last night."

Before Jim could answer, she declared, "If Nellie ever does that again, I will kick her out of this house! I want you to know that I have had other complaints about Nellie. But this takes the cake!"

Jim made an attempt to explain why Nellie had acted out, but he could see that the housekeeper was not in the least sympathetic. He left the house troubled. As he drove to work, he decided to call a meeting of all the Nellie Volunteers to discuss her problem.

The next Sunday, he, Nellie, and a good number of the Volunteers stayed after the church service to hold a meeting. He told them about the incident. He also gave them Nellie's explanation.

One volunteer said, "But Jim, we can't be there all the time!"

Another complained, "I can't finger spell. I am also hard of hearing. So, when I go to pick up Nellie, I can't talk to her. Sometimes she tries to talk to me, but her voice is so low and raspy that I can't understand what she is saying. It is really frustrating, for both of us."

Others expressed similar frustrations. One of the new volunteers piped up, "I think Nellie needs a companion! Someone who will live with her who can finger spell."

Jim explained that he had approached every agency he could think of to try to make provisions for such a companion. But all the social agencies in the area had refused to offer any financial assistance.

He concluded, "Due to the lack of funds, I have not even been able to provide a part-time companion for Nellie."

The discussion continued, but there seemed to be no solution.

Finally, one of the volunteers suggested, "Since there seems to be no obvious answer, I think that we should turn this matter over to God! Why don't we ask God to send the companion that Nellie needs?"

Jim agreed, but said, "It seems like we are asking God for a miracle."

The meeting ended with prayer.

Two weeks passed and Nellie's situation remained the same. It had been four days since she had the last visitor with whom she could talk. So she decided to vent her frustration in the same premeditated manner. This time she could be heard two blocks away.

Periodically, thereafter, she let the world know about her frustration. It did not take Nellie long to figure out that if she raised a rumpus, the harassed boarding home staff would call Jim. He always came right away, or he would contact someone else to come and talk with her. It also did not take long for the neighbors to voice their complaints about Nellie's howling. At first, their complaints were addressed to the manager of the boarding house. But soon the neighbors resorted to calling the police and their city council representatives. Each time Nellie threw her temper tantrum, Jim came and talked the boarding home staff into giving her another chance. But the time came when the administrator of the boarding house confronted Jim.

She explained, "The staff is concerned about our facility passing the state licensing review. If we fail a licensing review, we cannot remain in operation. Any neighborhood complaint creates a very serious situation for us. I'm sorry, but I must ask you to find another place for Nellie to live."

Jim promised her that he would begin looking immediately. He was upset and admonished Nellie with angry fingers.

"You must not do anything to disturb the people here, or the neighbors. Look at what you have done. Now I am going to have to find you another place to live!"

In all innocence, Nellie asked, "Why can't I come and live with you?"

Thrown off balance, Jim chose his words carefully, "You cannot live with me because there isn't any room in my apartment, and there would not be anyone home with you during the day. It would not be safe for you."

This explanation satisfied Nellie for the moment. But Jim had no idea how he was going to find a new home for her. The next Sunday, after church, he related the boarding home's decision to the Nellie Zimmerman Volunteers. They already knew that Nellie had been having tantrums, but they were steadfastly loyal to her.

One volunteer exclaimed, "Hey man, what would you expect! How would you like to be blind and deaf? To sit in your room for days at a time, not being able to see anything, or hear anything, and not be able to talk with anyone? Who wouldn't go nuts? Who wouldn't feel like yelling at the world?"

Everyone agreed.

Another person expressed regret, "I did not realize the seriousness of the situation. I wish I had gone to see Nellie more often. We shouldn't have left it all up to Jim!"

Jim was surprised and grateful that, in spite of her behavior, the group remained steadfast in their support of Nellie. But nobody had any suggestions for where Nellie could live.

Because he was already inundated with his job, church services, and other community and social activities, Jim decided that the best way for him to spend more time with Nellie was to take her with him to as many places as he could. Nellie was delighted! Now, she could get away from the boarding house on a regular basis. It allowed her to spend more time with Jim. Moreover, in Jim's company of friends, Nellie was an instant social success and the center of attention wherever she went. Although tiny in stature, she stood out in any crowd because of her regal bearing and her beautiful snow-white hair. She greatly enjoyed socializing with many of the Nellie Zimmerman Volunteers, including all of the people who had been providing transportation for her. She also made new acquaintances.

Participating in these activities helped Nellie to feel less frustrated with her situation. It gave the boarding home staff respite from her care, and the worry about the possibility of another tantrum. And Jim bought himself some additional time to search for new housing.

When their church, the Assembly of God, announced its Bicentennial celebration to be held on July 4, 1976, Jim told Nellie several days in advance that she would need to dress up for this special event. Filled with excitement, she planned very carefully the outfit she would wear.

Jim picked her up for the celebration right on time. When they arrived at the church, it was very crowded with a mixture of both deaf and hearing people. Nellie was the only deaf/blind person there. After the formal portion of the celebration was over, there was a congregational dinner. After dinner the crowd continued to socialize. People were milling around, talking and laughing.

Jim had to hang on tight to Nellie as they moved around the room. He found it was hard work to keep moving, shield her from being crushed by the crowd and, at the same time, keep her informed of all that was going on. With Nellie in tow, he spelled into her one hand while he maneuvered through the crowd, introducing her and greeting his many friends and acquaintances.

While they were still standing in the middle of the crowd, he felt a sharp tug on his coat tails. From somewhere behind him, came a loud, harshly spoken demand from a woman whose voice he did not recognize.

"Let me talk to Nellie! I want to talk to Nellie! Hey, let me talk to Nellie."

Hanging tightly onto Nellie's hand, he glanced backward through the crowd, but was not able to locate the owner of the loud, demanding voice.

He thought, "My, what a rude woman."

Again came a hard tug on his coat tails and a loud demand from somewhere behind and to the left of him.

"Hey, I want to talk to Nellie! Let me talk to Nellie Zimmerman!"

He turned around, looking over the crowd, muttering under his breath, "Who is this woman? What does she want? Where is she?"

Finally, Jim caught his first glimpse of the owner of the voice. He was startled. Before him was a slender, attractive young woman with dark hair, sparkling eyes, and a big smile. Her appearance stood in sharp contrast to the harsh demanding tone in her voice that had prompted his first impression of someone obnoxious, loud, domineering, and rude.

"Hi," she said with a delightful smile, now speaking in a normal tone.

"My name is Emily Street, and I have been wanting to meet you and Nellie for such a long time. I was so afraid that you would get away in the crowd, and I wouldn't get to meet her."

Jim recovered quickly, and with his most charming smile, spoke pleasantly in return.

"Hello, I didn't know what to expect when you pulled on my coat and spoke to me from the crowd."

He then finger spelled into Nellie's hand, "Emily Street, a nice lady, wants to meet you. She wants to talk to you."

Emily took Nellie's hands between hers and spelled into them, "Hi, I am Emily Street, and I have been wanting to meet you."

Nellie smiled her sweetest, most disarming, innocent smile. With her raspy voice, she responded, "I'm pleased to meet you. But you made your 'H' wrong."

Emily laughed delightedly at Nellie's response to her greeting. Jim was surprised that Emily understood what Nellie said to her. Then he noticed the slight tilt of Emily's head, a characteristic of someone hard of hearing. He decided that Emily had read Nellie's lips rather than having heard and understood what she had said. If she was hard of hearing, this also helped explain the booming rudeness of Emily's voice when she had first addressed him.

There was no mistaking Emily's sincerity in wanting to be friends with Nellie. There was an instant magnetism between them. For Jim, it was heart warming to see Nellie and Emily together. He left them alone. The two women left the crowd, went over to one side of the large room, and sat down on a bench, where they talked for more than an hour.

Jim took advantage of the respite that Emily gave him to mingle freely with his friends. When he returned to them, Emily told him that she had first heard about Nellie from friends in the deaf community. She had also read some articles about them in the *Canton Repository, Massillon Independent*, and the *Akron Beacon Journal*. She had become fascinated by Nellie.

Curious, Jim asked, "Tell me a little bit about yourself."

"I'm not deaf. But I have been hearing impaired since I was eleven. I went to Malone College and there I learned sign language. I became a Certified High School teacher, but after five years I had to quit because I couldn't hear the student's questions. Then I became a companion for Sue Franklin, a blind woman with cerebral palsy. I helped Sue get through her studies at Malone. Now I work at the Philomatean Society Group Home for the Blind in Canton. I have also been active in the deaf community, and just started coming to church here."

Emily fished in her purse for paper and pencil, and wrote down her name and phone number.

She said, "You will let me know if there is anything at all that I can do for Nellie, won't you?"

Without hesitation, Jim told Emily, "I need a friend for Nellie, a companion who can communicate with her and take her for regular outings."

Jim also told Emily about his need for alternate housing.

He explained, "I would like to see Nellie in her own apartment, with a companion, but I don't know how this can be worked out. Several organizations have made pledges toward Nellie's living expenses, but what she receives is only enough to pay for her rent at the boarding home. I haven't been able to raise money to pay for even a part time live-in companion."

Emily was excited by the challenge of befriending Nellie. She promised Jim that she would pick up Nellie the following week for a special outing. She also agreed to help in any other way that she could.

Emily kept her promise. The following Wednesday, she picked up Nellie after work. Even though she had been on her feet all day, working as a nurse's aid at the Philomatian Society, she stopped by and took Nellie shopping. Emily enjoyed helping Nellie pick out some evening snacks she could have in her room. But shopping for food made them both feel hungry. So Emily took Nellie out for pizza. As they waited to be served, finger spelling, laughing and joking, they got along famously.

The waiter came by to ask them, "And what would you two like to drink? Coke? Seven Up? Dr. Pepper? Root Beer?"

Emily related the question to Nellie. Then they laughed, and answered simultaneously, "Beer!"

Emily clarified, "Not Root Beer! Real beer!"

While waiting for their pizza, Emily suddenly burst out laughing. She spelled into Nellie's hands, "I wish my Mom could see us sitting here; she would have a hissy fit! She is a good Baptist, hates all drinking, and she hates for me to have anything to do with deaf people."

"Why?" Nellie asked.

"Because my grandmother was deaf, and my mother despised her. She never could accept my hearing impairment."

Back in her room, later that day, Nellie included her new friend in her evening prayers. She thanked God for allowing her to meet Emily.

Almost in awe, she said, "My prayers have been answered! You have sent me a true friend. She may be only twenty-seven and I may be seventy-one, but I feel like she is my sister. She is the sister I never had, but longed for all these years. Thank you, Jesus!"

After their first outing, Emily stopped by at least once a week to take Nellie for an excursion. Sometimes Emily would bring other friends along. Sometimes they simply went to shop or to eat out. There were special excursions that included visiting public parks, going to the petting zoo, and visiting Emily's friends.

At the public park playgrounds, Nellie loved to sit in the swings and be pushed.

Emily admonished her strongly, "If you have something to say, use your voice. Don't let go of the chains. Don't talk with your hands. You have to hold on to the chains with both hands or you will fall. When I push you and you swing real high, you are about ten feet off the ground."

Nellie was delighted. It was like being a child again. She loved the "middle feeling" she got when she lowered her head, giving herself over to the movement of the swing and the feel of rushing air around her. Back in her room, Nellie was quiet in her thoughts as she remembered the happy times of long ago when her father or her companion took her to a park to picnic and play....

Nellie particularly enjoyed the day when Emily took her shopping for a fur coat. She had a great time touching and feeling all the different furs, and learning about their styles and colors. Finally, she chose a beautiful full-length gray synthetic fox fur coat. Nellie was delighted with her purchase and even took it to bed with her that night so that she could stroke and pet it with her long, sensitive, loving fingers.

Another time, Nellie enjoyed visiting the McKinley Museum. As they walked around inside the huge hall, and through several smaller rooms, Emily spelled into Nellie's hand, giving her a vivid description of each display. At the end of the day, Emily asked the museum curator for special permission to have Nellie try on President McKinley's top hat. Permission was granted. Nellie drank in the feeling of importance as she put on the tall hat. The sight of this petite woman wearing the oversized black top hat, with her long snow white hair was impressive, and turned many heads of the people around them. As Emily drove Nellie home with one hand on the steering wheel and the other finger spelling into Nellie's hand, they both laughed as Emily described how spectacular Nellie looked in McKinley's hat.

While the two women were becoming fast friends, Emily also volunteered to help Jim find a better living arrangement for Nellie. Of course, Jim had no idea when he enlisted her to help in his search for a new home, that this was equivalent to releasing a tiger on the community. She vowed to use every means at her disposal to achieve the desired results. She covered most of the ground that Jim had traveled the year before when he sought help for Nellie's release from the State Hospital. She contacted all the State, Federal and private agencies that provided services to the blind. But they would not help with living expenses in any way.

One day she approached the administrator of the Philomatian Society in Canton where she worked. She knew that the society provided housing for the blind, but they did not have any deaf/blind residents. However, Emily did not see any reason why they could not serve as a home for Nellie.

Emily's hopes were dashed. The administrator had already heard about Nellie's howling tantrums at the boarding home.

Emily was shocked when the administrator quipped, "Are you referring to Nellie Zimmerman, that animal that no one can live with? Don't even ask me!"

Already lovingly attached to Nellie, Emily was disgusted by this comment. But before she got to her car, her disgust turned into outright rage. She was more determined than ever to help Nellie find a better place to live.

Emily also contacted the Vocational Services for the Blind in Canton. She knew that this agency was supposed to provide help with housing and training for the blind. But the caseworker steadfastly refused even to meet Nellie.

He insisted, "Nellie is too old to qualify for our services. Besides, she has a double handicap; we cannot take on cases of those who have no prospect of employment. It makes no difference to us that she now lives in the community."

Emily responded, "You've got to be kidding me!"

The caseworker quipped, "As far as I am concerned, Nellie would have been better off if you and your 'Do Gooder' friends had left her at Massillon State Hospital."

Infuriated, Emily reported the results of her efforts to Jim. Only then did she discover that when Jim had previously approached these agencies the same people had dismissed his request for their assistance as if it were absurd. But Emily was not one to take "No" for an answer. She was determined that somehow she was going to prove the professionals wrong.

Almost a year after Jim and Nellie had met Emily, the boarding home administrator called Jim at work.

"I know this is Friday, but I need to see you as soon as possible!"

Jim answered, "I'll come by to see you right after work. What is the problem?"

She snapped, "I'll tell you when you get here!"

Then she banged the receiver in his ear. Obviously, she was upset.

Jim had an uneasy feeling when he arrived. The administrator ushered him into the office.

Before he could sit down, she began: "Jim, I am giving you formal notice. You have less than thirty days to make alternate arrangements for Nellie."

She went on, "'We can no longer keep her here. The State Inspector has notified us that if we want to keep Nellie, we have to install a sprinkler system in her room. We just can't afford to do that. Besides, too many complaints from the neighbors about Nellie have been registered with the State."

In an obvious effort to soften the blow, she admitted, "Nellie's behavior has improved dramatically. We haven't had an incident of howling for several months. But the damage has been done. I'm sorry, but we have no choice but to ask her to leave."

She then handed Jim Nellie's eviction papers.

When Jim appeared in her room, Nellie was surprised. Immediately, she guessed that something was wrong by the subdued manner in which he greeted her.

He spelled into her hands, "I have received an ultimatum."

She listened to him with a somber look on her face, but showed no sign of being unduly upset as he told her of the thirty-day notice.

Instead, she smiled, patted his hand, and said, "Jim, don't you worry. Jesus will find a way for us to overcome this trouble. Remember, all things work for good for those that love God."

Jim looked at her in amazement, and thought, "What a person of faith!"

It was clear that Nellie was not afraid. There wasn't the slightest hint that Nellie felt any guilt about her role in causing their dilemma. Before Jim left, Nellie made it plain to him that she had no regrets about leaving the boarding home and going to another place to live.

She said, "I will pray for something better."

Jim left her and drove home, alone with his thoughts. Nellie was confident, but he was not. He had put himself and his reputation on the line by rescuing Nellie from the State Hospital. Since then, he had spent a great deal of time, and emotional and physical energy to support Nellie in her quest for independent living. He had seen this day coming for a long time, and had explored every possibility he could think of to make better arrangements for Nellie. But he had come up empty handed. Now he felt completely exhausted. His spirit took a nosedive.

Jim prayed, silently, "Lord, what am I going to do? I have failed! After all the community organizing and media publicity, how will I ever get over the embarrassment of failure? How can I find a suitable placement for Nellie? God, help me to get through this!"

Jim was in deep thought while he drove along State Highway 62, south of Canton. He passed through Navarre and headed out into the hilly Amish country. But he could not find peace of mind. Finally, he was so distraught that he stopped at an abandoned schoolhouse that was being converted into a Mennonite church. He decided to stay there and pray until he received an answer, and could see a way out of his dilemma.

For the entire weekend, Jim spent every waking moment in meditation and prayer, asking for God's help, and seeking Divine guidance.

On the second day, after becoming concerned because they had not heard from Jim, and not knowing where he was, Emily and a friend went looking for him. They, too, drove south on State Highway 62, through Navarre, and out into the countryside. Although they were just following a hunch, they finally found him sequestered in the unfinished church.

When they asked Jim what he was doing, Emily sensed an unusual hesitation on his part.

She said, "Come on Jim, it isn't like you to keep your thoughts to yourself! Talk to us!"

Jim was so tired he could not think straight, and he didn't know where to begin. The awkward pause continued.

But then he had an inspiration: "When in doubt, just dive right in."

So he said, "You know, I told you before that we would soon need a new place for Nellie to live. Her need for a new place is right now. We have been given formal notice by the boarding home that she has to move in less than thirty days. This happened much faster than I anticipated. I've tried everything. I just don't know what to do!"

After listening to him, the women went home, made sandwiches, and after adding some soft drinks, brought back a "care package" to Jim. Still, they could not talk him into leaving the unfinished church, so they left him to continue in his prayers through yet another night.

That same evening, Emily was tossing and turning in bed. She shared Jim's agony. She also kept thinking about all the heartless comments she had endured as she went from agency to agency. It seemed as if nobody was willing to help Nellie.

As Emily's anger rose within her, suddenly she heard a voice, "You're the one!"

"I'm the one what?"

Suddenly, she felt a great weight lift off her chest. A feeling of peace washed over her. Her mind was crystal clear.

"Yes, Lord, I know that I am the one! I am the one who is supposed to take Nellie in! Why not? She can live with me!"

The next day, Jim finally left the unfinished church, found a phone and called Emily.

He asked, "Can you meet with me to talk about Nellie?"

"Sure." Her voice boomed in his ear, "When? Where do you want to meet?"

Then Emily answered her own questions, "How about tonight at the Chicken Shack? How about 6:00 o'clock?"

When Jim arrived at the Chicken Shack and took his seat at her table, again he hesitated.

Emily looked at him in surprise, "Well, what is it?"

Jim was dejectedly shaking his head as though he had given up all hope.

"I still don't have a place where Nellie can live."

Emily gave him no chance to continue.

With a delighted grin on her face, she spoke in her loud, rapid-fire manner of talking, "Oh Jim, don't worry another second about it. I'll take Nellie to live with me. Now, that's settled! Come on, man, perk up! She'll be just fine with me!"

Jim's jaw dropped; he was astonished by the spontaneity with which Emily volunteered to take Nellie. He felt as if a great burden had been lifted from his shoulders.

He sighed with relief, and said, "Thank you, Jesus! Emily, you are a God-send, the answer to my prayers!"

But almost immediately, his feeling of relief gave way to worry over the feasibility of this solution. He had known Emily for almost a year. He knew there were stark differences between the two women's personalities. He wondered if they could really live together. While Nellie seemed quiet, neat, tactful, careful, and slow to act, Emily was a complete contrast. Emily was impulsive, loud, excitable, tactless, untidy, and careless in the treatment of her personal possessions. He could not help smiling when he mentally compared the two.

From experience in working with the deaf/blind, Jim knew very well that it would be difficult for the two women to live together. He felt as if it was his duty to impress upon Emily the extent of the problems she would encounter with Nellie.

Long ago, Emily had developed a severe case of "selective hearing." Even when she heard perfectly what someone was saying, she appeared to only discern the words that echoed what she wanted to hear, and effectively screened out everything else. Emily had experienced Nellie's wit and charm. They had shared many good times together. But Jim knew that this "fun side" was the only side of Nellie's personality that Emily had ever seen.

He felt obliged to tell Emily about Nellie's "other" side.

"You know, Nellie has more needs than any person I have ever known. She has been subjected to such traumatic emotional and physical deprivation that she is starved for human companionship and attention. She is jealous of anything that takes my time away from her. I know that she will be just as demanding of you, or any other caregiver. I'm not saying that this is a fault. It is not a character defect. Nellie can't help it. But Emily, what I am trying to say is that Nellie will not be easy to live with!"

Emily glared at him.

She said, "Jim, don't give me all this psycho-babble! I'm going to take Nellie in. She needs a place to stay. She needs a companion. I think this is what God wants me to do."

"I'm just trying to tell you, Emily, that Nellie will want to occupy all of your time. Your life will no longer be your own, and she will try your patience to the limit! Are you really ready for that?"

Emily laughed, "Oh, Jim, we'll be fine! You worry too much."

Sensing Emily's determination, Jim secretly rejoiced. But the social worker inside him still could not rest. He wanted to be sure that placing Nellie with Emily would work out.

To play the devil's advocate, he asked Emily, "Do you know why Nellie is being evicted from the boarding house?"

"Yes, I know about Nellie's standing on the back porch and yelling at the world in the middle of the night, but the fact that no one in the boarding home learned to finger spell and to communicate with Nellie makes me mad, too! Come on, Jim, I can finger spell. There won't be any such behavior if Nellie lives with me."

"Will you be serious? How do you know it will work?"

Emily flippantly dismissed him and his warnings.

"What's not to work?"

But Jim's widened eyes and raised eyebrows finally prompted an angry response from Emily.

Loud and obstinate, she scolded him, "Now you listen to me, Jim. Nellie needs a place to live. I will provide a home for her. As long as she agrees with this plan and it is what she wants, what could go wrong? Nellie and I will get along just fine!"

=   =   =

Chapter Six

OIL AND WATER

Even though it was past 9:00 O'clock when Jim and Emily left the Chicken Shack, they drove directly to the boarding house to tell Nellie. When they arrived, Nellie was sitting alone in her room. Her face lit up with a big smile when they touched her on the shoulder to let her know that they were there.

She spoke out loud, "Why it's Jim and Emily. What are you two doing here?"

Jim rapidly finger spelled, pressing down hard to emphasize each letter, into Nellie's hand, "We have a question for you! How would you like to live with Emily? Emily has decided that she wants to invite you to live with her!"

Nellie grinned from ear to ear and bounced up and down in her seat, her raspy voice cracking with emotion as she exclaimed, "Oh, Emily! Can I really come and live with you? Will I really be living in my own home with you? I can't wait to get out of this place!"

Nellie's excitement was contagious. With Emily grinning like a Cheshire cat, Jim could not help but match their excitement. Then Nellie's face took on a serious expression.

"Emily, I have visited your apartment. I know that it is small and you have only one bedroom. There won't be room for me. So where will we live?"

Without giving them time to answer, she went on, "When can we move? How will we move? Do we have enough furniture? Do we have enough dishes, pots, pans, and other kitchen stuff?"

With Nellie positioned in the middle, they held a three-way finger spelling discussion about what would be needed. They decided that the first order of business was to find a suitable apartment, and that they would begin their search for one the very next day.

The next afternoon, Emily came with a newspaper tucked under her arm. She had already circled a number of "Apartment for Rent" ads. She read them to Nellie, who was delighted to help decide which ones they should consider.

Almost immediately, they found one that sounded perfect for their needs. It was inexpensive. It was the right size. Located at 1612

Tuscawaras Drive, in Canton, it was close to the inner city, and just a few blocks west of Interstate 77. Emily did not waste any time in calling the number given in the ad, and they made an appointment to see it.

The landlord showed Emily, Nellie and Jim the apartment. It was a third floor flat above a small retail store. There was another apartment on the second floor. The stairway leading up to the second floor was attached to the storefront. A door opened to what was the roof of the business. A deck-like balcony ran across the top of the storefront, leading to the second flight of stairs. When they entered the apartment, Emily led Nellie around the good sized living room, the dining room, the kitchen, the bathroom and a large bedroom. She also took her outside on the balcony built on the roof of the second floor apartment and overlooking the street.

After further exploring the kitchen, its stove, refrigerator, counter top, sink and cupboards, Nellie said, "It's perfect!"

With their three-way conversation, using finger spelling, they agreed that Nellie would get the one bedroom. The dining table would be placed in the living room and Emily would convert the dining room into her own bedroom.

The three of them were standing in the living room of their newly chosen apartment when Jim finally summoned the courage to ask how Emily and Nellie could afford to pay the rent.

He looked expectantly at Emily. Emily swallowed. She felt that he was waiting for her to agree to take full financial responsibility for their living expenses. But before she had time to respond to Jim's question, Nellie waved a raised hand to get their attention.

"Yes, we do have to decide how we will pay for everything."

Nellie's voice was empathic, "I know that Emily must be the one to handle all the money. But I have my Social Security SSI benefits. Emily will have the money from her job. We will pool our money, make out a budget, and Emily will pay all the bills."

Jim was taken by surprise. Until now he had looked upon Nellie as a person who needed to be taken care of by others. Now she was asserting her capability to be responsible for herself. He saw her in a completely new light.

Smiling, proud as a father, he said, "That is great! I like your 'take charge' attitude."

Emily was surprised, relieved and pleased that Nellie had spoken up without hesitation and offered to pay her own way. It made her feel like they would be true partners in their new venture. Without further discussion, Emily and Jim agreed to Nellie's proposal. Together they made the arrangements with the landlord and rented the apartment.

On the way back to the boarding home, Nellie asked, "When do you think that we can move? Can we be ready by tomorrow?"

Emily laughed, "Just hold your horses! We have to get the utilities turned on in our names. We have to clean up the apartment. And we have to pack all of our stuff. How about trying to move in next week?"

As soon as Emily arrived home, she contacted as many friends as she could think of. Telling them the good news, she proceeded to ask them for help with the big move. About thirty-five people, including several of her acquaintances and many of the Nellie Volunteers would help. Emily scheduled work shifts and assigned jobs. There was a wonderful party atmosphere as all the helpers made short work of the cleaning and packing tasks.

In order to contain their excitement, both Emily and Nellie put their energy into cleaning and packing. Six days later, all Nellie and Emily had to do to complete the move was to wait for morning to arrive. The two women had a hard time waiting. Emily was so wound up about this monumental change in her life that she was unable to sleep. Nellie also tried to sleep, but could not. Finally, she got out of bed and patiently sat in her chair for the remainder of the long night. Every once in a while, she grinned and hugged herself in delight. Her thoughts were spinning.

"I can't believe it! I will actually live in my own home with a companion! It's going to be great, living with my good friend! It seems like an impossible dream!"

She also thought, "I'm going to be able to read in my new home, play my head games and do my crafts. I'll be able to shop for groceries. I will cook entire meals. Clean my own home. Handle my own money. I'll be free! Free to be me!"

The sun rose hot on the fifteenth of June 1977. Using a borrowed truck, Jim and several strong male volunteers came to move Emily into her new apartment. Emily was moved first so she could get everything ready for Nellie. Once in the apartment, she worked swiftly. Having unloaded Emily's few belongings, the men went to pick up some additional furniture that had been donated by the Nellie Zimmerman Volunteers, their church, and other interested friends. By noon the apartment was beginning to take on an inviting and cozy atmosphere.

After a lunch break, the men went to pick up Nellie. She was ready and waiting for them. Her mind was in high gear. The men were amazed when she climbed the stairs to her new home just one time, then told them exactly how many steps were in each flight. From that time on, without hesitating, she could quickly navigate the distance from the street, up a flight of stairs, across the balcony and then up another stairway to the apartment door.

While the men put Nellie's few boxes of possessions on her bed, Nellie was completely absorbed in learning about her new living space. She began by counting her steps as she felt along the different walls and found all the open doorways. She paced back and forth, from the living room to the kitchen, to her bedroom, and to Emily's bedroom. It didn't take long for her to know the exact distances between the different rooms and where the furniture was located in each of them.

Later, after she had put away her belongings, with Emily's help, Nellie explored every facet of the apartment. By the end of that first day, she knew every inch of their new home and where everything in it was located. Then, she was ready to go outside.

But Emily was exhausted.

She protested, "We have done enough for one day. We're going to eat and then rest. Exploring the neighborhood can wait until tomorrow.

After they had finished supper, Nellie paced the apartment, happily hugging herself and speaking out loud, "This is my home! I am really home! I really am home!"

That night, when Nellie finished her prayers of thanksgiving for this marvelous, magical day, she was overcome with emotion.

"Life here is going to be so different, so wonderful, so lovely. I can't believe that Emily is going to be my companion. She will be with me all the time. No more living in silence! No more waiting for days to have someone come around to talk with me."

As tired as she was, Nellie began planning for the next day. "It will be fun to explore our new neighborhood with Emily. Once I get my bearings, I will be able to go wherever I want to go."

Then a fantasy crept into her head.

"While I am out with Emily to tour the neighborhood, I'll learn some landmarks. Then I'll be able to walk around the neighborhood all by myself. I won't always have to be dependent upon Emily, or anyone else, to go outside with me! I'll be able to walk free!"

The next morning, immediately after breakfast, Nellie asked Emily to take her for a walk.

Nellie explained, "I want to know what is outside the apartment. I want to learn all about where we live."

Emily was very willing to comply with Nellie's request. She, too, wanted to learn all about their new neighborhood. They soon discovered that their apartment was located in one of the city's oldest established neighborhoods. It was an even mixture of private homes and rental properties. They also discovered that there were a wide variety of businesses and office buildings within a few blocks of their apartment.

The first business they discovered was a small grocery store. Emily walked in, approached the cashier, and said, "Hello! We just moved into the neighborhood. I am Emily Street, and this is my friend, Nellie Zimmerman. She is deaf and blind."

Laughing, she continued, "But with a little help, I'll bet she'll be able to get around in this store just as well as you can. And she will probably know where everything is located even better than you do."

The cashier extended her hand to Emily, welcoming them.

"Hello, Emily, my name is Mary. Let me go and get the owner. I'm sure that he will want to meet you and show you around the store."

"Just a minute," Emily said, and spelled the clerk's name into Nellie's hand.

Nellie smiled, reached out her hand and said, "Hello, Mary, it's nice to meet you."

The clerk shook Nellie's hand, and then left them to find the owner. When he appeared, wearing a crisp clean white apron, he greeted Emily and waited for her to introduce him to Nellie.

Then he suggested, "You know, I would be pleased to show you around the store, but if Nellie knows the things she wants to buy, all she has to do is write them down on a list and give it to the cashier. Then either I, or one of my clerks will go and pick out the things she has asked for. I tell you, it's no problem! We have some senior citizens who phone in their order and we fill it for them. We also have other handicapped people that we do business with this way! Don't worry! We pick out good stuff! We will always pick out good stuff for you!"

As the grocer talked, Emily had spelled all of his words into her hand. Nellie said, "Thank you! It's nice to meet you!"

But Emily said, "Oh, sir, that is really nice of you, but it won't be necessary. I don't think that Nellie will be coming here by herself, without me. And I can pick out the things we need just fine! But thanks for the offer. Would you show us around your store?"

The owner agreed. Emily offered Nellie her arm so she could lead her, and the two of them followed the owner. Emily stopped often to spell into Nellie's hand all that he said. Nellie confirmed what Emily was telling her by touching the dry goods and the fruits and vegetables. By the time they had finished the tour, indeed, Nellie, who had been counting her steps, had a complete mental picture of the layout of the store.

Back at the cash register, Emily spelled in her hand, "Nellie, would you bring some milk, some bread, and a bunch of bananas?"

To everyone's amazement, Nellie did as she was asked. Moving silently and gracefully through the store, she appeared just a few moments later with a grin on her face and the requested three items in her basket.

As they left the store, promising to return, Emily and Nellie continued their tour of the neighborhood. Within a few blocks, in addition to that first store they found another small grocery store, a bakery, a butcher shop, a dry cleaner's, and a shoe repair shop. They also found a number of specialty fashion boutiques. Whenever Emily saw a store where they thought they were likely to shop, she introduced Nellie to the store clerks and owners. Most of the managers and their clerks gave them a positive and encouraging response.

Nellie was pleased to meet so many new people. Emily was impressed with how favorable the people in the neighborhood responded to Nellie. As a gesture of good will, Emily taught many of their new acquaintances how to touch Nellie on the shoulder to let her know they recognized her and how to finger spell, "Hi, Nellie." into her hand.

Emily was particularly encouraged when the owner of the bakery responded by saying, "I am delighted. Now I can greet Nellie by name, in sign language!"

Back at the apartment, Emily gratefully removed her shoes to give her tired feet a rest. "I feel great!" she thought, "I think that important connections were made today. Shopping will be a lot more personal in this neighborhood."

Then a sobering thought came to mind, "It will help ensure Nellie's safety if, God forbid, she ever ventures out without me."

They went to church on Sunday, but in the early afternoon, Emily took Nellie for a longer walk. They discovered that within walking distance, there were even more opportunities for shopping, including a large indoor shopping mall, several small strip malls, and an IGA super market. Also, they found Aultman Hospital.

As they stopped by a nearby McDonald's to rest their feet, and to get a bite to eat, finger spelling to each other, Nellie said, "The more I learn about our neighborhood, the better I feel about living here with you. It is just ideal. We have everything we need close by. And, I really do like this Big Mac, even if it takes a lot of nerve to eat it because it's so messy."

On Monday morning Emily got up almost as early as Nellie. As she prepared to go to work as a nurse's aid at the Canton Country Lawn Nursing Home, Nellie was thinking to herself, "This is great! I will have the whole day to myself. I'll be free to do whatever I want in my new home!"

Emily saw Nellie grinning to herself as she ate her breakfast, and reaching over, spelled into her hand, "What is so funny?"

"Nothing," Nellie said, "I'm just thinking about what I am going to do today."

Without thinking about what she was saying, Emily spelled, "Now, Nellie, you be good!"

After breakfast, Nellie bathed and put on one of her nicer dresses. She and Emily had been so interested in getting to know about their neighborhood, that some of their things were still packed in moving boxes. So, Nellie began her day by puttering around the house, finding places to put all her clothes, books, and crafts. Next she felt like cleaning up the apartment. She put on an apron and began by washing every dish in the cupboard, including all the glasses, silverware, and the pots and pans. Then she went to the broom closet, got a bucket, some detergent, and a scrub brush, got down on her hands and knees and washed the floor. By the time she was finished, the place sparkled. When she stood up, she smiled to herself as she checked her clothes. She had done all those dishes without getting one spot of water on her apron, and she had washed the whole floor without getting wet!

After lunch, Nellie decided that she wanted to cook dinner for Emily. She decided to make spaghetti and to serve it with a salad. Emily had shown Nellie where all the food was and what was in the refrigerator. Nellie felt around with her sensitive fingers, found the spaghetti and the sauce. But she could not find any hamburger to put in the sauce. She found lettuce and tomatoes for the salad, but no radishes or carrots. So Nellie decided she wanted to go shopping.

As the owner of the corner grocery store had suggested, Nellie sat down and wrote out her short shopping list. She wrote with large letters, using her left forefinger for a guide to keep her lines straight, and leaving about an inch between each word. With the list in her hand, Nellie found her way down the stairs and to the sidewalk. With an air of complete self-confidence, she lifted her head and squared her shoulders. With her palms facing forward, and her fingers pointing upward, she stretched out her arms in front of her to feel any obstacles in her way, and proceeded, walking dead center down the sidewalk!

As Nellie marched down the sidewalk on that hot, steamy June afternoon, her neighbors in the apartments next door were outside, sitting on their porches. Nellie could neither see them nor hear them.

But if she had been able to hear, she would have heard them talking to each other, "Bill, what is wrong with that old lady? Look at the way she is walking! Hey, Miss, are you OK? Hey Miss!"

"Mary, I don't think she can hear you. I think that she is deaf!"

"Yeah, Bill! And the way she is walking, I don't think she can see anything either. Man! I don't believe it. Where do you think that she's going?"

As Nellie made her way to the corner, she drew near an elderly couple, coming from the opposite direction. Looking up, they stepped aside to get out of Nellie's way. They stood off the sidewalk, on the grass, near a tree, and watched her walk past them. Speechless and transfixed, their expressions changed from amazement to concern.

But when Nellie arrived at the entrance to the store, having counted her steps, she abruptly turned and went inside. She stood silently in the doorway and waited to be greeted by the cashier. When the cashier looked up, she was startled. After she recovered, she approached Nellie, touched her on the shoulder, and hesitantly spelled into her hand, "Hi, Nellie!"

Nellie's face lit up as she handed over her grocery list and said in her low raspy voice, "I only need a few things."

The cashier looked at the list and within a few minutes returned with the three items Nellie had requested. When Nellie had paid for her purchase, she returned to the apartment without incident and set about cooking supper. She was excited. She had learned how to cook when she was just a young girl, but she had not fixed a hot meal since her father's death. She lit the gas stove and went right to work.

When Emily entered the apartment, weary from her long day of work, she was astonished. She found the table set. The aroma of homemade spaghetti hung in the air. And Nellie was standing by the stove, stirring the sauce.

Emily gave Nellie a big hug and spelled into her hand, "Oh, Nellie, You really shouldn't have. But it smells wonderful! What are you making?"

Nellie replied, "Oh, just a little supper."

Then Emily looked at the big pot of boiling water, and saw the gas flames licking the bottom of the pot. Fear and sadness shadowed her face.

Nellie could not see Emily's expression of sincerity and sorrow as she again spelled into Nellie's hand, "You really should not have done this!"

Emily ate dinner with mixed emotions. The scene of the sightless and deaf Nellie standing by the stove, with the open gas flames licking the bottom of the pot frightened Emily. She could also see that Nellie was very excited about what she had been able to do all by herself.

Emily agonized, "I hate to steal Nellie's joy, but I can't have her cooking when I am not around. It just isn't safe!"

After supper, Emily took Nellie out on the balcony. Nellie took a deep breath of the sultry summer air and said out loud, "I love this balcony! I can smell the hamburgers being cooked on the grill next door. I smell someone baking pizza. And someone else is baking pie! An apple pie! This is a wonderful neighborhood. This is a wonderful apartment."

Then she both finger spelled and mouthed the words at the same time, "I feel the vibration of the traffic. Emily, tell me what you see."

Emily paused, trying to think of how to describe what she saw and the words to use. "Well," she said, "Tuscawaras Street runs east and west, and traffic is heavy. The big vibrations that you feel probably come from large tractor trailer rigs, the great big trucks that are like moving vans."

Nellie cocked her head sideways, as if she were listening. Then she giggled, "Oh, Emily, I'm feeling the trucks now and I can tell which way they are going. Some are going east and there is one that is going west. With the bottoms of my feet, the back of my neck, in my fingers, and in my head. Through my whole body, I can feel the vibrations they make as they drive past us."

The two stood there silently, drinking in all the smells and vibrations of the neighborhood.

Emily broke the silence, spelling into Nellie's hand, "Yes, it is a wonderful apartment. And it is your apartment. But I don't want you to use the gas stove when I am not here!"

"Why not?" Nellie asked in all innocence.

"Because it isn't safe. You can't see or hear the flame. You couldn't tell if something is burning or boiling over. It's too easy to get hurt. So promise me you won't do it again."

By now Emily was pressing down hard as she formed her letters. Nellie knew that she was upset.

So she said, "OK! OK! I promise."

But secretly Nellie thought, "I'm just glad that Emily didn't find out about me going shopping by myself. She would probably be even more upset!"

In spite of her intuition, Nellie still was very excited about being free and having her own home. She felt that she had a right to do what she wanted to do, and to go where she wanted to go!

Three days later, Nellie stepped out on the balcony after Emily went to work. As she inhaled the fresh morning air, she could smell the aroma of the nearby bakery. She decided she wanted to buy a loaf of fresh baked bread, some dinner rolls, and a half dozen donuts. She wrote down her list, slipped on a clean apron and tied a scarf over her long hair. Next she counted her money and put her change purse in a large cloth shopping bag. With the bag hanging from one arm, she set out for the store. Walking with her hands stretched out in front of her and counting off her steps, she knew exactly where to turn to enter the bakery.

The bread and donuts smelled heavenly as she stepped inside the door. She stood still, breathing deeply, drinking in the baking aromas. When she could stand the suspense no more, she walked to the counter.

The baker noticed her, walked around the counter, touched Nellie on the shoulder and finger spelled into her hand, "Hi, Nellie."

Nellie smiled and held out her list for him to take. He filled the order, picking out a variety of donuts.

Once back in the apartment, Nellie brewed some coffee and sat down to taste her goodies. They tasted just like they smelled, heavenly!

But as Nellie reveled in the sweet creamy flavor of one of her filled donuts, she thought, "I don't know if it tastes so good because it is good, or because I went out all by myself and bought it. Freedom is sweet!"

Nellie still felt quite pleased with herself, but when Emily returned home, one of her neighbors stopped her on the sidewalk and said, "I just want you to know that I saw Nellie out on the sidewalk today. I think she went to the bakery."

When Emily entered the apartment, she hugged Nellie and spelled into her palm, "I'm hungry. Can I have some bread to make a sandwich?"

Nellie gave her a loaf of store bought sliced bread.

But Emily spelled, "I don't mean this bread! I mean the fresh bread you bought at the bakery today."

Nellie frowned and protested out loud, "What?"

But she knew she had been caught.

"Who told you this," she pouted.

Emily responded with a lecture, finger spelling into Nellie's hand, "Nellie, I don't want you to go walking around the neighborhood alone. It is like cooking on the stove. It is not safe! You will have to wait until I get home, and then we can go shopping together."

She pressed down hard in Nellie's palm for emphasis, "Do you understand? Do you promise?"

Nellie answered like a child, raising her voice, "OK! OK! I promise."

But like a rebellious child, she was just saying "OK" to get Emily off her back. Secretly, she had no intention of keeping her word.

In spite of Emily's worry about Nellie's cooking and going shopping alone, the apartment was full of joy and laughter. Emily enjoyed Nellie's company. Nellie kept the apartment spotless and they both had fun cooking together. Emily looked forward to the weekend and the chance for an outing. On Friday, they met Jim and a few of the other Nellie Volunteers at the Pizza Hut in their neighborhood. Then on Saturday, they drove to the IGA Supermarket to stock up on food for the coming week.

When they entered the store, Emily brought a shopping cart. She placed Nellie's hands on the push bar and led by pulling the cart forward through the long aisles. Emily stopped every few feet to discuss what she was looking for. By spelling into Nellie's hand, she included her in deciding on which products and brands they should buy. Emily soon discovered that unlike herself, Nellie was a math whiz. She could instantly figure out, in her head, the unit prices of competing products.

When they got to the fruits and vegetables, Nellie had a great time touching and feeling all the fresh produce. Emily enjoyed watching Nellie pick up, smell, and squeeze the apples and oranges. Nellie caressed the fuzzy peaches. When she got to the bananas, Nellie picked up a loose one. Then she squeezed it to see how firm it was.

Emily was laughing as she spelled into Nellie's hand, "Gently, don't squeeze the banana so hard, you'll bruise it!"

Just then the produce manager came over to Emily and said, "What you touch you must buy!"

Emily acted as if she did not hear him, and went on finger spelling and interacting with Nellie. Since Emily did not respond to his words, he guessed that they were both deaf. So he followed along behind them and watched, with one raised eyebrow, as they continued their playful exploration of his department. Nevertheless, he kept his peace with them and allowed Nellie to touch everything even though they only put a few items into their cart to buy.

Emily could hardly contain herself. As soon as they sat down in the car, she burst out laughing. With flying fingers, she told Nellie about the produce manager and the trick that she had played on him. Emily described every detail of the scene.

"You should have seen yourself! When you picked up the tomato and smelled it, you looked like someone in perfect bliss. But the produce manager seemed absolutely horrified. I thought his eyes were going to pop right out of is head! Nellie laughed too, until the tears came streaking down her cheeks.

As Emily crawled into bed that night she said to herself, "I have never had so much fun with a friend as I have had with Nellie today! I am going to be sore from laughing so much!"

Likewise, Nellie blessed Jesus for sending her such a wonderful companion. She fell asleep dreaming about going to church in the morning, with Emily by her side, and telling her friends about their adventure at the IGA store.

As time passed, for the most part, the living arrangement between Emily and Nellie was pleasing to both. Emily felt especially good about having made her commitment to Nellie. It satisfied her to see how delighted Nellie was to be able to do even the smallest thing. Nellie loved to wash the dishes, cook dinner, or just to sit on their balcony, breathing in the night air and feeling the vibration of the traffic on the street below.

Every morning, Nellie collected the mail and put it in a box on top of the refrigerator. Then, periodically, Emily could go through all the mail, pay the bills and balance her checkbook. Six weeks after they moved in, Emily again sat down at the dining table and began writing the necessary checks. But when she had written them all and got around to balancing her ledger, she discovered that she was in the red by $53.00! It was clear that she would not be able to mail the checks until she transferred some money from her savings account. Emily was surprised and troubled.

As she looked over her checkbook register, she could see that the initial expense of settling into the apartment had taken more money than she had anticipated. The greatest drain on their finances had been the rental deposit, and the mandatory deposits she had made in order to get the utilities turned on. But even all the minor necessities to set up housekeeping now seemed to add up to a goodly sum. Emily had already dipped into her own savings by several hundred dollars to cover just the basic living expenses.

While the rent was just over one hundred forty dollars a month, the utilities were another seventy-five. Paying for their food, gas for the car, and other necessities had cost another one hundred and seventy five dollars. It was clear that even if they cut back on what they spent on their food and entertainment, the combination of Nellie's Social Security and Emily's paycheck would not be enough to make ends meet.

Emily sat back in her chair and thought, ruefully, "Well, I do have my small inheritance from my grandmother. I guess that I am willing to use some of it to help out, but this is money that I wanted to invest!"

Then she thought, "If my mother ever finds out that I have dipped into my inheritance to finance living with Nellie, she will go berserk. Mom hates it when I associate with deaf people. She already went nuts when I told her that I was going to live with Nellie. She hasn't spoken to me since the day we moved in, but I'll bet she would break her silence if she found out."

Emily cringed at the thought of enduring another of her mother's vehement tirades. She shuddered, "I guess I'd better not use up my inheritance. I will just have to find a way to supplement our monthly income."

Emily decided to call Jim. She invited him to come to the apartment. He arrived the following Saturday afternoon. Emily told him that she had been forced to dip into her small savings in order to make ends meet.

Jim frowned, "You should have told me sooner! I have money donated by the Nellie Zimmerman Volunteers, our church and other organizations which can be used for special purposes."

"Yes, I know," Emily responded, "But what is special about paying for electricity. Or food, or gas in the car?"

Nellie joined in by sitting between the two of them. They had a long three-way discussion and decided the simplest thing to do was to take in another roommate to share the expenses.

The next day all three of them went to church. After worship, Jim gathered the Nellie Volunteers together for a meeting. He told the group about the financial dilemma and the plan to find another roommate to help share the expenses. Everyone agreed that this was a good idea and promised to help search for a suitable person with whom Emily and Nellie could share the apartment.

Three days later, the phone rang. A soft-spoken woman asked, "Are you Emily Street? Are you still looking for another roommate? My name is Nancy. I am blind and live with my parents, but I am looking for my own place to stay. I have a job working at the concession stand in the

Federal Building, so I can pay my own way. And all I need is a safe place to live."

Emily thought that Nancy sounded like a good prospect. She told Nellie that a young blind woman had called to inquire about living with them. She also explained that although this woman could not see, she could hear.

The next day, one of Nancy's friends brought her to the apartment. Immediately, Emily could see that Nancy was an attractive young woman with shoulder length dark brown hair, dark, wrap-around sunglasses, and a white, collapsible blind cane. She was polite and self-confident. Having been greeted, she was shown around the apartment and finally ushered to a seat at the table. Nancy was disquieted by the hush of silence. She could not see that Emily was describing her impressions to Nellie by spelling into her hand.

After a few minutes of discussion the women made up their mind to accept Nancy into the household.

Nancy was relieved when Emily broke the silence with a laugh. "Nellie and I agree. You are perfect. Would you like to live with us?"

In order to make room for Nancy, Emily volunteered to sleep on the living room sofa and to let Nancy have the dining room for her bedroom. They agreed that they would each pay a third of the rent, utilities, and food bills. Each would be responsible for the care of their clothing, and for supplying their own toiletries. Also, everyone would take a share in general cooking and cleaning chores, but each would be responsible for her own laundry and personal space. After taking another look around the apartment, Nancy agreed that it would make an ideal place for her to live. Emily spelled to Nellie all that was said.

After reaching this agreement, Emily invited Nancy to stay for dinner. They all got along famously as they bustled around the kitchen. Laughter filled the air as they sat around the dining room table and shared the stories of their lives.

As Emily crawled into her bed in the dining room for the last time, she grinned to herself. Even though she had to give up her bed, she was very pleased with this arrangement. She thought the plan would solve two problems. It would resolve their financial problems and, also, at least for a few hours of each workday, it would relieve her anxiety about leaving Nellie home alone and unsupervised. She knew that whenever Nellie needed an item for cleaning the apartment, or something to help her prepare their evening meal, she would still be too impatient to wait for her to get home to go shopping.

Nellie was now a familiar figure in the neighborhood. Three store owners had reported that once in the store, while the clerks were getting the items on her list from the shelves, Nellie would place her money on the counter. Then they packed her purchases into her shopping bag, and placed it on her arm. With her shopping completed, Nellie proudly headed back home. In spite of Emily's disapproval, she was going shopping alone at least once a week. Clearly, Nellie thought she was capable of getting where she wanted to go and taking care of herself. But Emily could not help imagining what might happen if Nellie tripped on the uneven sidewalk, or stumbled out onto the street, or got lost. She also worried about Nellie being taken advantage of.

"What if one of the neighborhood kids tries to trip Nellie, or tries to snatch her shopping bag or purse? Or, God forbid, what if Nellie gets mugged?" she thought.

Each time Emily discovered that Nellie had ventured out alone, she severely admonished her. But secretly she knew that this was a no-win situation with Nellie. Emily thought that it would be worth sacrificing her bed and her privacy just to have another person in the apartment to keep an eye on Nellie.

"It might seem like the blind leading the blind," Emily thought, "But at least Nancy can hear!"

Before she fell asleep, Emily decided that she would ask her boss to put her on the second shift. That way she could be home with Nellie during the day, and Nancy would be with Nellie after work in the evening. Little did Emily know that the personalities of Nancy and Nellie would mix like oil and water.

A struggle between them began as soon as Nancy moved in the next day. Emily helped Nancy to find places for all her things.

Then she took her aside and said, "I know that we did not discuss this when you agreed to move into the apartment, but I wonder if you would be willing to help Nellie when she is cooking? She can't hear if something is boiling over or burning, but you can!"

Nancy agreed, so Emily went on, "I also wonder if you would be willing to accompany Nellie if she wants to go shopping when I am not home. I don't like it when she goes out alone. She knows exactly where each store is, but since you can hear, you could help by talking with the store owners and clerks."

Smiling, Nancy agreed. She willingly agreed to "take care" of Nellie when Emily was not at home. But being asked to play a supervisory role over Nellie inflamed in her a feeling of superiority . Unconsciously, Nancy looked down on people with a more severe handicap than her own.

She reasoned, "I am blind, but this old lady is blind and deaf! So I am better off than she is. I can take care of her!"

As soon as Emily told Nellie about the agreement with Nancy, she could tell that she was offended.

Without speaking the words out loud, Nellie told Emily, spelling slowly and emphatically with one hand, "I can take care of myself! I am seventy-two years old. I don't need a baby sitter!"

The friction between Nancy and Nellie increased throughout the day. Most of the time Emily and Nellie communicated by finger spelling to each other. This was a *silent* communication. Late in the afternoon, Nancy heard Emily walk into the living room and take a seat on the sofa. Then she heard Nellie come in and sit down next to Emily. Since the silence in the room was broken here and there by a laugh, or by a few spoken words from Nellie, Nancy knew they were talking, but she was not included in the conversation and she could not hear what was being said. Nancy felt unbearably jealous. It was obvious that Emily and Nellie were good friends.

When she could no longer stand it, Nancy interrupted their conversation by walking over to Emily, tapping her on the shoulder and saying, "Don't you think it's time for us to start supper?"

After supper, Emily and Nellie were sitting at the dining table, having a cup of tea and talking with their hands again. Nancy heard them laughing and having fun.

So Nancy interrupted their conversation by walking up to Emily, tapping her on the shoulder and saying, "Hey, Emily, guess what happened yesterday at work!"

She then began to tell Emily about an amusing encounter with a new customer at her concession stand. At first, Emily thought that Nancy was being rude. Then it dawned on her that Nancy was jealous and looking for attention. Emily realized that to be fair, Nancy would have to be included in all of their conversations.

But Emily's thoughts rebelled at this, "I don't want to have to interpret everything for both Nancy and Nellie. I want Nancy to be able to talk directly to Nellie."

Knowing that Nancy did not know how to finger spell, she said, "Hey, Nancy, that was a great story! Why don't I teach you how to finger spell and then you can tell Nellie about it yourself."

Emily's suggestion rubbed Nancy the wrong way and she walked off, saying, "Oh, that's OK. Maybe some other time."

Under her breath, silently, she said, "I'm not deaf, so why should I want to learn deaf talk?"

Nancy's feeling of jealously deepened the next day when Jim stopped by for a visit in the evening. After greeting Nancy and Emily, to be polite, he briefly looked at the way Nancy had arranged her room, and then spent his time talking silently to Nellie. All Nancy could hear of their conversation was an occasional laugh or a verbal outburst. Again, she tried to butt into the conversation, but Jim brushed her attempt aside and went on visiting with Nellie.

The next afternoon, when Emily came home from work, Nellie finger spelled to Emily, "I think we need to buy some more coffee, tuna fish, and macaroni."

Emily suggested, "Why don't you go to the store with Nancy?"

The two women left the apartment together. When Nellie got to the sidewalk, she took hold of Nancy's hand, placed it on her arm, assumed her usual posture and began to walk down the block with her hands stretched out in front of her. But Nancy did not trust Nellie's ability to lead her. Before they got to the end of the block, like a stubborn mule, Nancy stopped, dug in her heels, and refused to go any farther.

Nancy let go of Nellie's arm. She unfolded her white cane, took Nellie by the hand and proceeded to tap-tap her way down the sidewalk. Nellie tried to withdraw her hand and to take hold of Nancy's arm at the elbow as she was used to doing when she walked with Emily. Nancy batted her hand away, reestablished her grip on Nellie's hand and, like a mother dragging a slow hesitant child, kept Nellie off balance as She pulled her down the sidewalk. Nellie had a hard time counting her steps as she was dragged along, but she managed to keep her concentration in spite of her rising temper. When she reached the right number of steps and knew she was standing in front of the grocery store, she stopped, and with a violent twist, slipped out of Nancy's grip. Once free, knowing that

Nancy could not see her or the store entrance, she silently walked to the door, opened it and stepped inside, leaving Nancy standing alone on the sidewalk.

Furious, Nancy listened for any sound that Nellie might make which would tell her where she was. Finally, she heard the bell on the door of the store as Nellie went in. So tapping with her white cane, she found her way to the entrance.

Realizing that she had not brought a written shopping list, Nellie waited impatiently for Nancy to come into the store. When she arrived, they bumped into each other. Nellie took hold of Nancy's hand and put it on her arm.

Then the clerk came over, touched Nellie on the shoulder, and in his customary way, spelled into her hand, "Hi, Nellie."

Nellie spoke in her low raspy voice, "This is my new roommate."

Nancy heard Nellie's introduction and drowned out the rest of her words, saying in a loud peppy voice, "Hi, I am Nancy! It's nice to meet you! I am blind like Nellie, but I can hear, so you can talk normal to me."

Once the women had paid for their groceries, they returned to the apartment walking separately. Nellie carried her shopping bag over one arm and walked in front of Nancy, with the other arm outstretched. Nancy followed, tapping along with her white cane. When Nellie knew that she was standing in front of the stairs leading to their apartment, she stood still on the sidewalk until Nancy bumped into her with her cane. Then Nellie took her by the hand and led her to the bottom step of the outside stairway. The two women climbed the stairs in silence. Nellie handed Emily the groceries. Neither of them said a word to Emily about their trip.

As the days passed by, Emily was mystified by the fact that the two women seldom ventured outside when she was away.

Finally, she spelled to Nellie. "Why don't you take walks with Nancy when I'm not home?"

Nellie scowled at Emily, "I can't be bothered with having to take care of Nancy and myself, too."

Her raspy voice cracked with emotion as she added. "I'll wait for you to come home so you and I can go together."

It was clear to Emily that the level of conflict between the two women was escalating.

Two weeks later, Emily went ahead and requested a reduction in her hours and began working the second shift. This meant that Emily could be with Nellie during the greater part of the day, but she had to leave at 2:30 pm. Nancy, on the other hand, was off work at five, arrived home by 5:30 pm, and could be with Nellie all evening. This meant that on weekdays, Nellie was only left alone for about three hours.

However, much to Emily's surprise and frustration, this change increased the intensity of the conflict between the two women. Nellie was even more determined to use her three hours of 'freedom' to do whatever she wanted, to cook, or go shopping alone, if she pleased.

When Nancy arrived home from work, she would try to find out where Nellie was and what she was doing. This was a challenge because Nancy could not look around the apartment with her eyes. She had to search for Nellie with her ears. But whenever she caught Nellie cooking by herself, or discovered that she was not home, she would tell Emily about it.

Nellie resented feeling that Nancy was put in charge of her. She despised Nancy even more for being a tattletale. One day, in order to be obstinate, Nellie deliberately baited Nancy. When Nancy came home from work, Nellie was extra quiet to make her think that she was not home.

When the silence had been maintained for more than two hours, Nancy began to suspect that Nellie was home and that she was playing a trick on her. She began to make a room-to-room search for Nellie.

Nellie had two ways to tell exactly where Nancy was: by smelling her fragrant perfume and by feeling the vibration of the wooden floor as Nancy walked around the apartment. Nellie could glide, as silent as a ghost, across the floor and escape detection by Nancy. For the impish Nellie, hiding from Nancy in this way was great fun.

Nellie repeated this game two or three days a week. So Nancy never knew what to expect when she came home from work. She was quite perplexed and disquieted by the "silent treatment" she received from Nellie for hours on end. In her growing frustration, she became even more determined to tap her way around the apartment with her white cane to find Nellie.

Unable to admit that she could not keep track of Nellie, Nancy kept her mouth shut and did not complain about Nellie's game. But one day, when Emily was home and Nancy came home from work, she saw

Nellie hiding from her and sneaking around the apartment. She watched as Nellie walked right by Nancy, undetected. But rather than thinking that Nellie was being funny, Emily thought that she was being mean.

Emily caught Nellie by the arm and scolded her, speaking out loud as she spelled into her hand, "Stop that, Nellie! Nellie, how do you like it when people walk by you and don't make any contact? How do you like it when you know that they are there, but they act as if you are not there? You know better than to be mean to Nancy just because she is blind. Be nice!"

For emphasis, Emily pressed down hard on the last couple of letters of each word.

Nellie appeared contrite, but said facetiously out loud, "OK, I promise to make a lot of noise from now on so Nancy will know exactly where I am."

Nancy overheard this and smiled, knowing that Nellie had been caught.

As Emily suspected, Nellie was as true to her word about not playing hide and seek as she was about not going shopping alone. Finally, Nancy decided that it was too much trouble to keep track of Nellie's whereabouts. Thoroughly disgusted with the whole situation, she ignored Nellie.

When Nancy stopped playing Nellie's game, Nellie found a new way of vexing her.

She remembered her words to Emily, "I promise to make a lot of noise from now on so Nancy will know exactly where I am."

Nellie delighted in doing housework. Because it was the first time in her life that she had lived in her own home, her passion for cleaning bordered on a 'compulsion' disorder. Day and night were the same to her. Almost every night, in the wee hours of the morning, she would silently get up and quietly start doing her chores. Now, the impish Nellie started banging things around in the kitchen, making a big deal of washing and stacking all the dishes in the cupboard, and talking to herself as she scrubbed the kitchen floor. She enjoyed thinking that while Emily could sleep through a hurricane, Nancy's hearing was highly sensitive. Just knowing that made it great fun for her.

Nellie grinned. Like a mischievous child, she thought, "Ha, Nancy can't even come out here and tell me to be quiet because she doesn't know how to finger spell."

The next morning, Nancy complained to Emily about Nellie making noise all night long.

But Emily dismissed her comment saying, "Oh, come on, Nancy. She couldn't be that bad. I didn't hear anything."

Emily's flippant response only served to further alienate Nancy. After a week of putting up with Nellie's antics, she decided to fight back.

She announced to Emily, "Since Nellie is doing her housework at night and disturbing my sleep, I am going on strike. I will only do my own laundry and clean up my own room. But I am not going to cook, or wash dishes, or do anything else around here. I pay rent to stay here in this apartment, and I don't think its fair that Nellie can keep making noise all night long."

Although it did not bother Nellie to have Nancy out of the kitchen, it bugged Emily to see Nancy sitting down, doing nothing, while she and Nellie were bustling about cooking supper for her. It also perturbed Emily when Nancy left things lying around the living room and did not pick them up and put them away. Now, Emily's resentment toward Nancy began to grow.

One Friday evening, Emily announced that several friends were stopping by for a visit on Saturday evening. The next morning, while Emily and Nellie cleaned up the apartment, and then made special cookies for the party, Nancy remained on strike. When they went to get more food, soft drinks, and party supplies, Nancy refused to go along.

Later, when Jim and their friends arrived for the party they, too, could feel the tension as sparks flew between Nellie and Nancy. Even though friends were visiting, neither of them tried to conceal their resentment. Instead, they each spent the entire time complaining about each other. Not knowing how to deal with the unpleasant situation, and embarrassed for the two women, they did not stay long.

Jim was the last to leave and he remarked, "I hope that time will heal the friction between Nancy and Nellie."

Two days later, while she was driving to work, Emily began to talk to herself. She made a list of the things that bothered her about Nancy.

"It hurts me that she refuses to learn how to finger spell. At first, she made a half-hearted attempt to learn, but now she does not even pretend to want to know how to talk to Nellie. I feel used. Both Nellie and Nancy treat me as if I am hired help, someone who can see for them, and fetch and carry. They expect me to drive them everywhere, and to do whatever they want. I feel caught in the middle and have to act as a referee. If only we could go back to the way it was before Nancy came."

With those thoughts Emily realized that their arrangement was precariously close to falling apart. She knew that they needed Nancy's money to keep their leaky financial boat afloat. She decided that the best thing to do was to call a conference and try to "talk out" their differences.

That evening, Emily called Nancy and Nellie together for the conference. She sat between them and finger spelled for Nellie, and spoke out loud for Nancy.

She began by saying, "Two months ago we agreed to live together because it was beneficial to everyone."

She went on, "Nellie, we can't afford to live here without having Nancy to share the expenses. And Nancy, if you can't get along with Nellie, you will have to move back home and live with your parents. I know that things have gotten out of hand, but we have to find a way of getting along with each other."

Nancy jumped in, saying, "I don't think that it's fair that Nellie has the biggest bedroom. I want the big bedroom or I won't stay here. Besides, if I am sleeping in the bedroom in the back of the apartment, away from everything, it won't bother me so much if Nellie wants to wash dishes in the middle of the night."

Emily passed along Nancy's comment.

In a surprisingly graceful way, Nellie answered, "If it will help us to get along better, I am willing to switch rooms. The dining room is big enough for me and all my things."

Immediately they got up from the table and started moving the furniture around. An hour later, Nancy was relaxing in her new room, and Nellie had already put her belongings into their new places. And as Emily crawled under her blanket on the sofa, she sensed that an unspoken truce had been made between her two roommates.

When the tension in the apartment eased, Emily felt comfortable in inviting Jim and their friends to visit. On the following weekend, the apartment again vibrated with a party atmosphere. Emily was thankful for the peace that settled over their home.

=   =   =

"Kitten"

Chapter Seven

CAT CALLED KITTEN

In the midst of the unnatural peace between Nellie and Nancy, a kitten appeared at the apartment.

Emily wanted to do something special for Nellie, because she had been so cheerful about giving up her spacious bedroom. But it was not easy for her to come up with the perfect gift because Nellie already had everything she needed.

One night she awoke from a dream with an inspiration.

"A cat! Nellie needs a cat!"

A few days later Emily attended a meeting of the Canton Pilot Club. She knew that the club had taken an interest in Nellie's story, so she explained to the group that Nellie had never had a pet and she thought that it would be nice if Nellie had a pet cat. This suggestion caught their interest and, immediately, one of the young women offered to donate a four-week old kitten as a gift to Nellie. The group decided that when it was time to take the kitten to the Animal Hospital for its shots, and to be de-clawed and "fixed," they would pay all the medical costs. Emily was to give them the veterinarian's bill and they would take care of paying it. Emily agreed to provide the necessary supplies, including the litter box and feeding dishes. Everyone agreed that it was a perfect idea.

A week later, the young woman delivered the tiny pet. It was a gentle, playful little female "tiger" kitty. All three of the roommates were delighted with their new little friend.

Before Emily could establish that the kitty was for Nellie, Nancy asked, "Who is going to take care of it?"

Once Emily placed the kitten in Nellie's lap and guided her hands to hold and gently stroke her, she grinned. Enraptured, Nellie didn't say a word. She sat perfectly still. She felt the kitten's rapid heartbeat. In response to her continued stroking, the kitten began to purr. A confused expression crossed Nellie's face as she felt this new kind of vibration.

Emily spelled to Nellie, "That's its motor running. A cat will turn on its motor whenever it is happy."

With a delighted grin on her face, Nellie sat and petted the kitten. Her sensitive fingers traced its face and head and lingered a little longer as she was feeling its perfect little ears. Gently, she explored the curves of its tiny body. Then she stroked its long tail. When she got to the end of its tail, she gave it a gentle pull.

Nellie couldn't suppress her giggle when the little thing raised its rear end as she finished the onward sweep of her hand, out to the end of its tail. Then joyfully, she placed her hand back on the kitten's head and began the petting ritual over again. For the first time in her life, Nellie experienced the maternal feelings that come with caring for another living creature.

When Emily first placed the tiny kitten in Nellie's lap, she held her breath, "What if Nellie is too rough with the tiny kitten? What if she doesn't take to it?"

But by watching the sheer delight spread across Nellie's face, Emily quickly realized that Nellie would be careful and protective of their new pet.

Remembering Nancy's question, Emily simultaneously said out loud to Nancy and spelled to Nellie, "Whoever wants to keep this kitty is going to have to take care of it. The kitty needs somebody to feed it, give it water, and change the litter box."

Nancy said nothing.

But to Emily's delight, almost childlike in her enthusiasm, Nellie asked, "Oh, can I keep the kitty? I promise to take good care of it! I'll feed it! I'll give it water! And I can change that 'whatever it is,' too!"

Laughing over Nellie's excitement, Emily led her into the kitchen and by touch, showed her two small, heavy, ceramic bowls.

She explained into Nellie's palm, "One of these bowls is for dry cat food, the other bowl is for canned cat food."

She then guided Nellie's hand to feel a larger stoneware bowl and a small china dish and spelled, "This big one is to be used for water and the small one is for the kitty's evaporated milk. She will need that because she is still a baby!"

Nellie grinned as Emily showed her how to find and measure out the dry and canned cat food.

Emily warned her not to fill the water bowl too full and explained, "Run the tap water until it gets cold. Then slide your finger into the bowl."

Nellie reached over and put her finger in the center of the bowl and touched the bottom.

She asked, speaking out loud, "Oh, you mean like this?"

"No, Nellie, you should slide your hand along the side of the bowl until you feel the top edge with the second knuckle of your second finger. Then fill the bowl until you feel the cold water touch the tip of your first finger. Now you will be able to set the bowl down on the floor without spilling any water."

Next, Emily showed Nellie how to pour the evaporated milk into the smaller bowl, using the same method.

Nellie smiled as she licked the sweet tasting milk off her finger, then she giggled, "Emily, the kitty is tickling me!"

The kitten had stayed in the living room with Nancy, but came running into the kitchen when it heard the electric can opener. Now in its excitement, it was pacing back and forth, brushing up against Nellie's ankles.

Emily spelled to Nellie, "Let's see what kind of food the kitty likes best."

They placed the four bowls on the kitchen floor close to the wall, well out of everyone's walking path. Nellie gently followed the kitten with her hand as the tiny cat checked out the canned cat food, but ignored it for the moment and began lapping up the milk.

Emily spelled, "I know you will remember to feed the kitten twice a day. But don't over-feed her or you will make her sick."

She went on to say, "Our kitten is still a baby. She will have to be potty trained just like a new baby."

Nellie laughed and raised her chin as her sightless eyes widened. Then she nodded her head vigorously, her white curls bouncing around her face. Her raspy voice broke under the strain of her excitement.

She exclaimed, "Yes! Yes!"

Emily took Nellie to a corner of the bathroom.

She spelled into Nellie's hand, "You stand here for a minute."

Nellie stood as though rooted to the spot, waiting. Emily picked up the kitten's new litter box and held it up for Nellie to touch. She then guided Nellie's hand to feel the depth of the clean litter inside the box. With Nellie's hand holding onto the box, Emily slowly lowered it and replaced it in the corner.

Then she spelled, "This is the kitten's bathroom. We call it a litter box. The kitty will have to be trained to use the litter box."

Nellie looked puzzled, but didn't ask any questions.

As clearly as she could, Emily continued to explain, "The kitten is going to make mistakes. When this happens, take her and put her in the litter box. Then hold her there for a few seconds. She will soon get the idea."

Nellie grinned as she again nodded her head vigorously, and exclaimed, "Yes! Yes! I understand."

The kitten had been delivered on Sunday. The next morning, as she left to go to work, Emily felt confident that Nellie had understood what she had been taught about the basic care of the kitten.

On Tuesday, Emily came home from work to find a frustrated, wildly screeching Nellie, and a diapered kitten. She had made the diaper out of a piece of cloth torn from one of Emily's old blouses. Emily had to catch the frantic kitten before she could remove the diaper. She grabbed the kitten by her tail and pulled her up into her arms. She discovered that the cloth was pinned so tightly around the kitten's tiny middle that she wondered if it had suffered internal injuries. She sat down and quickly unpinned the diaper. Then she watched, with relief, as it scampered away from them to hide. The kitten seemed to be all right.

As she soothed and calmed Nellie, Emily didn't know whether to laugh or cry.

Emily lifted her eyes toward heaven and prayed, "Lord, help me."

She sat next to Nellie on the couch and asked, spelling into her hands, "Why did you put the diaper on so tight?"

Nellie spelled back and also said aloud, "The first time I pinned the diaper on the kitty, it wriggled out of it right away. So I fixed it so it would stay on!"

Painstakingly, Emily began again to explain how to potty train the kitty.

Emily asked her, "Do you know what I mean when I say that the kitten will make mistakes?"

Nellie looked puzzled and slowly shook her head.

"No, I don't."

Chagrined, Emily explained, "Making a mistake means the kitten might sometimes wet or mess either on the floor, under the beds, or somewhere else in the apartment instead of going to the bathroom in its litter box. Do you understand now what I mean?"

Nellie nodded and repeated back to Emily exactly as she had spelled it into her hands.

Emily saw the kitten warily peeking out from under Nellie's bed. She felt sorry for the timid little thing.

Then the thought occurred to her, "Nellie has never been around a baby. She has never been around children, or had any kind of pet. She probably has no idea how fragile and vulnerable they are and how important it is that they be treated gently in order for them to turn out nice."

So, communicating with her fingers she explained, "The kitten is a little baby, a little living creature. It can easily be hurt. It also has feelings. A pet must be able to trust you. You can only earn that trust by being gentle and patient when the kitty makes mistakes."

Again, Nellie nodded and repeated back to Emily everything she said. Emily breathed a deep sigh of relief.

She spelled to Nellie and said out loud, "Good. Everything should be all right now."

The next day, Emily came home from work, parked her car and started up the steps. Before she got half way up the stairway, she could hear Nellie. Again, she was wildly screeching and banging things around. Emily rushed into the apartment and found Nellie in the bathroom, down on her knees in front of the toilet bowl. She was holding the poor little kitten under the water, furiously washing its rear end. Then she proceeded to flush the toilet while the kitten was still immersed in the whirl of water.

Elbowing her way along the bathroom wall, Emily roughly took the kitten away from her. Thrown off balance in the struggle, Nellie tumbled down hard on the floor; she was so angry she was spitting unintelligible words.

Ignoring Nellie for the moment, Emily reached for a towel and began to rub the frightened kitten dry. She saw that she had barely arrived in time to save the kitten from being drowned!

Nellie got to her feet, clamped her lips shut, turned around, walked into the living room and sat down on her hands in her chair. She sat there for several minutes before she pulled her hands free. Then she sat, rigid, with her arms folded over her chest. She refused to say anything.

Emily released the slightly damp kitten and looked around the apartment. There was no sign of any mess anywhere. Whatever mess had been made, Nellie had already taken the time to clean it up before she tried to bathe the kitten in the toilet bowl. With the kitten dried off, and safely placed on a cloth on the couch, Emily could only look at Nellie in amazement.

She reached for Nellie's hands and asked, "What happened? What did the kitten do that made you so angry with her?"

Nellie screwed her face up into a scowl and screeched at Emily.

"No, No, I will not tell you. I will not talk about it."

She was so furious she was shaking.

Later that evening, when Emily thought she had given Nellie enough time to calm down, she asked, "Why were you trying to drown the cat? What did she do to make you so mad?"

Nellie again withdrew her hands, began waving her arms crazily in the air above her head, and exclaimed, "I told you I don't want to talk about it!"

Emily wisely decided to leave her alone.

But when Emily went to do a load of laundry, she found one of Nellie's aprons with a tiny spot of brown on it. She guessed that the kitten had soiled itself and later it had rubbed its little rear end on Nellie's apron while sitting in her lap. Only then, with a sigh of relief, did Emily realize that Nellie was not trying to drown the cat, but was only trying to wash its dirty bottom.

Then she said out loud, "Oh Lord, she couldn't see that the cat's head was under water. She couldn't hear it coughing and sputtering. I know she didn't mean it! Thank you, Lord; I got home just in time to save it."

All seemed to go well the next day.

On Friday, Emily came home from work to an unusually quiet and peaceful apartment. She didn't notice that the kitten was nowhere to be seen.

On her way home, Emily had made a quick stop at the neighborhood store, and she had carried two large bags of groceries up the two flights of stairs. She sat them down on the kitchen counter. After storing the milk and juice in the refrigerator, she put a package of hamburger in the freezer. When she turned around to pick up a package of chicken parts, she heard a muffled sound as the freezer door began to swing shut behind her.

"That's odd." Emily said, "I thought I heard the kitten."

She looked around the kitchen but saw no cat. Then she said out loud, "It must be behind the refrigerator."

She reopened the freezer and moved some items to make room for the chicken. Her hand brushed against a tiny furry body! Startled, she stared, as the little kitten managed to voice a weak, scared, "Meow."

As Emily pulled the shivering kitty out of the freezer, she noticed that frost was already forming on its fur. Holding the kitten close to her chest to warm it, she questioned both Nancy and Nellie. She made them both touch the frost bitten fur. But neither of them would admit to putting the cat in the freezer. Neither of them seemed to know how long the kitten had been in there.

Emily watched a worried look cross Nellie's face as she touched the tiny ice crystals in the kitten's fur.

Then Nellie reached out her hands and asked, "Can I have her?"

Nellie took the tiny kitten and cooed over it, rubbing its little body to warm it. She held it close in her arms for over an hour. From the way she was stroking the kitty and putting her cheek on its fur, Emily could see that Nellie loved the chilled creature. It was clear from her behavior that she was innocent of any intentional wrong doing.

Later Emily noticed some meat on the counter, thawing in preparation for supper. It dawned on her that the kitten must have jumped from the counter into the freezer when Nellie opened it to remove the frozen meat.

The kitten had been with them about two weeks when they decided she had to have a name. Since everyone already called her "the kitten," they simply chose the name, "Kitten."

The little cat was a lover, held no grudges, and feared nothing. After surviving that first week, minus at least three of her nine lives, Kitten was inseparable from Nellie. She followed her everywhere. When Nellie sat still, Kitten would settle down close to her, waiting patiently until she moved again. When she moved, Kitten followed her and stuck her nose into everything that Nellie did.

One day Jim and a few friends stopped by for a visit. Emily let them in. Nellie was not aware that they had arrived. She was in her room working on weaving large, colorful potholders, one of her favorite crafts. The little group of friends stood transfixed in the doorway, watching as she continued her work. Leaning forward, she was bending low over the craft material. Kitten leaped to the back of her chair, walked across her shoulder and, down her back. They watched the cat make a half circle to get into an acceptable position and lie down on Nellie's back.

Everyone marveled!

Jim laughed, "Her back makes a perfect shelf for the cat to lie on."

Nellie stopped working, and began to slowly straighten up. They watched, spell bound, as Kitten exactly matched Nellie's movements, slowly getting to her feet, walking up her back, and settling on her shoulder. Perched on Nellie's shoulder, Kitten took a ride as Nellie crossed the room.

Jim and his friends stayed quite a long time that evening. They couldn't resist picking up the little cat to pet or play with her. But whenever they sat her back down on the floor, she always returned to Nellie and resumed her special perch on her shoulder.

The very next day, Emily enjoyed a day off from work. She watched as Nellie prepared spaghetti for dinner. Kitten walked into the kitchen and began to rub around Nellie's legs. Nellie reached down, picked up the little cat, placed it on her shoulder, and continued browning the hamburger. Emily thought she saw the cat "smile" as it settled down on Nellie's shoulder.

As the cat grew, she tolerated Emily and Nancy. She allowed visitors, especially Jim, to fuss over her, hold, and stroke her. But Nellie was the one with whom she truly bonded.

Kitten was always deliciously content when she was with Nellie, whether she was beside her on the couch, resting on her lap, positioned on her back, or perched on her shoulders. Even Emily, who was hearing impaired, could hear Kitten's deep rumbling, contented purr.

Nellie began to expect the cat to come to her whenever she was working in the kitchen, and Kitten expected to be lifted up so she could get on Nellie's back. It didn't matter whether Nellie was preparing food, making cookies, or baking pies, she learned not to wash her hands in preparation for cooking until the cat was settled in its special position. She would stretch out full length with her long tail curved around one shoulder and her head resting on the other.

Nellie loved and enjoyed Kitten. By the same token, without a doubt, Kitten adopted Nellie. She seemed to know that Nellie could neither hear nor see her. No matter what task was occupying Nellie's attention, the cat was in close physical contact. Kitten liked to be petted and would approach other people with a loud meow, expecting to be picked up. But she never cried or meowed around Nellie. Instead, Kitten would either rub around Nellie's legs, or announce her presence by jumping up to land softly in her lap. Then the cat would climb gently up on Nellie's back, or even on top of her head. Nellie would laugh, reach up, and gently place Kitten on her shoulder.

=   =   =

Chapter Eight

THE FIGHT

The coming of Kitten brought cheer to everyone in the apartment. However, when it came to differences in life styles, Nellie and Emily were complete opposites.

Even Jim thought so, and teasingly told their friends, "With Emily, if anything falls on the floor, it stays there. With Nellie, if anything is on the floor and not nailed down, she will throw it away."

He was telling it exactly as it was. Any piece of paper that Nellie got her hands on, if it wasn't in Braille, she considered worthless and threw it away. This included anything printed or written on paper, such as letters, newspapers, household bills, and personal notes. Since she could not read it, what good was it? She discarded it and that was that. Nellie was not stupid. Of course she knew better.

When confronted by Jim about this, she grinned, and said, "I'm training Emily to be neat."

It worked, too. Emily quickly learned to keep all of the household bills in her purse. Every other piece of paper that she wanted to keep, she tried to hide from Nellie. However, because Nellie was constantly cleaning and exploring every nook and cranny of the apartment, it seemed impossible to hide anything from her. Whatever was 'out of place' (this included hiding places) was subject to being thrown out. This obsession with "having a place for everything and everything in its place" became the focus of her life.

Nellie wanted the apartment to be neat and clean at all times. Anything out of place, a clutter, or a wet or dry mess having to do with food and drink was an aggravation to her. Whenever Nellie became frustrated, or angry, she would announce her displeasure to her hapless roommates with an ear-piercing, nerve-wracking screech. It did not happen often but when it did, it really bothered Nancy, who still "nursed" her resentment against Nellie. Nancy would put her hands over her ears to block out the sound and yell for Emily.

"For heaven's sake, make her stop. How can you stand that noise? Make her shut up!"

Emily's hearing impairment buffered her from the high frequency element of Nellie's screech. Therefore it did not bother her very much, and Emily thought Nancy made a big fuss over nothing. The unacceptable noise level in the apartment, coupled with Emily's lack of sympathy, was fuel that added to Nancy's growing resentment.

Nancy wanted to strike out in a way that would hurt her roommates. She developed a devious plan for getting even with both of them. Every weekend, Emily and Nellie went together to do the grocery shopping. Although jealous of the time Emily spent with Nellie, each week Nancy declined an invitation to go with them.

Without warning, Nancy began an offhanded attack that was designed to sabotage their weekly visit to buy groceries. When they arrived home from their shopping, Nancy promptly sat down at the kitchen table and proceeded to eat. She ate almost the whole week's supply of food in two days. By Monday almost everything was gone. She then complained long and loud for the next few days that there was not anything in the house to eat. After repeating this performance for two weeks, Nancy used the very situation she had created as a reason to refuse to pay for her fair share of the groceries. In order to defeat this attack on their food supply, Emily began to shop two or three times a week and to buy in smaller quantities. Although Emily did take Nellie shopping whenever she could, it ceased to be the carefree Saturday morning activity it once had been!

The success Nancy had encouraged her to think of more devious games to play. She began to make and leave little messes in the kitchen and bathroom for Nellie to clean up. Of course, Nellie complained to Emily about this.

When confronted about her lack of consideration for her roommates, Nancy responded sharply, "I clean my own room. I am not responsible for the rest of the house. And, I pay to live here."

Because Emily knew that, financially, they needed Nancy, she allowed the young blackmailer to get away with this behavior. All that Nancy had to do to set Nellie off on a volatile tirade was to leave a mess in the bathroom or kitchen. Most often the messes were in the kitchen. Nellie, unaware of the spills left on the table or in a chair, would get her clothes wet or soiled by either sitting down on a chair or brushing her arms across the table into some unknown substance or spilled liquid. When she felt a grainy spotting from some unknown food, or the wetness soaking through her clothes, she would become furious.

Nellie felt abused by Nancy, and rightly so. Deeply indignant, there was no hesitation on her part in using graphic and descriptive language in venting her displeasure. Nellie had been out of the State Hospital for more than a year, and with constant use, her voice was stronger and her speech was clearer and easier to understand, especially when she was angry. Nancy could understand everything that Nellie said. Since Nellie could not hear herself talk, she had no way of regulating the tone or loudness of her voice. The full impact of the degree of viciousness that she expressed was also lost on her. When Nellie was angry, she was both blunt and gross. However, to her, these were just words that, once said, were gone and completely forgotten.

Nancy nursed her hurt feelings and complained to Emily, but continued to play her games. Finally, she decided that because she outweighed Nellie by some eighty pounds, she could whip her in a fight. Not only did Nancy outweigh Nellie, but she was a young woman, in her early twenties. Nellie was in her seventies. Intent on attacking Nellie, Nancy waited for a time when Emily would not be home. When the time came, she was ready. She stood with her back against the wall by the doorway leading from the kitchen to the living room. Her keen hearing helped her locate Nellie, who was busily working, traveling back and forth between the kitchen and the living room. She had no way of knowing what Nancy was planning.

Nancy waited for her to come close, then she made her move. A savage shove knocked Nellie off her feet and she landed hard on the wood floor. In an instant Nancy was on top of her. Nellie knew immediately that it was Nancy who had shoved her and was now pinning her down. She was in pain and stunned by the very idea that Nancy would physically attack her. Nancy had used surprise to further her advantage over the older woman.

However, Nellie became instantly alert when she felt Nancy's fingernails digging into her shoulders. The advantage of surprise was over. From that point on, Nellie acted purely by instinct. She reached up with her right hand and got a good hold on Nancy's hair, pulling her head back and to the side as hard as she could. Unprepared for Nellie's quick reaction, Nancy immediately released her grip on Nellie's shoulders.

Nellie knew from her past experiences in the State Hospital that if she was to gain an advantage in a hand-to-hand fight, she had to hang onto the other person. She knew that if she let go, she would not likely be able to find her assailant again. As soon as she felt Nancy's grip on her shoulders release, she grabbed with her left hand to get a good hold on something and what she grabbed was Nancy's right breast! She desperately hung on, her claw-like fingers dug in and held firm.

With her right hand, she socked Nancy hard with a tooth-rattling uppercut that landed under her chin, rocking her backwards. She could not escape because Nellie held tight onto her breast. Nancy screamed in pain and anger! She frantically tried to pry Nellie's fingers loose from their hold, but she could not. Forced to use both hands to try to loosen Nellie's hold left her defenseless.

Nancy was screaming, thrashing around, trying to get loose and dodge the blows she could not see coming at her. Nellie was not making any noise, just breathing hard. The fact that Nellie was quiet served to further terrify Nancy. Then Nellie gave a savage head butt, hitting Nancy in the face with all her might. She got her square in the nose, and blood spurted all over both of them. Nancy yelped, screamed, and choked. She spat blood into Nellie's face. Nothing fazed Nellie. She still hung onto Nancy. She hit her again, this time on the side of her head, close to her eye.

Suddenly, both women felt strong hands pulling them apart. Jim had dropped by unexpectedly, and heard Nancy screaming before he had gotten half way up the steps. He flung open the door. Stunned, he stood there. It took him a moment to understand that he was looking at a deadly battle. Aghast, he rushed forward, yelling as he began trying to separate the two women.

"Nancy, stop it! Stop it now! Nancy, do you hear me, stop this, now!"

Nancy, wracked with wrenching, gulping sobs could only whimper, "Make her stop! Oh, please make her stop!"

He had no way of speaking to Nellie. He, himself, was dangerously close to getting in the way of her lethal fist. Finally, Nellie realized that it was Jim who was pulling on her. Still, it was all he could do to get Nellie to release her death grip on Nancy. When he finally got her to turn loose, he held Nellie tight, locking his arms around her body to stop the wild flailing of her arms.

As soon as Nellie let go, Nancy plopped down on the floor, and sat still, stunned. Actually, Nancy had stopped fighting right after Nellie landed the first blow to her chin. Jim helped Nancy get to her feet and then led her to the bathroom. He left her there to wash up. Meanwhile, he sat Nellie in a chair next to the kitchen sink, and sponged the blood off her face. Her long white hair was wildly tangled. Smoothing it back from her face as best he could, he was relieved to see that she had no cuts on her face. Evidently, the blood splattered all over her face belonged to Nancy. He then left the two women alone.

Jim settled down to wait for Emily. When she finally came home, she was astonished, concerned, and greatly relieved that neither was seriously injured. Nonetheless, she felt heartsick because this physical confrontation between Nellie and Nancy meant an imminent threat to their financial security, if Nancy decided to move out.

Jim tried to reassure her, saying, "You can't have this kind of stress in the apartment. If Nancy wants to leave, let her. You will find someone to take her place. You worry too much. Believe me, the money situation is fixable."

Comforted by Jim's words, she decided to postpone worrying until she was actually confronted with that problem.

In the aftermath of the fight, both women were a sight to see. Each had signs of having been in battle. Both had visible bruises. Nellie had two dark bruises where she had hit the hardwood floor. There was a bruise on her forehead where she had butted Nancy. Her worst injury was to her right hand, which was swollen to twice the size of her left hand, and her knuckles were badly bruised. In contrast, Nancy looked like she had been the victim of a vicious mugging.

Emily pressed Nellie to tell her what caused the fight.

"I don't know why Nancy attacked me. I had no idea what was going on."

She went on, "I learned a long time ago that if someone attacks you, until you know you have won, you need to hang on, and not let them get away from you or you won't know where that person is. And you have to fight to kill, or maim. Who knows whether or not an attacker wants to kill you?"

Emily's jaw dropped. From this one tidbit of information, she could only speculate about what must have happened to Nellie while she was in the State Hospital.

Surprisingly, Nellie did not hold a grudge against Nancy. Each of them treated the other as though the confrontation had never happened. Emily thought it was a Godsend that neither of the two women could see themselves, or each other. She was sure that no woman would have looked at all the damage that Nellie inflicted and then forgiven the injuries.

To Emily's astonishment, Nancy did not move out. However, from that day forward she had a new and healthy respect for Nellie. In the days that followed what Emily called the "fight of this century," an unnatural peace settled over the apartment.

=   =   =

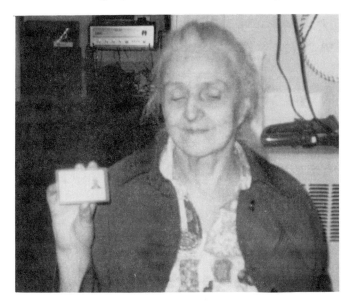

Nellie proudly showing off her first personal ID-card.

Chapter Nine

COLLEGE WOMAN

Three days after the fight, Emily came home to a house full of smoke. She snatched two potholders, grabbed a sizzling pot from the gas burner, and ran out the door onto the balcony. Smoke continued to billow out of the pot as Emily sat it down on the wood floor. When she turned around she heard Nellie and Nancy choking and coughing. She rushed into Nellie's bedroom. Without attempting to explain by finger spelling, she took Nellie's hand and firmly led her through the living room and on outside to the balcony.

As she crossed the living room, Nancy appeared, coughing and wheezing.

Emily called out, "Nancy! There's no fire, just smoke. Go out on the balcony!"

As the women coughed and gasped for a fresh breath of air, Emily looked into the pot and saw a whole, charred, stewing chicken.

She took Nellie's hand, and spelled, "What happened? Why is there a burned chicken in the pot?"

Emily saw Nellie's tears, but didn't know if her eyes were watering from the smoke, or if those were tears of fright and frustration.

Nellie finger spelled back, "I was trying to make chicken soup! Special chicken soup!"

Without comment, Emily went back inside, turned off the burner, and opened the windows to air out the apartment. Next, she returned to the balcony and tried to take the chicken out of the pot, but found that it had burned onto the bottom. Emily groaned and struggled to lift the bird, which came apart in the process. She held the sorry looking half bird in her hand. Again, she groaned as she looked at what was left of the chicken that was stuck fast to the bottom of the pot. She realized that cleaning the pot would be a major undertaking. She concluded that Nellie had let the pot boil dry.

After it had a chance to cool off, Emily placed the pot in the sink, filled it with water and left it there to soak. Then she suggested that they all go out to McDonald's for supper while the apartment aired out. But it was a sobering meal. All three women were subdued by their thoughts of "what might have been."

When Emily went to bed that night, she continued to reflect on the situation. She realized that most of the time, Nellie *could* safely handle cooking a full meal on the stove. However, when she was cooking something that took more than half an hour, she would think that she had time to do something else as well. Sometimes she would become preoccupied, misjudge the time, or forget about the food cooking on the stove altogether. More than once, Emily had come home to find the teakettle boiled dry, food burning on top of the stove, or a casserole smoking in the oven.

After a few near misses of what could have been full-blown disasters, Emily bought an electric crock-pot. She thought that this was an ideal solution. There was no open flame to worry about. The slow cooker had no hot surfaces on which Nellie could burn herself. And it was not likely to boil dry before Emily got home from work.

Since cooking food in the crockpot was a longer process, it required advance planning. So Emily helped Nellie plan each week's dinner menus in advance, and made sure they had everything on hand that Nellie needed to prepare the meals. She felt confident that if Nellie followed the planned menus, there would be no need for her to go out to the store alone, or use the gas range. However, Nellie often was inspired to cook something entirely different. When this happened, she would still go to the store alone and then prepare supper on the gas range.

In spite of her mishaps, it was clear that Nellie thought she knew exactly what she was doing in the kitchen. She saw no danger, either to herself, or to the apartment when she cooked on the stove.

Emily could not escape the feeling that an angel had been watching over them. She realized that she had gotten home just in the nick of time to save the lives of her two roommates. Then, "what if" fantasies filled her head as she thought of what could have happened if she had been too late. It was too much for her to think about!

As these thoughts went back and forth in her mind, Emily realized that Nellie was never going to change. She was impossibly independent and feisty. Emily concluded that it was simply too dangerous to trust Nellie not to use the stove when she was alone. Having wrestled for hours with the problem and with her terrible fantasies, Emily finally decided that she had no choice but to quit her job and stay home with Nellie full time.

While deciding to quit her job solved one problem, it created another. She had no idea how they could make up for the loss of income. She would simply have to use some more of her inheritance. If her mother found out, she would be furious!

Emily turned her thoughts to God, and prayed, "Dear Lord, you called me to take Nellie into my home! You know she needs a full time companion. You always said we should put following your will first and, if we did that, You would provide the things we need. I know it is my responsibility to provide for myself and for Nellie, but I don't know how I can do that if you want me to stay home with her. I don't know what to do. I don't know what your plan is for us. Therefore, I am going to turn this matter over to You. I know that with man it is *impossible*, but with You, God, all things *are possible!*"

The next morning Emily waited until after breakfast to talk with Nellie.

While they lingered over their morning coffee, Emily took Nellie's hand and finger spelled, "Last night's fire scared me, I would hate to come home some day and find the apartment in flames and you lying dead on the floor. I've decided to quit my job so that I can be at home with you all the time."

Nellie frowned and spelled back, "You don't have to do that!"

She cocked her head, raised her eyebrows, and went on spelling, "What did you say?"

Emily reiterated, "I have decided to quit my job so I can be with you, here, all the time!"

Nellie exclaimed out loud, "You mean you really want to be with me all the time? Oh, Emily, you are such a good friend. We will have a great time together!"

Nellie was ecstatic, bouncing up and down in her chair and squealing like a little girl.

When her friend had calmed down, Emily took Nellie's hand and spelled, "My decision to stay home with you full time means that I will have to quit my job. I don't know how we will survive, financially. We will still have your Supplemental Security Income and Nancy's rent. But we won't have my paycheck. For the time being, I will have to use my inheritance to make ends meet. But with our cost of living, it won't last forever."

It took a few moments for this information to sink in.

Nellie frowned and echoed Emily's last statement, "Your money won't last forever?"

Emily responded firmly, "No."

Then a peaceful expression crossed Nellie's face.

She smiled her sweetest smile and patted Emily's hand, reassuringly, "Emily, you always make things work out all right. God always makes things work out all right. Don't you worry, Emily, everything will turn out right."

Emily smiled as she listened to Nellie voicing her childlike trust in God, and in her. Nellie's words were the words of assurance that she needed to hear. The refrain from the old Baptist Hymn "Trust and Obey" echoed in her mind. From that time on, she stopped worrying about their finances and put her trust in God to provide.

The next evening Emily and Nellie were baking cookies and preparing the apartment for a party. As they worked side by side in silence, Emily noticed the bruise on Nellie's forehead. Reminded of Nellie's fight with Nancy, suddenly Emily realized that she really knew next to nothing about how Nellie managed to survive all those years and still maintain her sanity while at the State Hospital. She had never really talked with Nellie about it.

When the baking was finished, Emily ushered Nellie over to the sofa. Nellie knew that Emily wanted to have a serious talk.

Emily finger spelled into Nellie's hand, "Tell me how you spent your time at the State Hospital. What did you do all day?"

Nellie was pensive, thinking about Emily's question. It seemed like a long time since she had thought about her life at the State Hospital. Then her words began to flow as she went into great detail about how she spent her time.

"Well, I had my Braille Bible, that I read over and over again. After I read a passage or two in my Bible, I would mentally discuss them with myself. If I wanted more information, I would use the Concordance. I could run references until I was satisfied with my own understanding of the text.

Nellie paused, then continued, "I never tired of reading the stories of Jesus' life, his ministry and his promises to those who live a faithful life. I also spent a lot of time on the Old Testament Books. I loved to read the stories of Creation, and of the early patriarchs of Israel. Also, I worked to commit whole books of the Bible to memory. Then, I would recite these stories to myself."

She concluded, "Reading the Bible and committing it to memory kept my mind occupied for hours at a time."

Nellie's face was serene as she thought back to the pleasure her Bible study had given her during the years she lived at the State Hospital. Then a frown clouded her forehead as she continued describing her life there.

"I had no one else to talk to. So I learned to mentally talk to myself. I didn't dare speak out loud because I knew that some people say that if you talk to yourself, you must be crazy. I didn't want them to think that."

Nellie paused, smiled again and went on, "Besides reciting scripture in my head, I had a lot of other games that I played. There was my word game. I would choose one long word with lots of letters to use as a basis for my game. Then, I would imagine placing the letters out on a flat surface, like a game board, and see how many new and different words I could make from the letters of that one word."

"How did you keep track of the new words you made up?"

Nellie's fingers answered, "Oh, I remembered my word list as I went along. I had to, or I would have lost count of how many words I made up. When I wanted to make the game last longer, I would begin a second list, allowing myself to use each letter twice. When I did this, there were two lists to remember. After the game was over, I mentally reviewed both lists and counted the number of new words I had created. I was not satisfied unless my score exceeded more than fifty new words. Then, I dismissed the lists from my memory."

Nellie paused in her narration to nibble on a warm cookie.

Then she continued, speaking out loud and finger spelling, simultaneously, "Then there was my arithmetic game. This was another head game that I loved to play. Most of the time I did basic math problems in my head, usually starting out with addition, adding columns of three, four and five digits across and three or four lines down. I remembered the number combinations and what my sums were. To mentally check my work, I then added them from the bottom to the top, and would only be satisfied if my work was correct."

Nellie continued, "Next, I dreamed up problems in subtraction. These were at least five digits on the top line and four on the bottom. To check my work, I added my answer to the second line to see if I came up with the same answer as the top line. If I did, I knew I had done the problem correctly. Long division problems were a favorite, too. After I worked one of these problems, all I had to do was multiply my answer by the divisor and come up with the number of the dividend. I did multiplication problems, too."

Nellie was grinning as she took another bite of her cookie and eagerly went on, "But sometimes I would use some higher mathematics. I worked with decimals, fractions, and square roots. I invented logic puzzles, and even did algebra using two variables."

She laughed, and said, "Emily, don't you know that numbers are endless? Even in sign language you can count to infinity on one hand. I never got tired of playing arithmetic games. It was fun.

Emily could only shake her head in amazement at Nellie's mental faculties.

Then, she asked, "How did you decide what kind of game you wanted to play? Did you have a routine, a schedule, or did you just play whatever you wanted, whenever you wanted?"

"I had to have a routine," Nellie answered, with a nod of her head, "I spent a week or more on a particular kind of arithmetic game. Then I spent several days on my word game, and then I devoted my time to reading my Bible. After completing this schedule, which took about three weeks, I began all over again with my arithmetic games. This way I was always busy and had something to look forward to for the week to come."

The more Nellie talked, the more astonished Emily became.

"Heavens', I thought I was good in math, but I certainly could not do the kinds of problems Nellie is describing without writing them down. Do math in *my* head, like that? No way! This woman is a true genius."

It was late when they finally went to bed. Emily's question had opened the floodgates. Nellie had shared the secrets to her survival. But without seeing Emily's expression, she had no idea how much her stories and their indication of her intelligence had touched Emily's heart.

As Emily pulled up her blanket, her thoughts were spinning. From the beginning, she was aware that Nellie's IQ might be close to genius. She was impressed by how Nellie would count her steps and remember directions without fail. She already knew that Nellie had the ability to memorize about ninety percent of everything she read. Now, she realized that she had completely underestimated Nellie's mental capacity.

She thought, "Nellie's powers of visualization, problem solving, logic, retention, and memorization seem close to the supernatural!"

She remembered how Jim had said that the State Hospital not only labeled Nellie insane, but also profoundly retarded. In fact, so retarded that they thought no one could even communicate with her. This thought turned her stomach. From growing up with her own hearing problems, she knew only too well that people treated her as if she was stupid just because she was heard of hearing.

Suddenly, anger pressed down from the bridge of her nose and simultaneously rose from her belly through her chest and into her throat as she growled, "Deaf does not mean dumb!"

Then she heard a voice in the back of her mind, saying, "Help Nellie prove that deaf does not mean dumb!"

Emily answered, "Yes, God, I will tell the world about this woman's extraordinary intelligence. And I will help Nellie prove it!"

With that, a wave of peace washed over Emily. She felt that now she knew why God had brought them together.

The next morning Emily awoke bright-eyed and clear-minded. During the previous night, as a direct consequence of her righteous anger, she had decided that with the dawning of the new day, she would explore the possibility of Nellie going to college! She knew that Nellie had left public school before the third grade because of her deafness. But she was convinced that her friend had the necessary educational background and intelligence to go to college. She couldn't wait to prove that Nellie was smart enough to succeed.

Emily had earned two bachelor degrees at Malone College in Canton, Ohio. She knew that Malone operated under a Federal mandate to accept handicapped persons and provide educational opportunities to them. She felt certain that the school would be receptive to taking Nellie as a student. She promptly made a telephone call and learned from the admissions office that Malone was offering senior citizen classes that were free. A counselor explained that seniors could attend any class offered by the college for free, but that they had to be taken on an audit basis. Students taking classes through this program could benefit from the classroom instruction, but would not receive college credits for their work.

When Emily got off the phone, she breathed a sigh of relief. Although she thought that Nellie deserved a chance to go to college, she had worried about how they would pay the tuition. If accepted as a Senior Citizen, Nellie could attend classes free. She also thought that perhaps Nellie might finally be eligible for some financial aid from one of the federal or state organizations for the handicapped, if she were attending college.

Right after breakfast, she approached Nellie about the prospect of going to college. Nellie knew they were going to have a serious discussion. She knew it from the way Emily touched her arm and then guided her to the living room couch to sit down.

Emily sat beside her and reached for her hands, "Would you like to be a college girl?"

Nellie jerked her head upright, raised her eyebrows, and opened wide her unseeing eyes. Her snowy white hair bounced a little as she gave Emily her full attention.

"Where? When? How?" Nellie's questions came in rapid-fire succession. She didn't give Emily time to answer them.

Emily laughed delightedly, and spelled into Nellie's hand as quickly as she could, "Wait! Give me time to tell you, OK?"

Nellie nodded and forced herself to be patient. Emily explained what she had learned from the admissions office. A puzzled look crossed Nellie's face.

Nellie asked, "I understand that I can take classes for free, but how would I get there and how can I learn when I can't hear the lectures?"

Emily grinned, "I'm not working, so I can be with you all the time. I will drive you to and from the college, and I will go with you to your classes. You will know everything that is happening in class. I will finger spell to you everything that is said in the lectures."

Nellie was brimming with excitement as she asked, "When can I start?"

In her excitement, Emily stumbled over the letters she was forming in Nellie's hands, so she started again, "I believe we can get you in right away."

Emily found Nellie's excitement to be so contagious that her own excitement was rising to a dangerous high.

She gleefully pressed into Nellie's palm, "Calm down! Don't get your hopes up too high. I have to check all of this out. When I go to the college, I will take you with me, OK? "

Nellie clasped her beautifully eloquent hands together, and nodded vigorously, her hair bouncing like a teenager's as she exclaimed, "Yes, Oh, Yes! I would love to go with you. Together, we will find out about all of this!"

That same afternoon, Emily escorted Nellie to the Admissions Office at Malone College. The counselor greeted them warmly. He assured them that the college was very receptive to accepting Nellie as a student. He encouraged Nellie to enroll and to take advantage of their free senior citizen program. He assured Emily that she and Nellie would be afforded every courtesy. He also agreed to make any necessary adjustments to ensure that Nellie would be comfortable.

The counselor asked Emily to find out from Nellie what she was interested in studying. He had never seen finger spelling before and was touched by the way the two women communicated in silence with each other.

He was impressed when Nellie answered out loud, "I want to study history, literature, philosophy, and the Bible."

He could see that she had a wide variety of interests. Since Malone College was a church related Evangelical Friends school, it also intrigued him to know that she wanted to study the Bible.

Knowing that she was blind, he asked her, with Emily interpreting, "Do you know the Bible?"

"Oh, yes," Nellie said, with a laugh, "I wore out my first Braille Bible reading and memorizing the texts. But I haven't had a chance to discuss what I have read with other people. It will be exciting to study with real professors and with other college students."

Impressed by Nellie's eagerness to learn, the counselor was ready to enroll Nellie. He took them on a tour of the campus. Nellie was ecstatic as Emily described the buildings and classrooms to her.

When they returned to his office, he said to Emily, "Well, tell Nellie I am willing to enroll her as a student even though she has not officially passed second grade. If she wants to enroll for the fall semester, classes will begin after Labor Day. As a senior citizen, Nellie's tuition will be free. All she will have to be responsible for will be her books, supplies, transportation costs, and living expenses."

With those golden words echoing in their minds, the two women returned to their apartment. Emily couldn't wait to tell Jim about their plans. That evening when Jim came to visit, while Nellie bustled around the kitchen, Emily told him what they had in mind.

Instead of being pleased or happy for them, he totally disapproved, saying, "Oh, Emily, how could even think of trying to pull this off?"

Unlike himself, Jim began to get loud. "How could you do this to her? How could you raise such false hopes? I am enrolled at Akron University. I am studying Special Education. It is all that I can handle to keep up with my reading assignments. I can see and hear! How will Nellie be able to keep up when she is deaf and blind? I am young. I have all my senses. She is seventy-three years old. How can you even think that she could possibly stand up to the rigors of academic study and college life? And have you thought about how the young students might ridicule her?"

Emily said, "Now, Jim, you know me! You know that I hear only what I want to hear. I do not want to hear you talk this way. And you had better not talk this way to Nellie, either! Now, here she comes. You had better wipe that frown off your face, put on a smile and ask her what she did today!"

Sheepishly, Jim did as he was told.

Nellie sat down between them and excitedly told Jim every detail of their trip to the admissions office.

Finally Emily simultaneously spoke aloud to Jim and finger spelled to Nellie, "I think that having Nellie attend college is at least worth a try. If she succeeds, what a victory it will be for her! What a victory it will be for all handicapped people!"

Their contagious enthusiasm worked its miracle on Jim. As he left the apartment he could not wait to tell the Nellie Volunteers about their new project.

He turned to Emily and said, "What you are planning to do is truly wonderful. Without you there to translate the lectures by finger spelling, Nellie could not take advantage of this opportunity. I want you to know that I will give you my whole-hearted support in giving Nellie a college education. You have my promise that I will help you in every way I can."

The next morning, Emily called Jim and asked, "Now that Nellie has been accepted for admission to College, do you think that she will qualify for financial aid from any of the state agencies for the handicapped? We are going to need money for books, school supplies, and living expenses, especially since I won't be working."

Jim responded, "Well, I don't think there is much in the way of state or federal aid offered to the deaf. Typically, the only thing that deaf people can qualify for today is Social Security Disability and Nellie is already getting that. But, as you well know, there are many more services, educational grants, and scholarships available to the blind. Why don't we begin by approaching the Ohio Bureau of Services for the Blind?"

Encouraged, Emily hung up the phone. She told Nellie what Jim had suggested.

Nellie frowned, "But didn't you both talk to them before? Why should anything be different now?"

Emily answered, "Well, last time Jim and I were the only ones who were saying that you were educable and trainable. But now the college has said they believe that you are capable of doing college level work and study! Perhaps now, the agencies will change their minds."

Nellie smiled, "Let's go for it!"

Emily seriously pursued financial aid. She spent what seemed like countless hours, driving to all of the local agency offices, filling out applications, waiting for interviews, and answering questions.

Everyone at the deaf church was excited about Nellie's plans. The Nellie Volunteers held a reunion at the Chicken Shack. People were constantly dropping by the apartment to congratulate Nellie on her acceptance into college.

A week later, Emily opened a letter from the Ohio Bureau of Services for the Blind. Immediately she saw that it was a letter of denial, written on a standard form. Angry, Emily left the letter on the table and went out on the balcony.

Then she heard Nellie's raspy voice, "Emily, what does this letter say?"

Returning to Nellie's side, Emily did not mince any words as she spelled into her hand, "It is a letter from the Ohio Bureau of Services to the Blind. They said that it would be a waste of time for them to grant a personal interview with you. They said you are ineligible for any kind of subsidized educational program because you are too old. They said you are not even trainable because of your double handicap. They have no idea what a genius you are! How many of them can solve the kinds of math problems that you can do, even on paper, let alone in their head? How many of them with their college degrees can recite by memory the entire Book of Genesis or even the entire Sermon on the Mount?"

Over the next three days, Emily found four more letters of denial in the mail. The last letter even denied Nellie the most basic life skills instruction, including any training in the use of the universally recognized "white cane" for the blind.

The indifference to Nellie's needs made Emily furious.

As she read Nellie the last letter she finger spelled into her hand, pressing down hard with her fingers for emphasis, "Oh, I'm so mad, I could just spit!"

Nellie shook her head, "No, no, no, no, no, no!" as if, in so doing, she could shake off Emily's negative feelings.

Then, Nellie tried to soothe Emily, patting her hand and saying, "Don't worry, somehow we will find the money we need."

She went on, "Jim will be here today. He will know something we can do. Wait for him. He always helps us see the bright side of any problem."

Right then, Nellie's words of assurance were just what Emily needed to hear.

She laughed and spelled into Nellie's hand, "You're right, Jim can always pour soothing oil on our troubles. And he always seems to drop in just at the right time."

Sure enough, Jim showed up that evening.

When he read the letters, he said, "Emily, these letters look exactly like the ones I got two years ago when I was trying to get Nellie out of the State Hospital. They look like the same letters you got when you went back to them a year ago after we got her out. Let's face it; these people are never going to take a real interest in Nellie. They are never going to help Nellie, college or no college. And, I'm sorry to tell you, but the pledges originally made by the Nellie Zimmerman Volunteers have all dried up. It's clear to me that if Nellie is going to go to college, you two are going to have to do it on your own."

Inadvertently, Jim laid the ultimate challenge at Emily's feet. Emily quickly shifted from feeling sorry for herself and Nellie, into her stubbornness mode that she used when she knew she was right.

She knew that Nellie's success in a college setting would vindicate Jim's advocacy for her release from the mental hospital. It would also prove that, in denying Nellie any support for living in the community, denying her any participation in training programs for the blind, and in refusing to provide any financial aid for her studies, the various state and federal agencies had wrongly misjudged her. They had made her a victim of their unreasonable and blatant prejudice and discrimination. Emily vowed to herself that, with the grace of God, she and Nellie would prove all of them wrong, even if it took all of her inheritance.

The next day, Emily went again with Nellie to see the Admissions Counselor. When they arrived, the counselor handed her a letter of acceptance for Nellie. Nellie squealed with joy. But Emily soberly showed the counselor her letters of denial, and shared her anxiety about how they could afford to attend classes, even if they were tuition free. To her surprise, he assured her that the Malone College Administration would seek financial aid for Nellie.

Then he surprised Emily even further by asking, "Would you like to pray about this?"

Both Emily and Nellie were moved to tears as Emily spelled his prayer into Nellie's hand.

Then the counselor introduced Emily to the registrar, who responded by shaking Nellie's hand first, then Emily's.

He asked Emily to translate for him as he said, "I am pleased to meet our special new student! I understand you would like to study history, literature, philosophy, and the Bible. We have a number of courses in each of those departments. Let's go through the course descriptions and decide which courses you would like to enroll in."

Nellie made her selections. While Emily filled out the registration forms, the registrar said to her, "Let me assure you that we will make available whatever special services you think are necessary for Nellie. Do you need any special equipment or accommodations? We also have tutors if you find them necessary."

Emily spelled his words to Nellie.

Then Emily said, "Yes, I request that we be seated in the front of the room. I am partially deaf myself, and so I need to sit where I can hear enough of the lectures to interpret them for Nellie. Also, since I will be telling Nellie what the professors and the other students are saying through finger spelling, I will not be able to take notes for Nellie. If you would provide a tape recorder, I would like to tape the classes so that we can review them at home."

Nellie added, "I know that I am only auditing my classes and I will not be earning grades or credits, but I would like to take all the tests and have my assignments and papers graded."

The administrator laughed, "I think that we can fulfill all your requests. But your professors are not officially required to grade your tests and assignments if you are auditing their courses. You will have to speak individually to them about this. But since you are such a special student here at Malone College, I am sure that the faculty will be happy to evaluate and grade your work."

When they left the administration building, Emily tried to guide Nellie through the education halls and over the college grounds once again. However, Nellie already seemed to know exactly where she was going. In fact, Emily was grateful, because she felt as if she were walking around in a fog. She was so accustomed to fighting for every consideration from anyone, that she didn't quite know how to handle the college staff because they were being so gracious and helpful. She could not get over the fact that both their counselor and the registrar had prayed for them, and prayed for Nellie's academic success.

With the first day of classes fast approaching, Emily thought that it would be a good idea to introduce the professors to Nellie. After making the necessary phone calls, they dressed appropriately to make a good impression, and were soon ready to leave.

As Nellie climbed into the car she said, "I just love car rides!" Even though she had only traveled to the Malone campus twice, Emily was impressed because Nellie always seemed to know exactly where she was all the time. Obviously, on their two previous trips, Nellie had mentally counted "body leans" as they turned corners. She had counted right leans and left leans. She knew that a slight lean, either left or right, meant they were tracing the arc of a curve in the road. When Emily turned off their regular route to go to the bank, Nellie immediately became concerned and agitated.

"Where are you going now? This isn't the way. You aren't supposed to lean the car yet. We have to go straight a ways further before you lean the car this way. You will make us late!"

Emily was amazed by Nellie's constant mental alertness and said softly, to no one in particular, "You really are a genius!"

She spelled into Nellie's hand, "Don't worry, I am just stopping by the bank so that we will have enough money to buy your books."

When they arrived at the college, Emily introduced Nellie to her first professor. Nellie instantly made a good impression. She not only asked intelligent questions about the course, but she took a personal interest in her teachers. She inquired where they had gone to college, how long they had been teaching, about their church, and their families.

As they left each of their offices, each, in turn, said to Emily, "I can see why everybody has been telling me that Nellie is such a special student."

Emily was amazed by Nellie's social graces as she repeated the same performance with each instructor they met. But she was also impressed by the fact that all the professors already seemed to know who they were and what their special needs were. They all knew that Emily and Nellie had asked to sit in the front of the classroom and would be taping their lectures. Each of them also graciously agreed to grade Nellie's tests and term papers.

Next, they went to the financial aid office. Emily presented the financial aid officer with their monthly budget. It showed exactly how much income was needed for their basic living expenses. It also showed their income from Nellie's Social Security benefits and Nancy's contribution toward their rent and other expenses. But since

Emily had quit her job, it was clear that they needed considerable financial aid.

The officer reiterated that the school could not tap into traditional scholarship funds for non-tuition paying students.

However, he went on to say, "We have contacted some of our leading college donors and also a number of Baptist churches to see if they want to make special gifts to support Nellie's studies. It is too early to say how much support we can raise, but with God's help I am sure that everything will work out fine."

Emily was surprised to discover that the department had already gone beyond the call of duty to seek such alternate sources of financial aid for Nellie. It encouraged her to know that they were trying to live up to their promise to help. She was further comforted when the administrator offered to pray over the matter and asked God to bless their efforts.

Finally, they went to the college bookstore. Armed with the necessary book lists, Emily selected Nellie's textbooks. Nellie enjoyed hearing their titles as Emily spelled them into her hands. She also memorized each book by feel, weight, and smell so that she could instantly tell them apart.

But after Emily had paid for them, a puzzled look crossed Nellie's face as she asked, "How am I going to read all these books?"

Emily laughed, "Either Jim or I will finger spell them to you!"

On her first day of school, Nellie had been awake at least two hours before there was any hint of light in the September sky. By the time Emily opened her eyes and saw the morning sun glancing through the window, Nellie was already bathed, dressed, and reading her Bible in anticipation of her new classes. After breakfast, when it was time to leave for school, Emily looked around the apartment searching for Nellie. She was nowhere to be found. Then she looked out the window and saw Nellie already sitting in the car with her books in her lap, and her watch in her hand. Emily choked back her tears as she realized how excited Nellie was about becoming a "college girl."

As Nellie and Emily stood outside the door to their first class, a student approached them and shyly asked Emily, "Is this the deaf and blind lady?"

By her question, Emily knew that the rumor was out and that everyone would already know them.

She answered, "Yes, tell me your name. I will introduce you."

As soon as Emily spelled the student's name into Nellie's hand, her face lit up.

With a smile, she said in her raspy voice, "Hello, I am Nellie Zimmerman."

Emily breathed a sigh of relief as she realized that the ice had been broken.

Sure enough, the rumor had spread throughout the student body. Many of the students were spellbound watching Emily work with Nellie. They paid close attention as Emily carefully spelled the professors' words into Nellie's hands. After each class a number of students gathered around Nellie. They wanted to know what kind of "talking" that was and how it worked. Both Nellie and Emily thrived on the attention.

When it came time to go to the cafeteria for lunch, several students sat with them. They showed a growing interest in learning how to finger spell.

Emily explained, "It's fun to learn to finger spell. All you need to do is to learn the twenty-six letters of the alphabet, and then practice."

She went on to say, "However, it's easier for me than for Nellie. It is much easier for anyone to talk with their fingers than it is to read what someone else is saying. Would you like to know how to spell "Hi" so that you can greet Nellie yourselves?"

Nellie laughed, and her face lit up, when she was suddenly greeted by so many people who were trying to make contact with her through their fumbling fingers.

Then one of the students asked, "Wouldn't it be easer to use sign language?"

Emily laughed, "You are forgetting that Nellie is blind. I know the American Sign Language and the International Sign Language. But that won't help Nellie. She can't see the signs."

As they drove home Nellie was excited by the fact that so many of the students had taken an interest in her. She was even more excited about what the professors had said about their course of study in each class.

She told Emily with a laugh, "I have always loved books, but being able to discuss what I am reading with all those people, that will be so different, and so wonderful!"

After a full week of attending classes during the day and finger spelling the reading assignment to Nellie in the evening, Emily grew frustrated. It seemed that they were falling farther and farther behind in their reading.

As she crawled into bed after a particularly long translation session, Emily prayed, "O Lord! Help me!"

Early Saturday morning the phone rang, jerking Emily out of her deep sleep.

The shy voice on the phone asked, "Is this Emily Street? I read in the Massillon Newspaper that your friend, Nellie Zimmerman, is taking classes at Malone College. And I understand she is blind but can read Braille. Well, you don't know me, but I am Mrs. Bennett. I write Braille and I am willing to volunteer to transcribe Nellie's reading assignments into Braille."

Emily almost fell over with surprise.

When she regained her composure, she said, "Lady, you are an answer to my prayer! I am so glad you called! How soon can you start? When can we meet you?"

Later that evening, Mrs. Bennett stopped by to get to know Nellie. As for Nellie, she was beside herself with joy to know that she would be able to study independently. Emily agreed to buy Mrs. Bennett a second set of books. And, Mrs. Bennett agreed to send the transcriptions to Nellie, by chapter, through the mail. All that Mrs. Bennett requested was that Emily call her once a week and tell her Nellie's upcoming reading assignments. From that time on, Mrs. Bennett and a small circle of friends from the Akron area kept Nellie supplied with her reading assignments in Braille.

As the semester began to unfold, Nellie took to college as if it were the most natural thing in the world for her to do. Each one of her subjects was of vital interest to her. Nellie couldn't soak up all of the new information fast enough. She actively participated in classroom discussions. At home she spent hours in her bedroom, reading the Braille transcriptions of her texts. When in Emily's company, she talked constantly about their reading and their classes.

As planned, Emily tape recorded the lectures. These tapes became the basis of their home study in preparation for all of Nellie's tests. Emily played the tapes, finger spelling their contents to Nellie. Often their "cramming" for exams lasted well past midnight.

No matter how late their study sessions went, just as she had done when she lived in the boarding home, Nellie still woke up well before dawn. She always bathed, got dressed and was ready for the day a good hour and a half before it was time to leave for classes. Emily had no trouble getting Nellie from the apartment down to the car. Most of the time Nellie would already be sitting in the car, in a stew, afraid they were going to be late to class.

Clearly, Nellie was excited about, and completely committed to her "college girl" experience. As fall turned into winter, deep snow, icy conditions, sub-zero temperatures and bone freezing wind chill were no deterrent. Nellie eagerly walked the quarter mile across campus to the education building. The path from the parking lot to the class building sloped up and down. The sidewalk was uneven and there was a set of stone steps, descending to a level path that led to the classroom building. Nellie would walk briskly, confidently, and determinedly down this path, counting her steps. After the first week, Nellie knew exactly where she was and what to expect along the way. Out of habit, Nellie would hold onto Emily's arm as she walked. But she was so confident about where she was going, and so eager to get there, that she walked at least a half step ahead of Emily! Emily was hard pressed to keep up with Nellie. It looked as if Nellie was leading Emily, actually pulling her along.

Once in the building, Nellie let go of Emily's arm and walked independently to her classroom. Always well dressed, with her lovely, snowy white wavy hair, fair and flawless complexion, perfect posture, and graceful, flowing movements, she made quite an impression on the students.

Nellie was a "people" person, a natural charmer. Eager to get to know her fellow students, with Emily interpreting, she wanted to know the names of her new friends. She inquired about how they liked their classes. She also took the time to ask about their personal lives. What was most surprising was that when her new friends greeted her, sometimes two or three weeks later, even though she could not see them nor identify them by voice, Nellie would remember who they were and would call them by name. Somehow she recognized her fellow students solely by their scent, by their perfume or aftershave, and by the way they touched her as they greeted her. She also impressed her new friends by remembering exactly what they had talked about in their last conversations.

Nellie's professors marveled at her intellectual, academic, and social abilities. She was obviously pleased that she was able to take an active part in her classes, and she was always surrounded by a group of students whenever she and Emily ate in the cafeteria.

Emily gracefully accepted the invitations made by many of the students to meet them for dinner at the cafeteria, to join them for parties in their dorms, and to participate in other, on and off campus, social events. Emily found that, for the first time in her life she, too, was very popular. Students recognized what she was doing for Nellie. They were impressed by her devotion. They were continually intrigued by her ability to finger spell. They questioned her intensely about the kinds of problems that deaf, blind, and deaf-blind people face.

Whether in the cafeteria or in the dorms, Emily enjoyed being the center of attention as she taught interested students how to finger spell easy words like, "Hi" or "How are you?" so that they could greet Nellie. Also, she enjoyed playfully teaching them the exotic motions for certain words in sign language.

At the end of each demonstration, Emily would suggest, "If you want to learn how to finger spell or how to sign, the Canton Church For The Deaf, which meets at the Assembly of God Church that is located next door to our campus, has sign language classes after worship on Sunday morning."

But after three weeks of partying in the dorms on Friday and Saturday nights, on Sunday morning when she took Nellie to church she noticed that no one from the college student body came to church or attended the sign language classes.

She began to think that the students were acting like hypocrites. It seemed to her that these were people who showed an interest in the problems of the handicapped, but were never going to attend classes or learn how to be an interpreter. But, on the fourth Sunday, a handful of fellow students appeared in the church. Emily was ecstatic. She introduced them to several of her deaf friends. Following the service they went to the Chicken Shack for a late lunch. With Nellie in their midst, a 'cross fertilization' took place between a number of Nellie's deaf friends, and a few students from Malone College. They all agreed they should get together the following Friday evening and go out for pizza.

All week long Nellie and Emily looked forward to the festivities. On Friday night several people showed up at the Pizza Hut. Among the delegation from the church, Emily was delighted to see Vicky, who was deaf, with her friend Larry. Likewise, she was pleased to see a group of "normal hearing" students from Malone College, including classmates Michael and Michelle. When they had finished their pizza, Michael suggested that they go to their favorite special college student hangout near the Canton Center Mall, called the Pickle Barrel. There was also music and dancing. When they got there, Emily found the establishment to be crowded, and full of cigarette smoke. She also found the music to be very loud. Emily was frustrated. She could not hear what anyone was saying. She couldn't wait to escape and go home, just to have peace and quiet.

But when she spelled to Nellie, "Let's get out of here!" Nellie ignored her. Instead, she bent over and removed her shoes.

Then Nellie tapped Larry on the shoulder and spelled to him, "Would you like to dance?"

Larry spelled in her hand, "Sure!"

He took Nellie's hand and carefully led her out onto the dance floor. When Larry let go of her hand, she threw her arms up in the air, and began to dance, swaying to the music vibrations she felt in her feet and in her chest. As she swung her hips, her movements were graceful, feminine, and perfectly matched the beat of the music. Soon Emily, Michael, Vicky and Michelle joined the two. They formed a circle, dancing with each other. They were dancing in celebration of life, and of youth. For Nellie, she danced in celebration of "walking free."

Nellie was lost in the music. No one in the circle seemed to notice how odd it appeared to the people around them, who saw these college age kids dancing with the white haired, seventy-three year old Nellie.

When Emily and Nellie took a break and sat at their table, Emily spelled out, "What made you want to start dancing?"

Nellie answered, "I could feel the vibrations of the music through the floor."

Emily looked down and realized that what had sent Nellie to dancing was the vibrations in the hardwood floor of the Pickle Barrel. Emily kicked off her shoes and pressed her feet flat against the floor. She, too, could feel every drumbeat and vibration of the music. The rest of the circle of friends watched Emily shed her shoes. Then they all joined in the sock hop, and danced together for the remainder of the evening, and well into the wee hours of the morning.

When they finally left the Pickle Barrel and were standing in the parking lot, their ears still buzzing from the loud music, they all agreed that they had spent a fun-filled evening together.

Emily was so excited that she blurted out, "Why don't we make this a tradition! We should get together every Friday night for a celebration."

Hugs were joyfully passed around as they all agreed to invite more friends, and go dancing with Nellie every weekend.

During the first half of the semester, in spite of their partying, Nellie took her studies very seriously. She made arrangements to be allowed to take all of the quizzes and tests. Emily was not surprised that Nellie maintained a "B" average in every class.

When it came time for Nellie to take her midterm exams she doubled her study time. She spent hours reading her Braille texts and having Emily spell into her hand the lecture tapes. The night before her first exam she could not sleep. In the morning, after breakfast, Nellie took Emily by the hand and led her to the sofa. As Emily allowed herself to be ushered through the living room, she realized that Nellie had something serious to discuss.

To make sure that Emily understood her words, Nellie spelled as well as spoke aloud, "I know that you have heard all my lectures. Also, you are familiar with all my reading assignments. But I want to remind you that you are not the student. You are my interpreter. So I want you to tell me what the test questions are, but please don't try to give me the right answers."

Then she formed her letters slowly, for emphasis, and continued, "I don't want to cheat. So, now promise me. If you see me write down the wrong answer, don't tell me. Let me make my own mistakes."

Emily responded by squeezing Nellie's hand, giving her a hug and then, just for fun, finger spelled *on* Nellie's *forehead*, "Say no more!"

The professors handed out essay questions and "blue books," in which the students were to write their answers. After Emily had translated the essay questions, Nellie asked her to not talk to her except to tell her when it was time to stop writing.

The following Monday, Nellie's philosophy professor stopped Emily as she ushered Nellie to her class.

He said, "I am impressed. Nellie's writing slants uphill most of the time, but sometimes down. Nevertheless, her writing is perfectly legible and easy for me to read. I wish that all my students could write as readably as she does."

With these remarks, he handed Emily Nellie's blue book.

When Emily opened the front cover she shouted for joy.

Then she put the blue book in Nellie's hand and spelled into her other hand, "I don't believe it! You got an A+ on your first college essay!"

Nellie glowed with pride.

As Emily drove home, Nellie said, "Do you think that we should call Jim and tell him about my grades?"

"Good idea! You know, he is studying at Akron University. He has been busy with his studies, too. Jim knows what it takes to earn an A-Plus even if you are not deaf and blind!"

As Emily drove up to their apartment, she spelled to Nellie, "I see two cars in front of the store. One of them belongs to Jim. The other belongs to Michael."

Rushing up the stairs, they found both men sitting at the dining table. One had brought flowers and the other a bottle of wine. They were so caught up in their intense conversation that they did not notice the two women enter the apartment.

Emily spelled to Nellie, "Be quiet, they don't know we are here."

Nellie carefully sat her book bag down on the sofa. Following the scent of Jim's cologne, she silently glided up to stand behind him.

With a giggle, she couldn't suppress, she slipped her hands over his eyes, and said, "Knock, knock!"

"Who's there?"

"I'm A!"

"I'm A who?"

"I am an A Plus Student!"

Jim laughed, quickly stood up, turned to hug Nellie, and said, "Hallelujah! Merry Christmas!"

Emily heard heavy footsteps on the stairway. Suddenly, a group of Jim's friends from Akron University burst into the apartment carrying potato chips and other party supplies. No sooner than they had gotten settled down, when more footsteps were heard coming up the stairs. This time, it was Michelle and a several friends from Malone College. They had brought "carry out" food from the Chicken Shack.

Soon the music was blasting and a full-scale college party was under way. Students were sitting on the couch, leaning against the walls, and slouching on the floor. So many people were in the apartment that Nellie found it difficult to negotiate her way from the living room to the kitchen.

Nellie proudly presented Jim with her blue book essay. After congratulating Nellie on her grade, Jim began to read the essay out loud. A heated discussion of Nellie's perspective erupted. Soon it was apparent that the students from Akron University disagreed with what was being taught the students at Malone College.

A fierce debate followed. Emily and Jim took turns finger spelling the discussion into Nellie's hand. Soon the conversation moved to other subjects involving politics and religion. As Nellie joined in on the conversation and voiced her opinions, she felt as if she was being treated as an equal. The Christmas party continued until well after midnight. As it began to break up, Jim walked his friends out to their cars and returned with his sleeping bag.

Emily saw him come in, turned to Nellie and spelled, "Guess what Jim has in his hand."

Nellie laughed and said, "Hey, Jim, are you staying for the company or for breakfast?"

Jim didn't respond to the question, but he did have a big smile on his face as he unrolled his sleeping bag on the living room floor.

When everyone else had left, Jim stuck his feet into the bag, and propped himself up against the sofa. The two women joined him, sitting on the floor. They talked on toward the dawn of the new day.

Jim wearily spelled into Nellie's hand, "I hope all this was not too much for you!"

Nellie was moved to tears as she responded, "No, Jim, this was wonderful. After all the years I spent with no one to talk to, now to have intelligent people to spend this kind of time with me is a dream come true. I love going to college!"

With these words, Nellie excused herself and went to bed. Emily crawled up on the sofa and pulled up her blanket.

Then she said to Jim, "It's miraculous! Since the first day of classes, Nellie's attitude and personality have greatly improved. Her devious little games have ceased. She has stopped driving me crazy by going shopping alone. She has stopped teasing Nancy. There haven't been any more temper tantrums or ear-piercing screeches."

Jim laughed and sighed, "Yeah, I have to agree that your idea to enroll Nellie at Malone College was a stroke of genius. It was exactly what Nellie needed to give her life a meaningful focus. I'm sorry that I doubted you!"

He blew out the one remaining candle and added, "I'm sorry I underestimated Nellie!"

Christmas came and went, and winter turned into spring. Nellie threw herself into her studies. She also enjoyed the on-going Friday night celebrations at the Pizza Hut and the Pickle Barrel. Jim frequently brought his friends from Akron University to the apartment just to "hang out" and enjoy each other's company. But Nellie called a moratorium on parties during the week before her final exams.

By the end of the semester most of the students at Malone College had met Emily and Nellie. But on the last day of classes, they saw a group of prospective students, who were touring the campus. When the newcomers saw Emily with her long brown hair tied back, walking beside an older lady whose long snow white hair was blowing in the wind, they stopped and stared. As the two women approached, they made way for them on the sidewalk. They seemed puzzled.

As Emily passed by, with Nellie holding onto her arm, but walking half a step ahead, she heard one of them say, "I can't figure out which one of them is blind."

Another student said, "I don't think either one of them is blind."

Emily discreetly spelled into Nellie's hand, "You go ahead. I think I left the tape recorder in the car."

Emily let go of Nellie's hand just as they reached the top of the stone steps leading from the parking lot down to the Education Hall. Without missing a beat, Nellie walked confidently and gracefully down the steps and on toward the classroom building.

Emily turned to the prospective students and said, "This lady is blind and deaf. She can't see, she can't even hear her footsteps, but she knows exactly where she is and where she is going. It just goes to show you that, with God, all things are possible. By the grace of God, even a deaf-blind woman can go to college."

When the week of final exams came, Nellie was prepared. She turned in two major term papers and sat for her comprehensives. Again, Emily translated the essay questions. Nellie wrote her essays in the blue books that were provided. When the exams were over, she was surrounded by a large group of students. Everyone was relieved that finals week was over.

Then Nellie piped up and said, "Why don't we all celebrate! Let's all meet at the Pizza Hut and then at the Pickle Barrel on Friday night."

When Emily drove to the Pizza Hut the following night she found ten friends already waiting for them, including Vicky, Larry, Michael and Michelle. Later when she pulled into the Pickle Barrel's parking lot she could hardly find a place to park. There were many friends there from their church as well as from Malone. Immediately, Nellie was swallowed up in the crowd. Many of her new friends had learned how to finger spell. They were eager to talk with Nellie about how she did on her exams. They also wanted to tell her their own stories of success.

Emily stepped back and just watched as Nellie was surrounded. There were in the crowd both deaf and hearing persons, who were communicating with her through their fingers. Soon Nellie was invited onto the dance floor. Once there, she raised her arms, swayed back and forth and blissfully lost herself in the rhythm of the music.

Suddenly, a rather inebriated man tapped Emily on the shoulder and asked, "Hey, what's that old lady doing dancing with those kids?"

Emily turned to him and asked, "Do you believe in miracles?"

The man was puzzled. "Miracles? What miracles?"

Emily laughed, "That old lady is my friend. She is deaf and blind and she is going to college. And that is a miracle!"

He stared at her, with a puzzled look on his face. Emily turned with a flourish and joined the circle of friends dancing with Nellie. She too, raised her arms over her head and lost herself in the music.

=   =   =

Chapter Ten

TO TELL THE WORLD

After Nellie began attending classes, the Director of Community Relations approached Emily: "I am so excited about having Nellie as a student here. With your permission, I would like to write up a story about our special student for the newspaper."

"That would be wonderful!"

Emily lost herself in the experience of enabling Nellie's studies, attending classes, interpreting the lectures, and meeting with students. Each night she opened the *Canton Repository* and looked for the promised newspaper article. September and October passed, and November was quickly unfolding.

Late one night Emily carefully browsed the paper for a story about Nellie. Angrily, she crumpled up each page which failed to produce the sought after article. Soon the trashcan was spilling over with the balls of paper. Her search produced nothing!

Emily was restless as she stretched out on the sofa and pulled the comforter up over her head. She thought back to that night when Nellie had cheerfully told her about her mind games and how she used them to keep herself sane while living at the State Hospital.

Emily remembered, "I made two vows to God that night. The first was to prove that Nellie was highly intelligent by giving her the opportunity to succeed as a college student and the second vow was to tell the world about it."

Then she heard a voice in the back of her head say, "You have not seen Nellie's story in the paper because you promised me that you would do the telling."

Emily answered, "Of course, Lord, I should not have left it up to someone else. I'm the one who really knows about Nellie's life and achievements."

This conversation left her more restless than before.

Doubts and questions filled her mind as she talked on to herself, "I am no writer! If I wrote a story, how would I get it into the paper? What should I do? I feel like Moses who was afraid to speak!"

Then the inspiration came, "God sent Moses to Aaron, and he appointed Aaron to be his mouth piece, his reporter. You need to find a good reporter!"

In the morning Emily called the *Canton Repository* and asked to speak with someone in the newsroom. A reporter named Gary Brown answered the phone.

Emily jumped right in, saying, "Gary, two years ago, your paper followed a story about a deaf and blind woman named Nellie Zimmerman, who was living at the state mental hospital. Do you remember her story?"

"Yes, of course I do," Gary answered, "I wrote those articles about Nellie. Jim Schneck kept me informed about his struggle to have her released, but I haven't heard from him lately."

Encouraged, Emily pressed on, "Well, you'll probably never believe me, but Nellie is now living with me. She is doing fine. And now she is even enrolled as a student at Malone College. This woman is truly amazing and I thought you might like to write a story about what she is doing with her freedom."

A young, bright-eyed, enthusiastic reporter, Gary was eager to find good newsworthy stories. Immediately, he thanked Emily for calling. She filled him in on the details of how Nellie became a college student and what she was studying.

The next morning, just as they were about to leave for Nellie's classes, the woman from the Community Relations office called and said that the *Canton Repository* wanted to take a picture of Nellie, Emily and Jim at the college. Emily promised to contact Jim and agreed to meet the photographer at Malone College in the cafeteria.

Several days later a quarter page article, complete with a large photograph of the threesome appeared in the paper. Emily laughed as she read the article and saw herself quoted. As she also read the comments of various school officials, it was obvious to her that Gary had done his own investigation. Emily described the photo and translated the story to Nellie, finger spelling into her hands.

Nellie grinned, "Look! I made it into the paper! I can't believe it!"

That night Emily thanked God that she had been led to a reporter who would take an interest in telling Nellie's story. She vowed to continue to tell him about Nellie and her achievements. What she did not know was that Gary had sent the story to the Associated Press and the United Press International and that the story had been picked up by the *Akron Beacon Journal*, the *Massillon Independent*, and other papers as far away as Columbus, Ohio.

The story of Nellie and her new college career inspired many people from all walks of life. All the past publicity surrounding the fight for her release from the State Hospital had made the general public aware of the obstacles that Nellie had already overcome. The fact that she was now engaged in a successful college experience seemed amazing. Much to Emily's delight, Nellie had magically become an overnight heroine.

A few days after the article appeared in the *Repository* a psychology professor at Malone approached Emily and asked, "Would you and Nellie be willing to come to my class and explain what it is like for Nellie to be deaf and blind, and what it is like for you to live with someone who is deaf and blind?"

Without giving it a thought, Emily accepted the invitation.

But that night when she discussed the invitation with Nellie, Nellie was full of questions, "Who is going to do the talking? What will we talk about? How long should our talk be?"

Emily answered, "Well, I just thought that I would introduce you and then I could ask you some questions by finger spelling into your hand. Then you can answer them using your voice. That way the class can see how someone can communicate with the deaf and blind, and they can hear you speak. Sometimes people think that just because a person can't hear, that person can't speak!

Nellie's face lit up, "Yes! These are college students. We can talk with them just the way we do when we go visit new friends at the parties in the dorms. You know the kinds of questions they are always asking. And, it seems like I have answered them hundreds of times. I don't even think that we will need to rehearse!"

However, when it came time for them to give their presentation, Nellie was nervous.

As they drove to the College she worried, "Do you think that everyone will be able to understand what I am saying?"

Emily reassured her, "You just have to speak up. It is not always easy for people to understand you. But it is part of the experience of meeting you. Many of these students may never have heard the sound of a deaf person's voice. Your voice is different, but it is beautiful, just like the rest of you is beautiful."

Emily's words found their mark. As Nellie walked into the room, she was composed and confident. Emily brought two chairs and set them up in the front of the class. Once they were seated and introduced, the talk was a team effort.

She began by asking when and where Nellie was born. She spoke aloud, calling out the letters as she finger spelled into Nellie's hands. "W, h, a, t, what; i, s, is; y, o, u, r, your; n, a, m, e, name?"

A hush fell over the class as Nellie answered in her raspy voice, "My name is Nellie L. Zimmerman."

Emily continued, "H, o, w, How; o, l, d, old; a, r, e, are; y, o, u, you?"

Nellie answered, "I am seventy-three years old."

For the next twenty minutes Emily asked Nellie such questions as: Where were you born? Were you born deaf? Were you born blind? How did you receive your education? What are you studying at Malone College? How do you study? How do you like being a college girl?

At the end of the interview, Emily asked Nellie, "Is there anything else that you would like to tell the class?"

Nellie stood up and spoke with passion, "I hope that by telling my story and demonstrating what I have experienced, how God has intervened in my life, how my life has been enriched by friends, and how much I enjoy my studies, I have inspired you to become more sympathetic toward the needs of the deaf and the blind. I wish that all handicapped people, especially the deaf and the blind, might be given a chance to live in the community and enrich their lives through college level studies as I have been able to do! Those of us who are blind and deaf need people to believe in us and in our abilities. Give us a chance to prove ourselves!"

There was a moment of silence. Then the room erupted in applause. The students' questions that followed filled the rest of the class period. Both Nellie and Emily were glowing. After the professor dismissed the class, a crowd of students gathered around them and continued to greet and compliment them on their program.

The same evening, as they were washing dishes after dinner, the phone rang. It was a professor from Malone's social work department. He, too, wanted Emily and Nellie to give a presentation for his class.

Emily could not wait to tell Jim and Gary about this invitation! To that very day, no social worker or rehabilitation counselor had ever responded positively to her requests for help on Nellie's behalf. Now she and Nellie had a chance to make their case with future social workers. Nellie was so excited that she gave Emily a big hug.

"Do you think that this is a sign from God? They want me to talk about my experience, my needs, but I will speak to the needs of all deaf and blind people!"

True to his word, Gary covered the story about Nellie speaking to classes at Malone College. An article appeared in the *Canton Repository* along with a photo of Nellie and Emily sitting at the front of the class. Gary reported on how the audience responded to their program. He also reported that Nellie's answers to Emily's questions were completely unrehearsed and given in her own words. Gary also sent this story to the Associated Press and the United Press International.

As December approached, Emily sat down to pay the bills. With Nellie's SSI, Nancy's rent, and a gift from the Sunday School class at the Canton Church for the Deaf, she paid all the bills. But she was seventy-five dollars short of being able to pay the rent. It certainly looked as if she were going to have to dip into her inheritance once again.

As she stared at the checkbook ledger, unable to write the rent check, she prayed in exasperation, "O Lord, show me a sign, help me pay this bill!"

On the first evening of their Christmas break, a large party materialized in the apartment. In addition to their usual friends from the church and from Malone College, several new faces appeared including several students from the psychology and social work classes. Suddenly, the phone rang. Emily could hardly hear for all the noise of the party.

The voice on the other end of the phone said, "Is this Emily Street? I saw an article in the *Massillon Independent* about you and Nellie speaking at Malone College. I am the program chairman for the Fellowship of Christian Singles in Massillon. I have an opening for a program the first week of January. I wondered if you and Nellie could come and talk to us."

Not quite sure of what she heard, Emily yelled to the partiers, "Everybody be quiet!"

Silence fell upon the apartment as Emily asked the caller to repeat herself.

When Emily hung up the phone, she exclaimed to the silent but expectant crowd, "We have another speaking date!"

Everyone clapped and cheered their new heroines.

However, while Emily was acting excited on the outside, inside she was trembling.

When the crowd broke up, Emily confided in Nellie and Jim, "We have only conducted speaking engagements for two classes at Malone College. They were friendly audiences and we already knew some of the students. But now we will be talking to a group of complete strangers."

Nellie reassured her, "Yeah, but this gave us time to perfect our presentation before putting it to the acid test of speaking before absolute strangers. I think that we have nothing to worry about."

Jim added, "All that you have to worry about is that Nellie has to speak up and be herself and everybody will love you!"

The night before their presentation Nellie asked Emily to help her with her studies. They spent their time preparing for their Philosophy class and reading Plato's Discourses and comments on the nature of beauty.

Nervous about speaking to the Singles group and with her head full of Plato's philosophy, before Nellie crawled into bed she got out her Braille stencil, a piece of paper, and began to write down some thoughts.

As they drove to the church, Nellie was excited. She told Emily, "After you have introduced me and before you start your interview with me, I have something to read. It is a little speech I wrote last night."

When they arrived at the church, their host explained that the Fellowship of Christian Singles was an ecumenical group. About sixty people from a wide variety of churches attended their monthly meetings, and each month the meeting was held at a different church. Pointing out that they had an exceptionally large crowd, he then ushered them into a large fellowship hall with a stage at one end.

As Emily surveyed the assembly she counted about seventy-five people, none of whom she recognized. Emily felt nervous. Before she knew it, the chairperson was introducing them. As she ascended the stairs, with Nellie behind, suddenly Emily froze. In spite of all her years of experience as a schoolteacher, Emily was speechless.

Having been led up the stairs by Emily, Nellie put her arm around Emily's shoulder in a gesture of comradery. But she felt no motion. A puzzled look crossed Nellie's face. She put her hand between Emily's shoulder blades. Still, there was no motion. Intuitively, Nellie knew that Emily was not breathing, not talking. Instinctively, Nellie pushed Emily forward, and gave her a gentle pat on the back. Nellie's nudge awoke Emily from her stupor. But she felt like a robot as she introduced Nellie. But with a flourish Nellie took out her Braille reading. Tracing the letters, she recited:

> *The art of life consists of the ability to see the beauty in one's life.*
> *For without beauty life is a dead-end experience.*
> *Beauty, to me, is feeling the fur of a kitten, smelling a rose and tasting a good dinner.*
> *Beauty is feeling silk scarves, the coolness of one's bed sheets at night before one goes to sleep.*
> *Beauty is smelling the scent of the soap, the aroma of a fresh baked apple sauce pie.*
> *Beauty is tasting the cup of tea after breakfast, the many flavors of a Supreme Pizza on a Friday night and feeling the sauce dribble down your chin.*

Spellbound by Nellie's appearance, the sound of her unusual voice and the poetry of her words, the audience sat transfixed as Nellie and Emily began their usual questions and answers.

Following their presentation the audience asked questions for almost an hour. There was much laughter as Emily and Nellie shared both the funny and frightening stories of their life together.

Then, the chairperson announced, "Now, Emily and Nellie, it is our custom for us to pass the basket and take up a collection for our speaker."

As the basket was passed around the room the chairperson announced, "We have time for one last question!"

A woman stood up and asked Emily, "Did you write the speech which Nellie gave at the beginning of your talk?"

Emily laughed, "Oh, no, oh no, I could never write like that. I am just an old school teacher, but she is the one who reads and understands Plato and can write poetry like that. Sometimes the deaf and blind are more gifted than those of us who are 'normal'. That is the whole point of our program. Never underestimate what the handicapped can do! Expect them to be exceptional."

Nellie nudged Emily, "What is that strange vibration in the room?"

Emily answered, "It is applause! They are clapping for you and for your beautiful poem!"

Nellie grinned as she was presented with a bouquet of flowers.

As the two women drove home, exhausted from the evening, Nellie continued to caress and smell her flowers.

Suddenly she croaked, "What is this?"

Emily wrote into Nellie's palm, "I'm driving. It is dark. You will have to show me. Take my hand and show me!"

To Emily's surprise, it was the offering envelope.

When they reached home, the two women rushed up the stairs, with Nellie carrying her precious bouquet of flowers. Emily quickly opened the envelope and counted the bills into Nellie's hand. To their amazement, it came to exactly the seventy-five dollars they needed for their rent!

Emily and Nellie agreed that this was a sign from God. A sign that God must be pleased with what they were doing in sharing their story and speaking up for the rights and abilities of the handicapped.

A few days later, Emily received an invitation to speak to the evening meeting of a Methodist Women's fellowship group in Canton. Immediately, Emily called Gary Brown and told him about the invitation. He promised to cover the event.

When Emily and Nellie arrived at the church they were both pinned with corsages and seated at the head table for dinner. Following the meal, Nellie again began their presentation by reading her poem. Emily again conducted their unrehearsed interview, asking her usual questions, but adding questions about Nellie's religious background and her methods of Bible Study. At the end of the interview, Emily asked Nellie if she had anything more to say.

To her surprise, Nellie said, "I would just like to end our talk by singing a song. It is a hymn that often runs through my mind when I think about how God redeemed me from the State Hospital and set me free to live with Emily."

A murmur arose from the audience. "Can a deaf person sing? Oh, no! This is going to sound bad!"

Unable to hear or see the commotion, Nellie opened her mouth and began to sing.

> *O for a thousand tongues to sing my great Redeemer's praise, the glories of my God and King, the triumphs of his grace.*
>
> *Hear him, ye deaf; his praise, ye dumb, your loosened tongues employ; ye blind, behold your Savior come; and leap ye lame, for joy.*

There was not a dry eye in the place. The purity of Nellie's faith, in spite of all the things she had lived through, touched every heart.

After the program was over the chairwoman presented Emily with a check. Emily's eyes almost popped out of her head when she saw that it was made out for a hundred dollars. As they made their way toward the door two people approached them and invited them to speak to their neighborhood women's club. Then the head of the kitchen committee asked Emily if they would like to have the left-over food. Before she could answer, she handed Emily a large Tupperware container full of fried chicken. Then she came back with an equally large container of salad, baked beans and two bags of bread rolls.

As she drove home, Emily was so excited that she said, "How would you like to go to the Pickle Barrel? I feel like dancing!"

Nellie laughed, "Me too!"

As they sat at their table, getting into the music, Emily spelled into Nellie's palm, "God is great! God is good! You know, when I quit my job to stay home with you, I had no idea how we were going to make ends meet. You said that God would provide. And now look! Last week we made seventy-five dollars, and this week we made a hundred dollars. That is more money than I would have made working full time at the nursing home. I can't escape the feeling that God is calling us to make it our job to do these talks."

Nellie answered, "See, I told you that you and God would make it turn out all right. He has been helping us out all along with special donations from the church and from the college. And now look what He has done!"

Emily spelled back, "You know that old hymn, 'Where He Leads Me I Will Follow'? I think that we should go 'with him, with him, all the way' on this one. We make a perfect team. Let's make a toast! You take your beer mug, hook your elbow around mine, and we will drink together: partners in life, partners on the lecture circuit."

The two women drank their toast. Emily led Nellie to the dance floor and they both lost themselves in the music, as a new vision emerged of what they were called to do.

=   =   =

Chapter Eleven

THE LECTURE CIRCUIT

When an article about their presentation to the Women's Fellowship group appeared in the *Canton Repository*, complete with a picture of Nellie wearing her corsage, it seemed like the phone never stopped ringing. Since Nellie was still in school, Emily decided not to accept more than two speaking engagements per week. Soon the month of January was completely booked.

In addition to keeping Gary Brown informed of all Nellie's activities, Emily contacted the Associated Press and United Press International correspondents directly. Many newspaper reporters picked up the stories and continued to publicize Nellie's activities. Radio and TV news programs followed her progress in college. The extended media coverage added to the flurry of invitations to present their lecture.

As the semester unfolded their presentations continued to be unrehearsed and spontaneous. They also became more professional. With a format that was laid back, friendly, and open, they didn't hesitate to talk about their personal experiences and to laugh at themselves. This openness put their audiences at ease and made it easy for them to ask questions. At the same time, they continued to call for recognition of the rights and abilities of the handicapped. This made their presentations valuable material for religious, professional, fraternal, social, civic, and other organizations.

Almost overnight, they were in such demand that Emily was scheduling their public appearances months in advance.

Most of the time a dinner preceded their program. Their presentations usually lasted about forty minutes and afterwards they stayed as long as was necessary to answer questions. This meant their nights out on the lecture circuit, including travel time, normally took about four hours.

One evening when Jim dropped by for a visit, as the lecture circuit began to take off, Emily confided in him, "I have decided not to worry any more about our finances. I have resolved simply to pray to God for help when we need money to pay our bills, and to trust that the money will appear at the time it is needed."

She went on, "If we continue to fulfill God's call to tell the world about Nellie's life, I believe that God will take care of our material needs."

True to her word, Emily accepted all invitations to speak. She set no speaker fee. She never asked for money nor inquired how much they would be paid. With childlike faith, she trusted that God would take care of them and that they would receive some kind of honorarium, or a free will offering which would defray their travel expenses and contribute to their livelihood.

Sometimes they received twenty dollars, at other times, more than one hundred dollars. Often, Emily considered Nellie and herself to be twice blessed when their engagements included a free dinner and gifts of left-over food. Nellie considered such gifts a Godsend.

After weeks of juggling class schedules, squeezing in study time in between their speaking engagements, and studying hard for her mid-term and final exams, Nellie looked forward to the end of the semester.

Although she would never have told Nellie, Emily, too, breathed a sigh of relief when the semester was finally over. Enabling Nellie to be a college student had been fun and rewarding, but it had also been very time-consuming. Translating class lectures and personal conversations had been intensive work. She looked forward to having more time to herself.

Soon the two women settled into their summer routine of cooking, cleaning, and shopping. They also enjoyed giving their presentations two or three times a week.

Whenever they were not out giving their programs, it seemed as though Jim, Vicky, Larry, Michael, Michelle, Emily's blind friend, Sue, and others were always stopping by to party. They continued to meet their circle of friends for pizza and dancing on Friday nights. Everyone seemed excited about how God was opening the doors of opportunity for Nellie to tell her story.

Nancy continued to live in the apartment. During the day she worked at her concession stand, and in the evenings she mostly kept to herself. But whenever they had visitors she always came out of her room and joined the party.

Early one June morning, as the two women were buying groceries and running errands, Emily told Nellie, "I think that I will buy a scrap book and collect all the newspaper articles about you. So far, I have been saving them in a shoebox."

When Emily got home, she began to look over the articles she had saved.

As she read them, she became so excited about Nellie's activities and accomplishments that she spelled into Nellie's hand, "Do you remember how Jim used to send out newsletters to over two hundred people about the struggle to have you released from the State Hospital? I wonder how many of them have any idea of the wonderful things you are doing with your freedom? I think that we should send out our own newsletter to keep these good people abreast of what you are doing with your 'life on the outside'!"

Nellie nodded her head enthusiastically.

Emily continued, "Look, we get lots of newsletters for the blind, like the one we got today from the Helen Keller Institute. They always have interesting stories about what blind people are doing. Our newsletter can be in the form of a diary. We can focus on the highlights of our life."

Again Nellie nodded her head.

Emily went on, "Let's discuss what should be in it each month. I can write the articles and you can transcribe it into Braille so that our blind friends can read it. I can also use your help in putting out the mailing. You can help fold the newsletters and put the address labels on them."

Nellie responded, "When do we start?"

When Emily typed up their first monthly newsletter at the end of June, Nellie transcribed it into Braille. A friend of Jim's who owned a Braille press, agreed to mass-produce copies for the many blind friends who were on his mailing list.

When the day for preparing the mailing had come, Nellie eagerly folded the printed newsletters and began to stick on the address labels. Using Jim's mailing list, Nellie insisted that Emily read the names that appeared on each address label. As Emily spelled the names into Nellie's hand, she was touched by how many of them she knew. She was also surprised by how many of them she did not know.

When she licked the last label and lovingly placed it on her newsletter, Nellie frowned!

She said, "We forgot some important addresses. I have been receiving the Helen Keller Institute newsletter, and the newsletter from the American Federation for the Blind, along with several other Braille newsletters. I think that we should include them in our mailing."

Nellie went into her bedroom and got out the most recent Braille newsletters and read their addresses to Emily, saying with a laugh, "I'll bet that none of their subscribers have their own newsletter like I do!"

Writing the articles and putting the newsletter together added to their summertime schedule of activities. It took considerable effort and time each month. But the distribution of Nellie's newsletter not only allowed them to keep in touch with their extended circle of friends and supporters, it also led to even more invitations for speaking engagements. Many of these invitations were for appearances beyond the Canton-Massillon area.

By the end of the Summer, they had spoken to the Perry Rotary Club, the Friendship Circle at Grace United Methodist Church in Canton, the American Baptist Women's Group, the Y-Wives at the YMCA in Canton, the Alliance Kiwanis' Club, the Salem Mennonite Church in Wooster, Ohio, the Lions Club of Massillon, the Akron Pilot Club International, two Optimists' Clubs and three Women's Guilds.

As fall approached, Nellie realized that her summer vacation had been just long enough for her to feel the need for more intellectual stimulation. She also looked forward to again meeting with and hanging out with the college kids. She eagerly re-enrolled for classes at Malone College. She registered for classes in Speech, Ancient History, and two Bible classes. The first was on the Apostles and the other was on the Teachings of Jesus.

Emily reported Nellie's enrollment to Gary Brown and her contacts at the AP and the UPI. As this news was picked up by a wide variety of newspapers, and radio and television stations, again Emily's phone began to ring.

In addition to the usual civic organizations and church groups, Emily now received invitations to speak at area elementary schools and junior and senior high schools. She also received invitations to speak at many colleges in the area.

Early in October, Nellie was asked to give a presentation to the second grade class at the Whipple Elementary School.

As they made their way to the school, Nellie confided to Emily, "I am nervous! I haven't been around many young children. Do you think that they will like me?"

Emily spelled into her hand, "These kids will be your best audience yet! And even if they don't like or understand what you say they are going to love the cookies you baked! You'd better get ready for lots of hugs, because they are going to love you."

Emily was right. Nellie spoke to three classes that morning. After introducing Nellie to the first class and conducting an abbreviated interview by finger spelling, the children began to ask questions.

First a girl wanted to know what Nellie could see.

Their curiosity was raised when Nellie answered, "I can see light, but not shapes, or things like people or trees."

"What do you hear?" a boy asked.

They were astounded when she said, "I hear nothing. I can't even hear myself talking."

This sparked a series of questions Nellie had never been asked before.

"How do you know when you are talking?"

"How do you keep from walking into walls and doors?"

"How do you know what you are wearing?"

"How do you know what you are eating?"

"How do you know when you are asleep?"

The teacher asked what Nellie liked to do for fun. The children were surprised when Nellie reached into her bag and produced a potholder and a wallet she had made. They could not wait to come forward and feel a volume of Nellie's Braille Bible.

And they eagerly gobbled up the cookies that Nellie had baked for them, asking, "How do you know what you are putting into the cookie dough and how do you know how long to bake these cookies if you can't hear the oven timer beep?"

When it came time for her to say goodbye and to go to the next class, she found herself surrounded by kids. They all seemed to be trying to touch her. Some touched her beautiful white hair. Others touched her eyes, ears and mouth. Still others tried to hug her from all different angles.

When the teacher asked, "Who wants to lead Nellie to the next class?"

Every child raised his or her hand. The teacher appointed several guides. When Nellie left the classroom, she felt at least three children hanging on to each of her hands.

By the end of the morning Nellie was exhausted, but delighted by the response of the children.

As Emily drove home, Nellie said, "I hope I get to talk to more school children!"

Emily laughed, "You will! I already have two more elementary school appointments."

Of all the audiences to which they spoke on their lecture circuit, both Emily and Nellie felt that the most appreciative audiences were the children. Their question and answer periods usually lasted longer than any other type of audience. As they went from school to school the children had more and more questions: How did Nellie wake up from being asleep? How did she know if someone was behind her? How did she walk in a straight line? How did she pour a drink of water without spilling it? Did she really cook? How could she do that? How did she know if her dishes were clean?

In spite of the fact that the primary purpose of their presentation was to confront prejudice against the handicapped, especially the deaf and the blind, sometimes they were confronted by discrimination when they went out to speak. Not all of the people who invited them to speak were comfortable around Nellie.

On one occasion they were invited to speak to a civic club that met in the conference room of one of the banks in Alliance.

When the chairman wrote to confirm the date he very bluntly wrote, "Don't bring the blind woman."

Emily was furious.

Immediately, she called the program chairman and canceled the engagement, saying, "I never give a presentation without Nellie. If you don't want Nellie, you don't get me!"

When Emily spelled the contents of the letter into Nellie's hand and told her that she had canceled the engagement, she added, "Some people don't even know that they are being unkind; they are just very uncomfortable around any handicapped person. However, sometimes, people can be downright mean."

Another time, they went to speak to a civic club in Akron. Instead of being invited to sit at the head table with the officers, Emily and Nellie were seated at a separate table set up for two. Not long after that they went to speak at a well-attended church dinner in Canal Fulton. When they arrived their host seated them for dinner at a long table with eight place settings, but once they were seated no one came to join them at the table. Finally, when all the other seats were taken, the last two women asked if they could sit with them.

Emily responded cheerfully, "Sure, have a seat!"

Instead to sitting next to them, they left a seat empty between them. After brief greetings and introductions, the two women proceeded to have an intense private conversation as if neither Emily nor Nellie were even there.

As Emily encountered these situations, she became more aware that in spite of outward attempts to be open, accepting, and hospitable, prejudice sometimes ran very deep.

One evening after they had given their presentation to a women's group at a church near Brewster, Nellie told Emily, "I have to go to the bathroom."

Emily approached her hostess, who was talking with two other women, and said, "Nellie needs to use the lady's room. Can you show us where it is?"

The three women looked awkwardly at one another. Then one whispered something to the host.

The hostess smiled and said, "Sure, I can show you the way."

She escorted them down the hall, past a men's room, and a ladies' room. She then led them down a long flight of stairs into the church basement. Finally, she brought them to a small custodian's closet and opened the door. Emily stared in disbelief. Amidst the mops, buckets, cleaning supplies and old cans of paint there stood an old, grimy, unused toilet.

By this time, after their long walk, Nellie was having an emergency. So Emily showed her to the toilet and closed the door, all the time thanking God that Nellie was blind and could not see the room.

When she closed the door, Emily asked the hostess, "Why did you lead us way down here when we could have used the restrooms we passed by upstairs? This room does not even have a sink!"

Without batting an eyelash, her hostess answered, "Well, we didn't want her to use our restroom because we don't want to catch Nellie's disease."

As on other occasions, Emily protected Nellie from knowing how inhumanely she had been treated. But she never forgot the incident and it added to the fire of her passion to speak up for the human rights of the handicapped.

One Saturday evening Emily and Nellie were invited to give their presentation to Jim's signing class at Akron University. When they got there Jim gave Emily their honorarium in cash.

She gave the envelope to Nellie and finger spelled, "There is fifty dollars in this envelope."

Nellie promptly put it in her purse. But she left her purse unattended during the program.

As they drove home, Nellie suddenly started screeching.

Emily spelled into her hand, "What is the matter with you?"

Nellie wailed, "Somebody stole my money!"

Emily quickly pulled the car over to the side of the road and stopped. She looked through Nellie's purse. Sure enough, the envelope was gone.

Emily tried to calm Nellie down, but she fussed all the way home. Emily was upset too, because they needed the money to pay the gas bill.

As she crawled into her bed, she prayed, "O Lord, you gave, but someone else took the gift."

The next morning, they drove to the First United Methodist Church in Massillon to speak to a Sunday School Class. After they had been ushered into the classroom and were waiting for the class to gather, Nellie again opened her purse, felt around for the money, and then started moaning and groaning.

Emily asked with her fingers, "What is the matter?"

Nellie wailed repeatedly, "Somebody stole my money!"

Embarrassed, Emily pressed into her palm, "Stop that! Be quiet!"

But the class wanted to know what Nellie was talking about and why she was so upset.

Emily explained the situation. When the class was over, the group decided to take up a collection to see if they could make up for what had been stolen. She was astonished when she counted what was in the envelope.

Excitedly, she spelled into Nellie's palm, "Look! We have been twice blessed. Last night someone stole fifty dollars from us, but now we have been given more than one hundred dollars."

In spite of the occasional affront to their pride, Emily was convinced that the more they told Nellie's story to the public the more they received divine blessings. It seemed that if they had a need, all she had to do was to ask for it and the money would magically appear.

On occasion, Emily would invite other members of their circle of friends to accompany them to their presentations. One night in mid

December, she decided to invite Larry and Sue to accompany them to Akron University for a program.

While on the way home they were all laughing and joking about the evening and all the funny questions people had asked and all the funny answers Nellie had given.

As they made their way south on Route 77, suddenly they hit a chunk of ice and their tire went flat. Emily pulled off the road and stopped. Everyone but Nellie got out of the car and stood around looking at the tire. No one knew what to do since there was no spare tire.

It was cold. It began snowing, so they climbed back into the car to wait for someone to come along and help. After about 10 minutes, a white pickup truck passed them and pulled over into the emergency lane. A man got out and walked back to Emily's car.

Emily rolled down the window as he asked, "Are you having car trouble?"

When Emily explained about the flat tire he said, "Don't worry, I'll take care of it. Give me your keys so I can open the trunk. Just stay in the car and stay warm."

The man jacked up the car, unbolted the tire, threw the keys back to Emily through her open window and walked off with the tire.

To everyone's amazement he threw the tire into the back of his pick up truck and without a word, drove off.

Now Emily was really worried. She said to Larry and Sue, "We not only have a flat tire, but now we have no tire! I think that we are in serious trouble!"

For fifteen minutes they sat there as the cars on the road sped by. Suddenly, the white truck pulled up behind them. The man returned with the repaired tire and quickly replaced it.

He let the car down, put the jack back in the trunk and said through Emily's open window, "Be careful whom you trust!"

Before she had a chance to thank him, he said, "Now I don't want you to leave until I pass you by."

As everyone talked about what had happened, Emily waited for the truck to pass. But it did not. After a minute, she looked back. The rear window was covered with snow. She opened her window, stuck her head out, and looked back. The truck was gone!

Everyone in the car was amazed.

Larry said, "Hey, man, how did he get by us. This is a divided highway. He couldn't have turned around and gone the other way!"

Sue said, "Ooh! This is spooky!"

Emily added, "Was that a man or an angel?"

When they finger spelled all that had taken place into Nellie's hand she said, "This is another sign that God is with us whenever we go out to speak!"

As the fall semester came to an end, there continued to be extensive media coverage of the activities of Nellie and Emily. One article reported that they had spoken to more than one hundred forty different groups numbering from five to two hundred people. Emily carefully gathered the many articles and put them in her bulging scrapbooks.

=   =   =

Nellie prepares pies for a dinner party at their home.

Chapter Twelve

Life At Home

In the Fall of 1978 Gary Brown quoted Nellie in one of his articles, "I like to walk free. I like to go to the Belden Village Mall because it is safe and I can walk freely from one store to the next one."

In the same article he also quoted Emily, "I am single and in my late twenties. We have several friends who are my age and also single. Nellie is in her early seventies and fits in perfectly with us. When we want to run around, she runs faster than all of us!"

As Nellie enrolled for the fall semester at Malone College, she decided that she needed some new clothes to go back to school. Now that they had a little money from the lecture circuit, Emily decided to take Nellie to the Belden Village Mall. As Emily guided her from store to store, Nellie insisted that they browse through every dress shop.

Six hours later Nellie had a complete new wardrobe. As they reached the car to go home, the exhausted Emily was grateful to sit down. But Nellie was like the "Energizer Bunny". She would not stop talking, laughing and bouncing around in her seat.

Emily's fingers spelled into Nellie's hand, "What is so much fun about going shopping at the Mall?" Nellie answered, "The walkways are smooth. There are no cracks or uneven places on the sidewalks. There are no curbs, no steps, no doors to open. People are friendly, the stores are close together and they have so many things to explore, to touch and to try on! I love it! When can we go back?"

Touched by how much these little conveniences meant to her sightless friend, Emily promised that they would go back at least once or twice a month. So, shopping at the Belden Village Mall became a regular feature of their life together.

As Nellie went back to college that September, life in the apartment continued to be exciting and eventful. As the semester began to unfold, Nancy continued to live with them. Each day while Nancy went to her job, Nellie and Emily went off to college.

Nellie was a model student. She was extremely conscientious in keeping up with her studies. When Braille copies of the material were available, she eagerly took her books to her bedroom and did the reading by herself. Otherwise, with flying fingers Emily patiently read into Nellie's palms whatever printed material was necessary. Nellie's professors were impressed by how she completed and understood all her reading assignments.

Nellie felt like an upper classman now. She had never been one to be at a loss for words during class discussions. But now she was not afraid to voice her opinion whenever she disagreed with what her professors were saying. Emily always knew when Nellie was getting ready to speak up. She would straighten her spine, square her shoulders and snort.

One day her New Testament professor was outlining the ministry of Jesus.

Emily spelled into Nellie's hand, "Jesus preached the Good News, healed the sick, and cast out demons."

Nellie straightened up in her chair.

Emily spelled out "What is it?"

"He is not right!"

"Who are you to question a professor?" Emily said, to no avail.

Nellie raised her voice, interrupting the professor, and said, "Professor, you are only three quarters correct. You left out the fact that Jesus also raised the dead!"

Laughing good naturedly, the professor responded, "I stand corrected. True enough. Jesus also raised the dead. Nellie may not be able to see or hear, but she has a brilliant mind and certainly knows her Bible."

After class the professor approached Nellie. With the help of Emily's fingers, he said, "Thank you for your input. You are insightful."

Each day, when Nellie had finished all her schoolwork, completed her household chores, and had laid out her clothes and books for the next day, she would present herself to Emily and say, adopting the language of their college friends, "I'm ready to party!" Her idea of "partying" sometimes meant doing things by herself, such as doing her crafts or spending time reading her Braille Bible. Other times it meant doing something with Emily, like cooking and baking together, taking long walks around the neighborhood, or going shopping at the Mall.

One Sunday morning in late September, Nellie dressed for church and sought out Emily, declaring, "I'm ready to party!"

Emily looked up in surprise, and wrote into her palm, "OK? What would you like to do?"

Nellie answered, "Why don't we go out for breakfast!"

"Where would you like to go?"

"To Mc Donald's!" Nellie laughed.

"To Mc Donald's?" Emily asked.

"What is so special about going to McDonald's? We could go out to Friendly's or Sambo's."

Nellie grinned, "Because McDonald's has a Braille Menu!"

As they drove to a nearby McDonald's restaurant, Emily wrote into Nellie's hand, "What would you like to order?"

Immediately, Nellie answered, "I just love their Egg McMuffins!"

But when Nellie entered the restaurant, instead of ordering her Egg McMuffin, she asked the cashier for a Braille Menu. The cashier summoned the manager who went off to look for a copy.

Then Nellie turned to Emily and said, "Go ahead and order."

Just as the cashier was putting Emily's Egg Mc Muffin and black coffee on her tray, the manager returned with the Braille Menu. Emily led Nellie to a table by the window.

Nellie told her friend, "Go ahead and eat," and proceeded to read the entire Braille menu, tracing every line with her finger.

When Nellie had read every word, she looked up and said, "OK, I'm ready to order!"

"What are you going to have?" Emily asked with raised eyebrows.

Nellie grinned. "Oh, I'm going to have an Egg McMuffin, just as I said."

Emily led Nellie to the counter to place her order. Since she had already finished her breakfast, she asked for a refill of her coffee and picked up a newspaper. Not a word passed between them as Nellie savored every bite of her McMuffin, while Emily lost herself in her reading.

As they left the restaurant, Emily's fingers asked, "Why did you read the whole menu when you already knew what you wanted to order?"

Nellie laughed, "Well, I go to so many restaurants where I cannot read the menu. It is a real treat when I get to one that has a menu I can read. It is interesting to read for myself about all the things I can order, along with their prices."

Now that they had money from their lecture circuit, Nellie often wanted to "party" by going out for breakfast. Soon this became a regular part of their life together, especially on Sundays before church. Most of the time Nellie wanted to go to Mc Donald's, and every time they went, Nellie repeated the same ritual of reading the entire Braille Menu while Emily ate her breakfast. Soon Nellie discovered that she not only liked Egg McMuffins, but she also loved hash browns and apple pies. To her, breakfast at McDonald's was a feast.

Meanwhile, Jim had successfully established the New Life Group Home. It housed five young deaf, and deaf and visually impaired boys, who were former inmates from Apple Creek. Now that he had hired a capable staff, he enjoyed getting away from work.

While Nellie and Emily got back into the swing of college life, Jim began to stop by more frequently. Even though he would appear without warning, often on a school night, Nellie was always ready to drop whatever she was doing and "party" with Jim.

As the new semester began to unfold, their popularity as returning students grew on campus. Nellie and Emily had an active social life in and outside the classroom.

Late one evening three new friends from Malone College arrived.

As they walked in, they asked, "What's happening?"

When Emily spelled their question into Nellie's hand, Nellie answered, "This is the seventies. Our favorite pastime as college intellectuals is discussion, discussion, and more discussion. We're discussing world religions, capitalism and socialism, women's liberation, and solving world problems like overpopulation and the depletion of natural resources. Come and join us!"

Emily extended the invitation saying, "Whenever our discussion continues into the wee hours of the morning, or the weather turns nasty, you are welcome to spend the night here. Just bring your sleeping bag and find a place on the floor. You can sleep in. When everyone is awake, Nellie prepares a large breakfast. Usually she makes scrambled eggs, bacon and stacks of pancakes. So come on in and make yourselves comfortable."

The reputation of their apartment as a party house spread throughout the campus. More and more of their college and church friends dropped by to "hang out" in the evenings. Whenever their friends stopped by, Emily made sure that Nellie joined the party and was kept involved in all conversations, acting as interpreter, finger spelling the endless discussions. Nellie always had a strong opinion to voice. She was especially vocal in advocating the theory of treating the planet like "space ship Earth," and critiquing Alan Greenspan's influence on the national and world economy.

Nancy also joined these parties even though she often felt like an outsider. She was not a college student and didn't understand the jokes about what had happened in their classes. So Nancy took to jumping into the conversation with critical and snide remarks about Nellie and her opinions. Most of the time her comments were ignored, which made her feel even more jealous. Eventually, she would withdraw to her bedroom to sulk.

Both Nancy and Nellie were accustomed to people coming to "party" and staying overnight, sleeping on the floor. Since Nancy had to get up early to go to work and Nellie was an early riser by nature, the two blind women had to pick their way through sleeping bodies to get to the kitchen. Nancy usually had a quick breakfast of cold cereal before leaving for work. But the aroma of eggs, bacon and fresh perked coffee which filled the apartment as Nellie cooked breakfast for their guests drove Nancy mad with jealousy.

For her part, Nellie thrived on the compliments she received for her cooking efforts. After breakfast their visitors always took their leave, promising to come back.

As they made their exit Nellie would say, "You are all welcome!"

But when the door closed she would always turn to Emily, sighing, "I'm happy to see them come and stay overnight, but I am also happy to see them go."

Nellie was grateful that nobody stayed over for more than one night at a time. She thought the apartment was crowded enough with just the three of them. After the guests left, she would bring the apartment back into order and meticulously clean up their living space. Then all would be "right" again in Nellie's little world.

One afternoon in late October, when they had come home from their classes, Nellie asked Emily, "How about some beef stew for dinner?"

Emily spelled back, "Sounds delicious! But you'd better put in some extra meat and potatoes for Jim."

As Nellie prepared the enriched stew, the two women joked about how Jim was a typical bachelor and how all typical bachelors tried to drop by just in time to eat a well cooked meal.

Once the stew had been prepared in the slow cooker, Nellie turned her attention to her homework and Emily sat down to read the paper and pay the bills.

Three hours later, when she was done with all her reading, Nellie lifted the lid to the crock-pot, savored the smell and declared, "The stew is ready!"

At that very moment, as though he had ESP, Jim rang the doorbell.

Emily alerted Nellie, spelling out, "The door bell just rang. Guess who is here?"

Nellie laughed, "Jim must have a psychic nose!"

Nancy came out from her room as Jim sauntered into the kitchen and gave Nellie a hug.

With one arm still around Nellie's waist, he lifted the lid to the slow cooker and devilishly spelled into Nellie's palm as he spoke out loud for Emily's benefit, "Where did you get this 'mystery meat'?"

Without giving her a chance to respond he pressed on, "Don't tell me. Is it wild deer? Wild rabbit? Alley cat? I won't even touch it, until I see Kitten!"

Nellie laughed, walked across the living room and sat down on the sofa. The now fully-grown cat had heard Jim arrive and was peeking out from Nellie's bedroom doorway. Immediately, when Nellie sat down, she scampered across the living room floor, leapt to the back of the sofa with a single bound, walked across Nellie's shoulders, and arranged herself around her neck, with her head and tail draped down Nellie's chest.

With the cat perched on her shoulders, Nellie stood up, walked back to the kitchen where Jim was standing and said, "Go on! Touch Kitten. See if she is alive!"

As Jim reached out to pet Kitten, the little cat raised her head in expectation and began to purr.

Feeling the vibration, Nellie said, "See, Kitten is alive, her motor is running. So now are you ready to eat?"

They all laughed as Nellie, with the kitten still riding on her shoulder, served up the stew.

Nancy, who had been listening to their joking, took her seat at the table and quipped, "What's so funny? If I had asked, 'What is this mystery meat,' Nellie would have been insulted. I wish the stupid cat was in the stew!"

"Oh, shut up!" Emily snapped back, silencing Nancy.

After supper, Nancy withdrew to her room while Jim and Emily settled down on the sofa with Nellie between them. For hours, they held a three-way conversation, talking with their fingers into Nellie's hands. Finally, Nellie withdrew to do a little reading before bedtime.

As soon as Nellie left the room, Emily signed, "I need your help!" Jim signed back, "Let me guess. It's Nancy."

"Yes" Emily signed, "She has stopped pitching in with the chores and she is always making snide remarks about Nellie to me and even in front of all our friends."

Jim responded silently with his hands, "Well, at the New Life home, when we have a behavior problem, we write a contract between the staff and the kids. It spells out specifically what we expect, why we expect it, and the consequences of failing to live up to the terms of the contract."

Emily tucked this idea in the back of her mind and they

continued to visit.

After school the next day, Emily dropped Nellie off at the apartment and drove to the New Life group home to look at some samples of Jim's behavior modification contracts. By suppertime Emily had prepared her own draft.

She called both Nancy and Nellie to the table announcing, "We need to have a house meeting!"

To her amazement, without much discussion, Nancy signed the contract, which not only spelled out her chores and responsibilities, but also required her to respect Nellie's dignity and keep her negative comments to herself. But Emily was even more surprised as Nancy's behavior actually did improve. Even their visitors noticed the change and began to include Nancy more conscientiously into their conversations.

One Sunday morning in early November, Nellie presented herself to Emily, saying, "I'm ready to party!"

"Do you want to go to McDonald's?"

Nellie answered, "No, I want to go to a 'sit down' restaurant!"

They decided to go to Friendly's for breakfast and to invite Nancy to come along.

As she sat in their booth, Nellie felt chilled.

"I feel cold! I want something hot to eat!"

Emily spelled back into her hand, "They have good, hot, spicy chili. Why don't you order some chili?"

Nellie frowned, "Chili for breakfast?"

"Yes!" Emily answered, "They serve whatever is on the menu, twenty-four hours a day. You can order chili and pancakes if you want."

Nellie laughed, "That sounds good!"

In spite of the strange look she received from the waitress, Emily placed Nellie's order. To Emily's surprise, when the food was finally brought to the table, instead of putting syrup on her pancake, Nellie picked it up, dipped it in the chili, and took a bite.

A smile spread across her face as she smacked her lips, "Now that is good! Hot, spicy and good."

Emily tied a napkin around Nellie's neck to protect her Sunday dress. Nellie finished eating her chili with pancakes. And from that time on, Nellie always ordered chili and pancakes whenever they went to Friendly's.

With all their student discussions, Nellie had become politically aware. She decided that she, too, wanted to vote in the upcoming November elections. Well in advance of the deadline for registration, Emily took Nellie to the Stark County Board of Elections. She was appalled to discover that there were no Braille ballots provided. After discussing the matter with Congressman Ralph Regula, it was clear that Emily would have to assist Nellie.

Using the League of Women Voter's guide, Emily gave Nellie a run-down on the issues, on who was running for office, and the published details of each contender's background and qualifications.

When they arrived at the polls, UPI correspondent Ms. Armao was already there. Emily easily convinced the ladies working at the polls that she should be allowed to assist Nellie in voting. While Emily guided her hand, Nellie signed her name in the proper column in the large registration book. Emily then led her over to an open voting booth on the far side of the room and pulled the curtain.

For the next half hour, Emily finger spelled every question on the ballot. She also guided Nellie's hand so she could punch her own voting card.

When they stepped out of the voting booth, a UPI photographer snapped Nellie's picture. She was beaming, clapping her hands, and shouting.

"Now, I am one hundred percent American!"

As the fall semester came to a climax with Nellie's final exams, she was extremely busy with her studies. Emily was also tied up with spelling out the classroom lectures she had taped, and helping Nellie to cram for her exams. Suddenly, after Nellie had taken her last exam, all the pressure was gone.

The following Monday they stopped by the college to pick up her exams and receive her grades. Clearly, Nellie continued to do well in every subject. She was particularly pleased when Emily picked up her blue book and reported that she had earned a high "B" on her Philosophy final.

Emily began to read:

Discuss the following statement.
The non-correspondence between language and reality and between language and our perceptions of reality has many important implications for our everyday communication.

Nellie's discussion was as follows:

My world comes in hands. I feel with my hands. What my hands touch is real. I talk with my hands, and I feel noise with my head bones, hands and feet. I talk with all parts of my body. My behavior is my language as I talk with my hands. My language is a direct part of my reality. There is no difference between my reality and what I say because everything comes in one package for me. My perception is my reality. My hands tell me true. All my reality I usually get from language. Hand talk is directly in touch with what is, because my interpreter will give me little more than what is. I will do a better job answering this question when my Braille textbooks are done.

Emily saw that the professor had written on the bottom of Nellie's paper:

This is good even without your Braille books. You seem to really understand communication---Because that is your world!!

Just then, the professor stepped out of his office.

Greeting the two women, he said, "I hope Nellie will be in one of my classes next year." As Emily wrote his comment into Nellie's hand, Nellie smiled saying, "I hope so too!"

When they got home to the apartment, Emily exhaustedly sank into a chair. Then she looked at the calendar.

"Oh, my gosh," she spelled into Nellie's palm, "It's only three days until Christmas Eve!"

That night Jim stopped by. He helped them place the Christmas tree, which had been stored on the balcony for two weeks, into Emily's Christmas tree stand.

Nellie said, "I remember making paper chains to decorate the Christmas tree when I was a little girl. We also made pop corn strings."

Emily found some colored construction paper. Jim was amazed as he watched Nellie cut the paper into strips.

He marveled, "I can't believe how straight she can cut. I couldn't cut that straight, even though I can see what I am doing."

The three of them worked together to glue the strips into

intertwining loops. Then Jim helped Nellie to hang the chain on the tree. Next, Nellie made a batch of popcorn. She asked Emily for a needle and thread. Pressing her tongue into the eye of the needle, Nellie poked the thread through the needle's eye until she felt it come through with her tongue. Once the needle was threaded, she strung the popcorn together until she had a chain about six feet long. Very gently, so as not to make a mess, Emily and Jim helped Nellie to spiral the popcorn around the tree. Then Nellie repeated the process until the tree was covered from top to bottom with popcorn and paper chains.

Emily then got out some scented candles and placed them on the coffee table.

As Jim ceremoniously lit them, Nellie said, "It smells like the Christmas I used to know as a kid: the fresh scent of a live tree, the smell of popcorn, and the aroma of the candles."

For the rest of the evening they swapped stories about the way Christmas had been celebrated when they were children.

Finally, Nellie excused herself and went to bed.

After Nellie had left the room, Emily said, "I think that we should plan a big surprise for Nellie this Christmas."

After tossing a few ideas back and forth, Emily laughed, "I know. Why don't I wrap you up, Jim, like a present. You will be the 'big' gift. She will love it!"

Jim laughed, "Sounds like fun!"

"Of course" Emily went on, "We'll have to work hard to keep our surprise a secret. We'll have to be sneaky. Nellie will know by heart every gift that is near, under, or even on the tree. She has a keen sense of smell. You will have to take a shower and wash your hair without shampoo. No aftershave either."

Jim chimed in, "When I get here I'll have to walk as softly as a cat. Nellie can feel my footsteps on the wooden floor. She'll know immediately that I am in the apartment if I am not careful."

As planned, after Nancy left the apartment to spend Christmas Eve with her parents and family, Jim drove up. Silently he climbed the stairs and stepped through the open door into the living room. He could hear Nellie humming a Christmas Carol in her bedroom.

Emily was prepared. She had purchased extra wide Christmas paper and a wide red ribbon with a huge floppy bow.

Jim stood still as Emily wrapped him up, shoes and all, saying, "It's a good thing that Nellie can't hear the noise I am making with this paper!"

Then she commanded, "Lean back! I'll catch you and lay you down on the floor."

With her help he managed to lie down next to the Christmas tree without tearing the paper.

Meanwhile, Nellie was in her room waiting patiently for Jim to come so they could open gifts. As time passed and he didn't come, Nellie kept checking her faceless watch. By the time she came out of her room, she thought Jim was half an hour late.

Nellie was fuming. "It's not like Jim to be late! Where do you suppose he is? He surely didn't forget that it is Christmas Eve. Emily, what can we do?"

With Jim lying right there on the floor, wrapped up like a colorful mummy, Emily had to control herself.

She kept up the charade, spelling out, "He should be here any minute; but if he doesn't show up within the next ten minutes, we will go ahead and open the gifts."

Nellie looked stricken. She was very unhappy about the whole situation. Ten minutes passed.

Emily grabbed Nellie's hands and spelled out, "We are not going to wait any longer. We are going to open the gifts right now!"

Nellie was miserable.

"Oh, Emily, do you think we should?"

Emily was beginning to feel guilty for upsetting Nellie. But she was relentless.

She bore down slightly for emphasis on the last letter of each word as she continued to lead Nellie on, "Yes, we should! He knows better than to be late. I'll give you one of your gifts first. You go ahead and open it. Jim can open his gifts whenever he gets here."

Emily gave Nellie a small gift, placing it in her hands. Nellie set it down beside her, on the sofa, and stubbornly lifted her chin in defiance.

"No," she said, "I'll wait for Jim."

Acting exasperated, Emily firmly took Nellie's hands.

Her fingers flew as she spelled, "Well, you have one great big gift. It's in the way. Would you like to open it first? You will need to sit down on the floor to open it."

Nellie's eyebrows arched in surprise, and she tilted her head sideways.

She wondered, "I know every package that is under the tree. Someone must have brought in a gift without my knowing about it."

Too curious to protest any further, Nellie sat down on the floor. Emily helped her feel around among the presents on the floor. Together they moved some of the gifts out of the way. Then Nellie accidentally touched Jim, wrapped in the Christmas paper. She squeezed one of his shoes.

As the soft toe of the shoe gave way, she jerked her hand back and screeched, "What is that? What have you done? I don't want whatever that thing is!"

Nearly bursting out with laughter and shaking with glee, Emily calmed Nellie down telling her, "You need to undo the package by untying the big bow."

She guided Nellie's hands, making sure she touched only the bow. Then she helped her pull on it until it came undone.

Jim couldn't control himself any longer. He laughed out loud. Nellie could not hear him laugh. But she felt his body shaking as she inspected the wrapping paper to see where the package should be opened.

"Oh, my gosh, it's alive!"

The wrapping paper began to tear and Jim literally burst out of the package. Only then did Nellie realize that the "thing" that was alive was Jim! At first, Nellie didn't know whether to laugh or cry, whether to be mad at them for teasing her or to just be happy that Jim was there and that he was all right. After a moment, she regained her composure and smiled as she again took her seat.

"Jim, it was a fine joke." Nellie said, "Now, let's open the real presents."

The rest of the evening was full of joy and laughter as they opened Christmas gifts.

As Jim gave Nellie a hug and took his leave, she finger spelled into his hand, "Truly, you are God's gift to me! None of this would have been possible without you!"

After Christmas Emily noticed a marked increase in the friction between Nellie and Nancy. In spite of their contract, Nancy had again taken to making snide remarks about Nellie.

To make matters worse, when Emily asked her to pay her share of the January rent, Nancy quipped, "I know that all of Nellie's SSI benefits are turned over to you. But is Nellie really paying her full share? It seems to me that you are always asking me for money. Money for rent, money for the heat bill, for the grocery bill, for a tank of gas."

From that time on, Nancy began to fuss and complain.

Two days later, she approached Emily. "I think you over-charged me. You owe me two dollars and thirty-two cents. I paid more than my fair share for a tank of gas."

Taken by surprise, Emily asked, "When did this happen?"

"Some two months back." Nancy stated with a snort.

"You can't be serious."

But Nancy *was* serious.

She raved, "I am going to move out if you don't give me back my money this instant."

Emily was fed up.

She blurted out, "Fine! This settles it! Here, Nancy, take the two dollars and thirty-two cents. I will call your father and have him come and take you back home!"

"Good! You do that!" Nancy yelped back.

Before Nancy had time for any second thoughts, Emily placed the call. She helped Nancy pack all of her belongings until she was ready to go. An hour later, her father came to pick her up. Suddenly, Nancy was gone.

With Nancy out of the apartment, Nellie moved back to the big bedroom. Emily moved back into the dining room. Peace returned to the apartment.

A few days after Christmas Emily's mother had invited her to stop by for their annual New Year's Eve dinner. Emily was torn. Nellie was not included in the invitation. She knew that this was not a matter of innocent oversight. Nellie would not be welcome.

Ever since she had moved in with Nellie, Emily had been shunned by her mother. She had not been invited to any family gatherings for over a year and a half. She longed to feel accepted once again. Finally, Emily decided to accept the invitation.

As she stepped into her mother's house, the aroma of roast pork cooked in sauerkraut, their traditional New Year's Eve dinner, filled the air. The feeling of "being home" brought bittersweet tears to her eyes.

Her mother tormented her throughout the meal.

Speaking in an overly loud and condescending voice so everyone in the room could hear, she quipped, "And, where are you working now? How long are you going to live with that old deaf woman? Blind, too! I can't believe how you have dragged the family name through the mud with all these newspaper articles of your living with that Nellie!"

Emily choked back her tears. She felt like crawling under the table. When she could take no more, she abruptly stood up and excused herself.

She picked up her coat, and headed toward the door, but her mother blocked the exit and pressed on. "How much money have you wasted on that old blind and deaf woman? I have a right to know!"

Mortified, Emily retorted, "All you care about is money! Good bye!"

Tears of bitterness rolled down her face as she thought, "Why can't my own mother be proud of me and what I have done for Nellie? But I should have known better than to expect anything different."

Emily soon discovered that in spite of the money they were making on the lecture circuit, without Nancy's financial contribution to their cost of living, she had to borrow from her inheritance. At the end of the month she was stewing over how to pay all the bills.

Chewing on her pen and thought, "We have already given more than 200 lectures. The lecture circuit is drying up. We have to go farther away from Canton to find new engagements. We have to spend more money on gas. We're going to have to do something differently."

Emily concluded that it was time to find jobs where she and Nellie could work together. Unfortunately, it seemed that Nellie would have to forego her college studies.

Emily met with Jim and explained their financial situation. He quickly offered them a solution saying, "I am looking for help at the group home. If I can find funding for additional staff, you can work as a caretaker and Nellie can teach independent living skills to the boys. You know that there are two who are deaf and also legally blind. She will be a natural to work with them."

Emily was excited about the prospect of their working with Jim at the New Life group home. Acting on a tip from a friend she went to Goodwill in Canton. A caseworker named Linda Owen, who was familiar with the Title 9 program, explained that the State of Ohio would pay senior citizens for doing public service work. She went on to explain that Nellie's work with the boys at New Life could be considered a public service. All that was required was for Nellie to fill out the forms.

Emily was beside herself with joy, saying, "You are the first case worker who has ever been helpful to us!"

But as she drove home she was sobered by the thought that she would now have to tell Nellie that she needed to give up going to college and go to work. Early the next Saturday morning, Emily took Nellie by the hand and led her to the couch. She sat down beside her, reached for her hands and began to spell.

"Without Nancy's rent we are running out of money to pay our bills. We are going to have to find some new way to earn money besides doing the lecture circuit. Jim has offered us jobs with him at the New Life group home. I will be a child caretaker. You can work as a life skills instructor for his young deaf and blind boys. They need someone who can teach them how to take care of themselves. How to cook and clean, take care of their clothes, go shopping and manage their own money. They need someone to teach them everything they will need to know in order to live independently in the community."

Emily continued to spell out, "The case worker from Goodwill says that since you are a senior citizen, the State of Ohio will pay your salary. But this means you have to give up college and begin a new career. What do you think about this?"

Nellie sat still for several minutes while she thought about all that Emily had said. God had called them to share her wisdom and experience with the public through their lectures. Now it seemed that perhaps God was calling her to share her wisdom and experience, in a hands-on way, with Jim's boys. She could see that her life was about to change again.

Nellie turned her body toward Emily. She was smiling, her face radiant.

"I think the idea of our working together is wonderful. God bless Jim for offering us this work when we need it so badly. God has again answered our prayers. No, I don't mind giving up college. It is time for me to get a real job. It's time for me to become a working woman. We will be two working women together!"

=   =   =

Chapter Thirteen

WORKING WOMAN

Dawn broke late on the second Monday of January. Awake long before there was any hint of light in the sky, Nellie had bathed, dressed and eaten breakfast. It was her first day of work. She could not suppress her excitement!

Groggy from a short night of sleep, Emily soon joined Nellie at the table, groaning and slowly spelling into her hand, "Where is the coffee? Why are you awake so early?"

The contrast between the two women was amazing. Having been a public school teacher for five years, and having held a multitude of other positions in more recent years, there was nothing really exciting for Emily about starting a new job. But Nellie had never held any paying job. At an age when most people would have long been retired, Nellie was as excited as a teenager at the prospect of going to work and earning her own paycheck.

She spelled back, "I am awake because I can't stop thinking about my new job."

Emily smiled and wrote into her palm, "Are you nervous?"

"No!" Nellie said emphatically, "There is nothing to be nervous about! I know Jim. You and I have visited the group home many times. I know all the boys. You and I have already chaperoned them on shopping trips to the Belden Village Mall, and several other outings. Why should I be nervous?"

Nellie paused for a moment, then she spelled out, "But I wonder what will happen when we get there today. What will Jim want me to teach the boys first?"

Emily answered with the voice of experience.

"The first thing we will do is to have a staff meeting with Jim. We may not even do any work with the boys today."

Nellie was disappointed, and sighed, "Well, at least I hope I get a chance to teach the boys how to make apple sauce pie."

As Emily drove to the New Life Group Home located at 4733 Lincoln Way in Massillon, Nellie focused her mind on recollecting what she knew about the layout of the large two-story house. As she took her mental tour, she remembered that the front door opened into a large living room. It had a small alcove, which the housekeeper used as her room. There was a large, family-style kitchen and dining room. Off the kitchen there was another room that Jim used as his office and bedroom. Upstairs there were three large bedrooms and a bathroom for the four boys.

As Emily had anticipated, Jim met the two women at the door and ushered them directly into his office.

Spelling to both Nellie and Emily, Jim said "I am talking to you both with my fingers in order to get you acclimated to the work environment. We almost always use finger spelling to communicate with the boys."

Jim spelled on, "Welcome to the staff of the New life Group Home. We have been friends for a long time. You have helped me as volunteers before. But since you are full-time employees now, we still need to go over the purpose and goals for this home and to talk about your duties and responsibilities.

As you know, I first opened the New Life Group Home in 1977 when you, Nellie, were still living at the boarding house. The basic purpose of this home is to motivate, educate, and train our deaf and deaf/blind residents so they can live independently in the community. We provide housing for four teenage boys who are former patients of the Apple Creek Mental Hospital. They are all either totally deaf, or profoundly hearing impaired, and two of them are also legally blind. At Apple Creek they were labeled as retarded and non-trainable. My hope is to prove that the professionals at Apple Creek were wrong, and that these boys can live successful lives in the community in spite of the fact that they are deaf, or deaf and blind. To do this, I want these boys to live as if we were a family. They should be able to go to school and receive their education just like other children and youth in this community.

I have volunteers who serve as a policy making board of directors. I have a number of volunteers who help provide supervision for our special youth activities. Darlene is our full-time housekeeper and cook. She also takes care of the laundry.

Emily, your position is titled House Parent/Child Care Worker. Unofficially, you will be the house 'mom.' You will be responsible for getting the boys ready for the day, transporting them to school and other activities, and putting them to bed at night. You will help in the kitchen and eat with the boys. Your job is to help them to resolve their conflicts and learn how to get along with each other. You will also be their nurse. In addition to taking care of these kinds of daily details, I want to enlist your help in getting these boys enrolled in school.

Nellie, your job title is Teacher/Trainer. You will work along side Emily, but your job is to help the boys learn some important life skills: how to take care of their clothes, to dress themselves, to cook, to wash dishes and clean up after themselves. You will also teach them how to do crafts and to manage their own money.

I need to warn you that this will not be an easy job. These boys had it worse than you, Nellie! Much worse! When you were born, you could hear. All of these boys were born deaf. Three of them have never heard a sound. They have lived at Apple Creek since they were infants. They were kept there locked in a room. They were treated like animals. They were not even toilet trained. There were no bathroom facilities in the room. The staff just came in and hosed down the floor twice a day.

When I met the boys, they did not know how to dress themselves. They were not taught how to take care of their personal hygiene. They had no manners. To my knowledge, until I was hired, no one had ever tried to communicate with them. They were just pushed and shoved around and tied into their chairs with leather restraints."

By this time, Nellie was in tears. She turned to Emily and asked, "Is this really true?"

"Yes," Emily answered with her fingers, "I have worked at Apple Creek, and I have seen it, too."

Jim pressed on, "Like Annie Sullivan, who worked with Helen Keller, I had to break the communication barrier. But she only had one child to work with, and I had more than a dozen. How I did it, I will never know. But let me give you an idea of what I was up against. When your father taught you how to finger spell, you had already learned how to read and write. But these boys could do none of these things. I had to begin at ground zero.

These four have already come a long, long way. You can communicate with them by finger spelling. They have been living here for more than a year. I have spent the time trying to civilize and de-institutionalize them. They are beginning to learn how to act like normal human beings. I believe that three of them are now ready to be enrolled in public school. But the school board still has not agreed to let them attend. So our biggest project will be to get these kids enrolled in school.

Meanwhile, the boys still have a lot to learn and a long way to go. Your jobs will not be easy."

Jim paused, then he laughed "By the way, I call them boys, but you know that they are the size of grown men. The youngest is Ron; he is sixteen. Ted is seventeen. Ken is nineteen, Mickie is thirty-two. Our next resident will probably be a girl who is seventeen. Nellie, they are all at least half a foot taller than you and weigh about twice as much."

Nellie interrupted Jim, spelling out, "I have heard enough, enough bad stories. Now let me try to sweeten these boy's lives a little and give them something to grow on. How about making them an apple sauce pie?"

Jim smiled, as his fingers answered. "That would be wonderful; but instead of your doing it all by yourself for them, take one or two of the boys and show them how you make this pie. That will be your job today! Good luck!"

The staff meeting ended with a round of hugs. Then, Nellie asked Darlene to show her around the kitchen. After familiarizing herself with what was in all the cupboards, she searched out the ingredients to make the pie and mixed up the dough for a piecrust.

When everything was ready she found Jim in the living room and told him with her fingers, "I am ready to teach!"

Jim answered, "Let me call the boys. Let's see who is ready to learn."

Unlike the typical house parent, who would stand at the bottom of the stairs and call for the boys to come down, Jim had to go upstairs and spell out to each of the boys, "Come down. Come downstairs."

Like a herd of buffalo, the boys stomped down the stairs to the living room. Instantly, Nellie knew by the vibration of the floor that they were there. Jim met them at the foot of the stairs. With flying fingers he introduced the boys to the two women and explained what they would be doing at the home.

With confidence, Nellie stepped forward and spelled into one of the boy's hands, "Would you like to help me make an apple sauce pie?"

She received no answer.

Undaunted, she turned to the next and spelled out her question. He wrote back, "Get someone else to help you."

She approached the third, he replied, "No, I've never done that before."

And the fourth answered, "Get lost. Get someone else."

Disappointed, Nellie went back to the kitchen. She put her hand on the pie dough, took up the rolling pin and was about to start rolling out the piecrust herself, when Jim gently took the rolling pin from her hand.

Jim spelled into her palm, "I told you that you were not supposed to make this pie all by yourself."

Pouting, Nellie spelled back, "But I asked the boys to help me and they were all too busy or had some other excuse."

Jim smiled and caressed her hand before spelling out, "I told you this wouldn't be easy. Your job is to go back and ask, and ask again, until someone finally agrees to help you. Ask your question another way."

As Nellie walked back to the living room, she decided to take another approach.

Again, she made the rounds, speaking to each of the young teenagers with her fingers and saying, "Since nobody wants to help me make an apple sauce pie today, I guess we won't have one. Too bad, it sure would have tasted good, very good!"

This time she received no answer at all. Nellie went back to the kitchen thinking, "Are they giving me the silent treatment?"

Discouraged, she began to put the dough and the other ingredients back into the refrigerator.

As Nellie wiped off the counter she had cleared, one of the deaf and visually impaired boys came into the kitchen and bumped into the sightless Nellie.

Nellie gently explored his face with her hand and spelled onto his forehead, "Who are you?"

Copying her, he gently felt of her face, tracing her forehead, eyelids, nose, bone structure, her lips and her chin. Then, he wrote on her forehead, "I am Ron. Who are you? Are you the pie lady?"

Nellie took his hand and spelled in it, "Yes, I am Nellie. I am deaf and blind. And, I am the pie lady."

"I will help you make the pie," Ron spelled back, "If we can have it for dessert today."

Nellie answered with her fingers, "You'll get the first piece of pie tonight, if you help me. I will guide your hands, just follow me."

Nellie retrieved the ingredients from the refrigerator. Placing the dough on a breadboard, she ducked between his arms, picked up the rolling pin, and placed his right hand on hers. He copied, placing his left hand on hers. Then, Nellie began gently to roll out the dough.

Emily stepped into the kitchen. She was astounded by the sight of the tiny Nellie grinning, with the brawny Ron standing close behind her, with his arms and hands round her, looking very concentrated. Tears filled her eyes as she watch them work wordlessly. They were like poetry in motion.

Without letting them know she was there, Emily observed as Nellie finished rolling out the dough. She handed Ron the pie pan, letting him explore it with his fingers. Then she put her hands on his and gently guided them as he pressed the crust into the pie pan.

Nellie wrote into his palm, "Next we need to mix up the pie filling. It takes apple sauce, thickener, and cinnamon."

Nellie showed Ron how to pour the applesauce into a measuring cup with his right hand while dipping the forefinger of his left hand into the cup so he could tell when it was getting full. Ron grinned when he felt the cool applesauce touch his finger. He smacked his lips as he licked it off, but he didn't spill a drop. Seeing that the two worked so well together, Emily stole out of the kitchen and went to talk to the other boys.

A few minutes later Emily heard the oven door slam. Ron came bounding into the living room and, like a six year old, danced around the room chanting, "I made a pie! I made a pie! Nana, nana, Boo-boo, I made a pie!"

His joy was contagious. Emily and Jim both laughed as the young lad shook the house with his dancing feet.

Jim turned to Emily and said, "That's what its all about! Giving these boys a chance to feel like that! Knowing that they can do something!"

When dinner was served, Emily sat on one side of the table with Jim and Nellie. The four boys sat on the opposite side. Darlene came in, carrying the serving dishes with the meat and vegetables. Then she went back and brought a bowl with steaming hot baked potatoes.

Overwhelmed by the smell of the dinner and the pie still baking in the oven, Emily turned to Jim and said, "I can't believe how well this is going!"

Jim turned around to help Darlene set the gravy on the table. The moment he turned his back, Ted reached across the table, snatched a potato, stuffed the whole thing into his mouth, and with a vacant stare chewed and swallowed it.

Emily tapped Jim on the shoulder. "Jim, Ted just took a potato." Turning back around, Jim said, "Good."

"Not good," Emily insisted, "He just stuck the whole boiling hot potato in his mouth."

Instantly, Jim realized what Emily was saying. He sprang from his chair, and yelled "Emily, you stay here. Make sure nothing else happens!"

Jim grabbed Ted by the scruff of the neck, marched him to the kitchen, and stuffed a handful of ice cubes in his mouth. Ted spit them back out. Jim opened Ted's mouth. His lips, and the roof of his mouth were already blistering. Jim spent the next half hour applying burn cream to Ted's lips and putting the ice cubes back in Ted's mouth every time he spit them out. By the time he returned to the table to finish his dinner the food was cold.

Jim turned to Emily and said, "I told you that this job will not be easy."

Emily asked, "Is that what you meant when you said that these boys don't have any manners?"

"That's beside the point," Jim said wryly, "He did that to test you; he wanted to see if you were watching, to show you how tough he is. That is why he didn't cry out even though his mouth was on fire. These boys will do anything and endure any kind of pain to prove that they are wild, tough, and cool."

Exhausted from the long day, and sobered by the potato incident, as she drove home Emily spelled into Nellie's hand, "That was a baptism by fire! We were both tested! You passed the first test. You and Ron made a delicious pie. You won't have such a hard time getting volunteers to help you make the next one, but we will probably be tested like that in some way every day."

Tired though she was, Nellie spelled back, "Just remember the words of Paul, 'I can do all things through Christ who strengthens me'."

It did not take long for the boys to settle into a routine with Nellie and Emily. With the boys at home all day, Nellie had plenty of time to work with them. She was eager to teach. Jim soon recognized that hiring her was a stroke of genius. When the boys realized that she was both totally deaf and totally blind, they became receptive to being taught by her. As time went on they treated her with great respect.

The boys were most excited about learning how to cook. Nellie always worked one on one. She found that Ted and Ken, who were only deaf, learned quickly. But Ron and Mick, who were also almost blind, had to develop additional skills. They required more attention and encouragement. At the same time, they were more excited when they were successful.

As the days and weeks unfolded, Nellie continued to be as thrilled about being a "working woman" as she had been about being a college girl. She loved getting to know each of the boys. For the first time in her life, Nellie felt that she was doing something important and worthwhile.

She began by teaching the boys how to make desserts. Soon they had all helped to make applesauce pie, vinegar pie, pie made with custard, and everyone's favorite, chocolate chip peanut butter pie. Next, Nellie showed them how to make scrambled eggs with bacon, pancakes, and coffee cake made with Bisquick mix. She also taught them how to skin and strip the meat off a boiled chicken to prepare chicken soup. The boys had fun cooking Macaroni and Cheese with Tuna because it seemed so easy to make. But soon their favorite main dish to prepare was Chili Meatloaf. Nellie showed them how to make this dish by adding canned chili to the mix of hamburger, eggs, and cubed bread crusts. The boys loved to put their hands in the mixing bowl and knead the mush. Then they would chase the staff around the kitchen, threatening to touch them with their greasy hands. At the same time, Nellie taught the boys how to wash the dishes and clean the kitchen.

In order to reinforce their newly learned life skills and build what he called "a normal family atmosphere", Jim insisted that the boys take turns helping to cook the meals and clean up afterwards. The boys enjoyed working side by side with Nellie so much that he received surprisingly little resistance when he asked them to help out. They also took great pride whenever Jim complimented their work.

But from Emily's point of view, Nellie's next teaching effort caused a marvelous change at the New Life Group Home: she taught the boys how to organize their own clothes. It was Emily's job to help the boys get dressed in the morning. This task had proved to be quite a challenge with all four boys demanding assistance at the same time.

But after Nellie showed them how to organize their dresser

drawers, it seemed that suddenly the boys stopped whining, "Where are my socks?" or "I can't find my shirt!"

Instead, they quietly got dressed and then ceremoniously presented themselves to Emily saying, "Look at me!" or "How do I look?"

Meanwhile, as requested, Emily met with the Superintendent of the Massillon public schools to see if they would enroll the boys.

He denied her request saying, "Here in Massillon we do have some handicapped children in our schools, but we do not have any teachers who know sign language. Unless these boys can lip read, we can't enroll them."

When Emily reported this conversation to Jim, he groaned, "That is exactly what they told me. They are not going to change their minds unless we do what we did with the Massillon State Hospital. We need to stir up public opinion."

Emily decided to begin by sending written requests to the school administrators. To get public attention she also wrote letters to various local and state government officials. Then she sent a letter to the editor of the *Massillon Independent.* When her letter was published, it stimulated a number of readers to respond by writing letters to the editor in support of her position. Eventually, a reporter came and interviewed the staff at the New Life Group Home. When the reporter recognized Nellie, the interview resulted in two feature articles. One was about the boys and their fight to be admitted to public school, and the other was about Nellie working as a professional life skills teacher at the home.

While the school superintendent remained staunch in his position regarding the enrollment of the boys, once again Emily's phone rang off the hook with requests for Nellie to come and speak to various groups and organizations. But now those who called wanted to hear Nellie talk about her work at the children's home.

Jim seized the opportunity to have Nellie and Emily present their programs to benefit the New Life Group Home.

Jim explained to Emily, "I have three goals for these programs: to raise public awareness about New Life, to increase public pressure on the school board, and to raise funds for our operating budget."

Nellie proved to be just as adept at telling funny and inspiring stories about her work with the boys as she had been about telling the story of her own life. Many seemed to agree with the comment of one person from the Massillon Pilot's Club.

"What impressed me the most about Nellie's talk is that this woman is seventy three years old. Most people her age have long since retired. Here is this handicapped woman, both deaf and blind, and she is working full time and enjoying it."

The story about Nellie's work was picked up by UPI, and appeared in many newspapers. As a result, Nellie received many citations, awards, and honors for her work with the boys.

As Emily's campaign to get the boys into school gained momentum, Jim redoubled his efforts to teach them how to read. He had already begun this process before the boys were released from Apple Creek, but he realized that eventually, the school would require them to be tested before they could be placed in class. So, Jim set aside time each day and enlisted Emily's assistance in tutoring the boys. Jim's method was simple. He had a large set of letter blocks. He would spell out a word with the blocks and then point to the object or a picture. Once the boys had learned how to read a word, Jim helped them find it in a set of deaf sign language books that contained lists of words and their corresponding signs. Using these, they learned how to read "out loud".

Initially, this method of instruction worked fine. The block letters were very large and even the boys with visual impairments could read them. But when Jim tried to introduce his students to printed children's books, three of the boys had great trouble reading them because their vision was so poor. When they would practically put their noses on the page, it was still difficult for them to make out the words.

One day Emily was watching Ken try to read "See Spot Run."

She turned to Jim and said, "Say, Jim, I see that none of these boys have glasses. We have been told that three of them are legally blind, but have they ever been examined to see if glasses could help them?"

Surprised by her question, Jim answered, "I have no idea! Knowing Apple Creek, probably not. But even if they have been, I guess it should be done again."

Emily had noticed that there was an optometrist's office located in the shopping center right across the street from the children's home. The next day she decided to walk over and introduce herself to Dr. Channane. Without hesitation, he agreed to give the boys a full examination.

First, Emily brought Ron to see the doctor.

While Ron walked around the store, exploring the racks of frames, she explained, "We are told that this boy is legally blind. Obviously, he is severely visually impaired."

Dr. Channane frowned, "If his eyes are so bad, how come he can walk around this store without bumping into things?"

After a full examination, an hour later, Dr. Channane, with tears in his eyes, told Emily, "I can't believe that this young man had to walk around blind for sixteen years when all he needed was a pair of glasses. He is very nearsighted and has severe astigmatism. But his vision is correctable to 20/30. Almost perfect!"

As Emily placed the order for the glasses, she was both excited for Ron and enraged.

When she got home, Jim met her at the door and said, "What is wrong?"

Emily growled, "The system, the system! I can't believe they labeled this boy retarded and locked him away for 15 years, simply because he was deaf and needed a pair of glasses."

By the end of the week, they had discovered that Ted's vision also was almost perfect. He did not need glasses. Ken and Mickie were given prescriptions that also greatly improved their vision. Although they were not fully correctable, this meant that they were no longer legally blind. Even Mickie could now read books with regular print. He no longer had to hold them up to his nose, but could read them from about eight inches away.

With their vision improved, by the end of May, all the boys could read at least at the third grade level. They also had learned how to write, and use sign language.

As spring turned to summer, Jim called a special board meeting.

He explained, "I am committed to making the group home look good and blend into the rest of the neighborhood. I also believe that in order for our residents to move out eventually and live independently in the community, they will need to know how to properly maintain their own homes. Therefore, I want to make it a point to teach the boys how to do yard work."

Without hesitation, the board approved Jim's idea. He began by involving the boys in doing some light landscaping. They planted new bushes, expanded the flowerbeds, and planted a bright variety of flowers. Next, he taught them how to mow the lawn and trim the hedges. Once they got the idea that yard work was "men's work" they were eager to pitch in. They took great pride in manicuring the lawn and sprucing up the exterior of the house. Whenever they finished a project, the boys gave Nellie a personal tour of the grounds, testifying to all they had done.

In order to stimulate their social life, Jim and Nellie encouraged the boys to participate in the worship and activities of the Canton Church for the Deaf. They always looked forward to these outings because they met other deaf children and youth there. They also met children whose parents were deaf. Sometimes they were hearing, but they also knew how to communicate by sign language. It pleased Nellie that the boys enjoyed talking and joking around with people their own age, and with people who could understand them.

Of course, not everything they tried to do proved to be successful. Toward the end of July, Jim called his staff together to plan a special outing. Emily suggested that they might take the boys to the fair in Canal Fulton. Nellie also thought that this was a terrific idea.

When the day came and they arrived at the fairgrounds, the first thing the boys noticed was the crowd of children and youth. They followed the parade of teenagers to the amusement section of the fair. They all wanted to try as many rides as possible.

Mickie saw a big line of kids going into the "House of Horrors."

Nellie was standing next to Emily when Mickie asked her, "What is that?"

Without reading the sign over the door, Emily spelled back, "That is a Fun House."

That was all that Mickie needed to hear. In no time he had joined the line of youth and was out of sight. Then a doubt crossed Emily's mind. She knew that Mickie did not like anything scary. She knew that he loved to watch TV even though he could not hear the programs. With great interest, he would sit very close to the screen. But whenever anything scary happened, he would get up and leave the room. She knew that he had no idea what went on inside the House of Horrors.

She was just about to tell Nellie of her concern when she noticed that the whole fun house trailer was shaking. Over the loud speaker, Emily heard Mickie's wild howl. Moments later the manager came sprinting out of the trailer, waving his arms and yelling, "There's a real demon in there! A real demon!"

A split second later, the two hundred and ten pound Mickie came flying out of the trailer stuttering and spitting, with his hair standing straight up from his head. Emily could not help laughing as she saw him chasing the wide-eyed, terrified manager down the road. She left Nellie standing there and went after him. After Emily caught up with Mickie, it took a long time for her to calm him down.

When she returned to the perplexed Nellie, Emily told her what had happened. Nellie wisely said, "Let this remind you of how important words are to these kids. Whatever you write into their hand, they take literally."

As August rolled around, Jim called the staff together to discuss how to teach the boys some money management skills.

He began by spelling out, "One of the most important skills the boys need to learn is how to handle money and budget their resources. Our job is to teach them how to comparison shop and make responsible decisions."

He went on to announce that he had raised some special funds for the purpose of giving the boys an allowance so that they could buy their own clothes. Three times a year, each boy was to receive thirty-five dollars for this purpose.

Emily began, "Although Nellie and I like to go shopping at the Belden Village Mall, for the purpose of teaching how to do comparison shopping, and stretching their dollars, I think that we should visit places like K-Mart and Gold Circle."

"Wait! Wait!" Nellie interrupted, "You are jumping the gun. Before we talk about where to take the boys shopping I think they need to know how to handle money. They need their own wallets. I think that they will take good care of their wallets, and the money they have in them, if they make their own."

Upon Nellie's suggestion, Jim ordered for each boy a leather kit so he could make his own wallet. Each one had a different color. Jim also ordered a kit for Nellie so that she could demonstrate how to make them. Nellie showed the boys how to lace the parts together. They sat, mesmerized, as they watched her assemble the parts, feeling with her fingers for the pre-punched holes. They watched as Nellie threaded the lacing needle, using her tongue to tell when she had poked the lace through the eye of the needle. Soon the wallet was finished. The spiral of lacing around its edge was perfect.

Impressed, the boys went to work. Since they could see, they had a much easier time assembling the parts and threading their needles. But they had great difficulty poking the lacing needle through four layers of leather. Ken and Mickie both skipped holes. They became quite frustrated and upset when Emily insisted that they undo their work and try again.

When all the boys had finished, they had not only a divided billfold, but also a place to put their own photo, and a snap-pocket where they could put their coins. One by one, they went upstairs to further explore their prized possession.

Suddenly, all four boys came stomping down the stairs. Having discussed the matter upstairs, they surrounded Nellie and Emily, and begged, "Take us to K-mart. Please take us to K-Mart now."

"What for?" Emily asked.

"So we can go in the photo booth and get our pictures taken. We need pictures for our new wallets!" they answered in a chorus.

Nellie's intuition proved correct. Nothing that Jim, Emily and Nellie did with the boys made them feel more grown up and responsible than having their own wallets. They took great pride in having made them, and even though they kept no cash in them the boys always put the wallets in their pockets whenever they left the house.

In anticipation that the boys might be admitted to school in September, the day came when Jim gave them their allowances so they could buy their school clothes. Nellie and Emily showed Ken and Mickie, who both had trouble reading the different bills, how to fold them in different ways so that they could tell the ones from the fives and the tens. Then, Emily took the boys upstairs and helped them to make an inventory of their clothes. After trying on all their pants and shirts, each one made a list of what he needed. Then, Emily and Nellie took them to K-Mart.

As they climbed out of the car, Emily explained to the boys, "The purpose of this shopping trip is for you to practice how to spend your allowances wisely."

As they spread excitedly throughout the store, their eyes were bigger than their wallets. It was hard for them to resist impulse buying. Finally, after two hours and what seemed like endless consultations with Nellie and Emily, the boys returned to the house with their prized new possessions. They could not wait to show Jim what they had bought.

Ron, the youngest, proudly opened his bag and unveiled a pair of pants, a new shirt and a pair of high top, black and white, Converse All-Star's gym shoes. As he proudly showed Emily what he had in his shopping bag, she was troubled. She knew that he already had two pair of the same popular and expensive brand of shoes. She knew that they still fit him and were in fairly good condition. She also noticed that he had forgotten to buy a fall jacket that he would soon need for school.

Emily swallowed hard. Ron was so proud of his new shoes. She did not want to hurt his feelings. But she knew that it was her job to get him to reconsider his choices. She would have to persuade him to return the shoes and use the money to get the jacket he so badly needed.

She began by admiring his new shoes. Then, without a word of criticism about his purchases, she took him upstairs to help him put his new clothes away in his closet.

Nonchalantly, she spelled, "How many pair of shoes do you have? What brand are they? Do you really need three pair? Do you have a jacket to wear to school?"

Ron looked at Emily. His sad eyes told her that he knew what she was doing.

"Go away!" he said.

Ron pouted for the rest of the afternoon and all through supper.

Finally, he approached Nellie and complained, finger spelling into her hand, "Emily doesn't like my new shoes."

Nellie, who had been informed about the problem, spelled back, "That is not what I heard!"

Ron protested, "But she wants me to take them back."

"Why?"

Almost in tears, Ron answered, "Because she thinks I need a new jacket instead!"

Nellie turned her face away from him, as if she really didn't care, "Well, do you?" Nellie asked back with her fingers.

Dejectedly he answered, "I guess so."

Radiant, Nellie turned her smiling face toward him and spelled, "Ron, you are growing up. It takes a real man to admit that he has made a bad choice! But proving that you can make responsible choices is the key to graduating from this group home and living independently in the community. Do you want to be free one day?"

Suddenly, Ron realized why Nellie's face was so radiant. Like him, she had been locked away in a mental institution. Freedom meant so much to her! Sad though he was to take back the shoes, with Nellie's words echoing in his mind, he felt childishness slipping away. In its place a new sense of seriousness and responsibility emerged. Nellie had lit in him the spark of the hope of freedom.

Emily immediately sensed the change when Ron approached her, looked her straight in the eyes, and said, "I'm ready to go back to K-Mart."

With only a few weeks left to enroll the boys for the new school year, Jim requested for the third time to be on the agenda to address the Massillon School Board. Emily had written no less that six letters to the editor of the *Massillon Independent*. Several newspapers also covered the story of their struggle to have the boys admitted. With the support of a lawyer who had volunteered to represent them, Jim felt sure that the board would finally change its mind.

At the appointed hour Jim and the lawyer, accompanied by Emily and Nellie, arrived for the meeting. But instead of allowing Jim to address them, the chairman called the board into executive session and asked all visitors to leave the room.

The four of them decided that they were not going to leave the building until they had received an answer. They sat down in the hallway to wait for the board to reopen its meeting.

Smiling, Nellie asked, "Is this a sit in?"

A reporter from the *Canton Repository*, who also had been excused from the meeting, overheard Nellie's comment. She spent the next hour interviewing them.

Finally, the chairman of the board emerged from behind the closed doors and said, "We have considered your request. But we have reached no decision. The matter has been tabled until next month."

Jim was livid. But Nellie silently finger spelled to him, "Turn the matter over to Jesus. The Bible says that, 'They who wait on the Lord shall be satisfied'."

Two days later, an extensive article appeared in the *Canton Repository*. The same story was repeated by the *Independent*, and several other publications.

Within a week, Jim's phone rang. The superintendent on the other end of the line apologized for taking so long to get back to him. He explained that since Mickie was already in his thirties he was too old to be served by the public school system. But the board had decided that they would admit the other three boys to the public school system. He explained that since the neighboring Canton school system had a special education teacher who knew sign language, they had reached an agreement with the Canton school district to form a special countywide class for deaf students that could accommodate them. All the board required was that the boys be tested to determine if they were ready to go to school.

Nellie was overjoyed by the news. Their campaign had been successful. Dutifully, the boys took their tests. The tests showed that Ken's reading and writing skills were still at an elementary school level. Since he was now twenty years old and would only be eligible to attend school until he was 21, the staff made the decision to place both Mickie and Ken in a sheltered workshop. However, to everyone's amazement, Ron tested high enough in his reading and math skills to skip the elementary grades altogether. He was admitted to Timken High School as a freshman in a special education class. Although Ted's evaluation showed that he was reading at only a seventh grade level, it was determined that he should be placed in the same special education class with Ron. When they arrived at Timken High School on the first day of classes, Ted and Ron were ushered past the parking lot and across the street to a small square building that was used as the school's textbook depository. There they were led to a small room that had been equipped with black boards and desks. As they entered they were introduced to four other deaf children from the Canton area. One of them was also blind and another was sitting in a wheel chair. Their teacher proved to be adept in sign language. For the first time in their lives, they now were given the opportunity to receive a formal education.

Both Emily and Nellie had regular work hours and assigned duties, but they also were expected to handle emergency situations at the group home. This meant that they were "on call" twenty-four hours a day. Since it was a four mile drive through heavy traffic to get to the group home, they decided that it would be a good idea to move closer to their workplace.

One day Emily noticed a "For Rent" sign on a small two-story duplex located across the street from the group home. After discussing the matter with Nellie, they took a tour of the first floor apartment. It had two bedrooms and was well suited to their needs. They rented the duplex the next day. A group of their friends volunteered to help with the move and before they knew it, the women were busy making their nest in a new home.

One day in October, the boys received an invitation from a deaf couple to visit their farm and to pick fruit. The boys had never been on a farm. When they arrived, they were given a tour. Then they were told that the apples were ripe. They could pick all they wanted.

The boys donned shoulder bags and had a great time climbing up into the trees and picking apples. When they proudly presented Nellie with their loot, she showed the boys how to make applesauce. Emily suggested that they also make Bisquick pancakes to serve with the applesauce. The boy's faces lit up as they set to work preparing a feast.

That day a new tradition at the New Life Group Home was born. Saturday morning pancakes, served with home made applesauce. Sometimes the boys were so pleased with the meal they had prepared that, after they had just finished eating, they requested to have the same menu for supper!

Likewise, a new tradition that Nellie called "foraging expeditions" was born. Whenever the season and the weather permitted, Emily loaded up Nellie and the boys and took them to the farm. They enjoyed being outside in the fresh air. In due time they became experts in collecting strawberries, corn, apples, pears and walnuts.

By the beginning of November it was clear that Ken's placement at the sheltered workshop was not appropriate. The work was not interesting to him. Jim realized that Ken needed more of a challenge. Since he loved to work with his hands, Jim found a carpenter who was willing to take him on as an apprentice. Ken soon thrived under this new arrangement.

On Thanksgiving Eve Emily and Nellie had the night off. They decided to go to church. The pastor at the Canton Church for the Deaf talked about "Counting Your Blessings".

As they drove to their new home, Nellie finger spelled into Emily's hand, "I thank God that I can work. I thank God that I can be self-supporting. But most of all, I thank God that Jesus took my situation and made it a blessing for my boys."

"Yes," Emily spelled back, "Maybe that is why you had to be deaf and blind. Maybe that is why you had to live for so many years in the mental hospital. Only someone like you could know what it is like to be in their shoes."

With tears in her eyes, Nellie spelled in the dark, "I guess that is what Paul meant when he said, "All things work together for good to those who love God and who are called according to his purposes."

Nellie and Emily continued to work at the New Life Group Home for more than two years. During that time, Ron breezed through his studies and graduated from Timken High School. The rest of the boys also made progress toward independent living. Meanwhile, the story of Nellie's work at the New Life Group Home won her public recognition. In due time, Nellie became a national celebrity!

=   =   =

Emily translates award ceremonies - Nellie is the Pilot Club's
"Handicapped Professional Woman of the Year." Courtesy of Canton Repository

Chapter Fourteen

HONORS

It was a cold, gray day in early March of 1979. Weary from a long day of work, Emily heard the phone ring as she and Nellie arrived home. Dashing through the door, she snatched up the phone.

A moment later, she hung up the receiver, turned to Nellie and spelled into her hands, "The president of the Canton Pilot Club just called. You have been voted handicapped professional of the year!"

Puzzled, Nellie spelled back, "What does that mean?"

"It means that they want to give you an award to honor you for the work you are doing with the boys. They have invited us to a special recognition dinner, in your honor, at the Holiday Inn in Canton."

Surprised, Nellie asked, "They want to give me an award? An award like the ones they write about in my Braille magazines? Why? What have I done to deserve it?"

"Just think of it as getting an 'A'. You used to get A's for your studies at Malone College. Now the Pilot Club wants to give you an A for your work with the boys."

On March 9, 1979, an article with a large photo, written by reporter Amy Shriver, appeared in the *Massillon Independent* notifying the community about Nellie's award.

When Emily saw the article, she described it to Nellie, spelling out: "At the top of the page there is a large photo of you, with your long, snow white hair falling down your shoulders in loose curls. It shows you in the kitchen at work. You are making a pie, crimping the edges of the top and bottom crusts with a fork."

She went on, "The article quotes Jim saying, 'Nellie is a good cook. Pies are her specialty. There will be ten people from Akron University here for dinner tonight and Nellie is making pies for them. She will make the mashed potatoes, too. She's a big help'."

Nellie smiled and blushed a little as Emily read Jim's compliment.

Emily spelled on, "The article goes on to talk about your background and the reasons why you have been chosen the <u>1979 Handicapped Professional Woman of the Year</u> by the Pilot Club."

Nellie frowned, "This article makes it sound like getting this award is a big deal."

"It is a big deal!" Emily spelled back, "It's a big deal to me, because I had to sit there and listen to all those officials who said that you would have been better off if Jim had left you in the State Hospital because you were non-trainable and too handicapped to work. Now, two years later you have a job and are winning the Handicapped Professional of the Year award."

Nellie raised her right eyebrow, but said nothing as she took in the significance of Emily's words.

The following Sunday, before the service of the deaf church, a parishioner approached Nellie.

She identified herself as a member of the Pilot Club, and spelled into her hand, "You are such an inspiration!"

Then she handed Nellie an envelope and walked away.

Turning to Emily, Nellie spelled, "What is this?"

Emily's eyes widened as she opened the envelope, unfolded a copy of the newspaper article about Nellie's award and found five twenty-dollar bills.

A note was attached: "This is for you to get some new clothes for the banquet."

When Emily explained to Nellie what was in the envelope, her face lit up.

Spontaneously she exclaimed, "Oh, man!"

At the appointed time the two women, decked out in their new outfits, stepped into the reception hall at the Holiday Inn. Emily caught her breath. She could not believe how many people had come for the event. Among the crowd she recognized civic leaders, city officials, county commissioners, and even several judges.

After dinner the President of the Pilot Club, Marge Brizuela, opened the meeting by welcoming guests and recognizing the many dignitaries who were present. Nellie shook her head in disbelief as Emily spelled their names into her hands.

Emily's fingers continued to speak as Ms. Brizuela went on to say, "This is the Second Annual Award Banquet given by the Canton Chapter of the Pilot Club International, to honor the Handicapped Professional Woman of the Year. The purpose of this awards program is to select outstanding executive, business, or professional women of the Greater Canton Area in order to dramatize the abilities of handicapped people and recognize their achievements. Our theme for this evening is, 'A Salute to Nellie Zimmerman, 1978-79 Handicapped Professional Woman of the Year'."

Nellie continued to listen intently to Emily's fingers as the president went on to talk about her life and achievements.

She nodded her head as Ms. Brizuela concluded her remarks saying, "Due to her loss of hearing the woman we salute tonight was forced to drop out of school after the second grade. Yet at the age of seventy-two, Nellie was admitted to Malone College. Currently, Nellie teaches arts, crafts, and cooking at New Life Home, a group home for deaf and deaf/blind young men.

We also salute Nellie for her work in the community as an advocate on behalf of the deaf. Together with her interpreter, companion and friend, Emily Street, she is telling the story of her life to school children and to people in church and civic organizations throughout Northeast Ohio in the hope that the time will come when all those who are deaf and blind are able to hire the companions they need in order to live in the community and be all that they can be. And now to continue our salute to Nellie Zimmerman, I would like to invite to the podium, Mr. Jim Schneck."

Nellie gasped, turned to Emily and said out loud, "He never said anything to me about being here tonight!"

Jim began his presentation by talking about Nellie and the work she was doing at the New Life Group Home. He also gave the audience a brief lesson in finger spelling so that they could greet Nellie after the ceremony. Then Emily was invited to say a few words.

Finally, the president took the podium again saying, "The Pilot Club of Canton, Ohio, is proud to recognize Nellie Zimmerman as our 1979 Handicapped Professional Woman of the Year, realizing the almost overwhelming difficulties that life has presented her, and recognizing her courage in overcoming those obstacles. On behalf of the Pilot Club International and Sears, Roebuck and Company we present you with this trophy as a token of our appreciation, and recognition."

She then invited Nellie and Emily to come forward. Unexpected tears filled her eyes as Nellie received the trophy. Nellie was further moved as Judy Blair, Vice President of the club, presented her with a framed Certificate of Award. She also handed Nellie an embossed plaque with a copy of the certificate printed in Braille.

Nellie turned to Emily asking, "What should I do?"

A tearful Emily spelled back, "Thank them!"

With the plaque in her hand, Nellie was guided to the microphone. She wonderingly fingered the Braille and caught her breath. With trembling lips, Nellie read the raised dots out loud, "God bless you, Nellie. The Pilot Club salutes your courage and inspiration. We love you."

There was not a dry eye in the room. Then applause filled the banquet hall.

Nellie gave a heartfelt and gracious acceptance speech, closing her remarks by saying, "Most of all, I want to thank God. God has truly blessed me. And, tonight you have all blessed me! If there is anything I can do to help others, please let me know."

Nellie received a standing ovation as she was led back to her seat. Then Canton's Mayor, Mark Ross, addressed the gathering.

"This evening has been the most exhilarating experience I've had since I took office."

He then presented the Pilot Club International with a Certificate of Recognition saying, "This Certificate is in honor of Pilot Club International's efforts to recognize the accomplishments of the handicapped."

Next, Massillon Municipal Judge, Sheila Farmer, took the podium, applauding the Pilot Club for recognizing such achievers as Miss Zimmerman.

She then read a quote from Helen Keller and approached Nellie, finger spelling into her hands, "God bless you!"

Canton Municipal Judge, Irene Smart, also complimented the Pilot club for recognizing Nellie. Then Canton Municipal Judge, Donald Ramsayer, approached the microphone.

"I am very impressed with the Pilot Club and Miss Zimmerman. Her accomplishments make me realize that I have been given so much in my life and have done so little."

Aided by Jim's finger spelling lesson, at the close of the evening many persons stopped at Nellie's table to spell messages into her palms.

As the jubilant Emily drove her exhausted friend home, she asked, "What did all those people say to you?"

Nellie answered, "Most of them spelled, 'Thank you!' or 'God bless you.' But several of the more fluent wrote, 'Thank you for being such an inspiration!' One person even wrote, 'You have overcome such severe handicaps and accomplished so much. You are a blessing to us all'."

Nellie paused, "I have never been talked to directly by so many people."

Tears came to her eyes, "Do they really feel that way about me?"

Weary from the emotion of the evening, Nellie went to bed early. But she could not find sleep. She felt humbled by the whole experience. Her thoughts swirled. Bitter scenes from her past kept coming to mind as she remembered the words of admiration from those who had spoken to her tonight.

She thought, "How could anyone really know what I have been through? Yet, by the grace of God, I have survived. I have told my story. And now, God has turned my suffering into a blessing for others. It takes away some of the sting of what I have been through."

Her thoughts drifted back to her childhood. She saw herself walking through the woods. She heard her father calling her name and lost herself in dreams of happy days, living in the light of his love.

The news that Nellie had been awarded the Pilot Club recognition went out over the National Wire Services. Newspapers across the United States picked up on the story, including the *Akron Beacon Journal*, the *Cincinnati Post*, the *Chicago Tribune*, and the *Los Angeles Times*.

After Nellie received the Pilot Club award, Emily and Jim took a new sense of pride in her. When the April edition of the Apple Creek Mental Institute newsletter, *Apple Sauce*, was delivered to the group home, Jim saw that the front-page story was about Nellie and her award. Immediately, he gathered the boys around him and held a five-way conversation, spelling out every word. Like a relay, he passed the message to his right, and each boy passed it along until it got back to Jim. The boys were impressed. They too became proud of their association with Nellie.

One week later Emily found an oversized envelope stuffed in the mailbox. Upon opening it she was surprised to see that it contained a letter from the Stark County Commissioners, and a framed Resolution. Eagerly she ushered Nellie to the table and spelled out the words:

Adopted March 29, 1979

Whereas:	*Nellie Zimmerman has been profoundly deaf since the age of seven and legally blind since her early twenties, and*
Whereas:	*Nellie Zimmerman, despite handicapped disabilities has overcome tremendous burdens throughout her life and gone on to teach other handicapped individuals as so exemplified by her work at New Life Home, and*
Whereas:	*Nellie Zimmerman has been honored by the Pilot Club of Canton, Inc., as Handicapped Professional Woman of the year for 1979 for her outstanding achievements as a handicapped individual.*
Now,	*therefore, be it resolved: That the Board of Stark County Commissioners does hereby congratulate Nellie Zimmerman on her receipt of the Handicapped Professional Woman of the Year Award, and does hereby recognize and commend her for accomplishments as a handicapped individual and for outstanding service to the handicapped community in Stark County.*

Board of County Commissioners

Looking puzzled, Nellie responded, "I understand the words you read to me, but what do they mean?"

Emily laughed, "Yes! It is a funny way of talking, but government officials talk that way, with all those 'whereases', when they want to let people know that they are doing something very important. It's their way of saying they think you are an amazing person and that they agree with the Pilot Club that you deserve the Handicapped Professional Woman of the Year Award. They are congratulating you on behalf of all the people in Stark County."

"Really?"

Nellie sounded dubious, but Emily noticed that her friend straightened her spine and squared her shoulders. For the rest of the evening, she seemed taller, more robust, and more energetic. Even the next morning, Emily noticed that Nellie carried herself with a new sense of pride.

Three weeks later, the mailbox was again stuffed with an oversized envelope. It contained a framed Statement of Recognition from the Ohio House of Representatives. Emily could not believe her eyes. This document was very ornate, and included a portrait of the State Capitol and the State Seal. Its words touched her heart.

Excitedly, Emily spelled the words into Nellie's palms, pressing down vigorously for emphasis.

April 18, 1979
On behalf of the members of the House of Representatives of the 113th Assembly of Ohio, we extend recognition to Nellie Zimmerman for her remarkable accomplishments as an advocate for the needs of Ohio's handicapped, on the occasion of your being honored as the 1979 Handicapped Professional Woman of the Year by the Pilot Club of Canton .... You have surmounted unusual barriers to become an important and productive member of your community.

With Emily Street's companionship and help you have become a public speaker of renown in Northeastern Ohio, demonstrating through your own gifts and attainments, that handicapped Ohioans are important for their skills and achievements. Your willingness at the age of seventy-three to undertake teaching responsibilities at the New Life Home and your success in teaching the deaf boys at this home attest to the strength of your character.

Thus, with a great deal of pride, we congratulate you on being chosen as the 1979 Handicapped Professional Woman of the year and recognize you as an outstanding Ohioan.

As Emily spelled these last words, Nellie felt a tingling rush of white electricity which began in her palms, ran up her arms, across her shoulders, and down her spine. Nellie shuddered, "Ooh! Who? What? Why?"

Healing took place in Nellie's soul that day. She had never been one to dwell or brood on her past. But deep within, she knew that her family had cast her away. Like a helpless rag doll whose ears had been torn off and whose button eyes had been ripped out, she had been tossed out of the house and left in the dark. It always had seemed as if painful memories were not far behind her. They came back to haunt her at unexpected times and often in her dreams. Now it seemed that an ever-widening circle of people felt that she was not worthless, but special, someone to look up to and admire. Now the House of Representatives was recognizing her as an outstanding Ohioan. It filled Nellie with a new sense of pride.

The next day a reporter from CBS News in New York called. She had picked up Nellie's story from the wire service and wanted to do a news feature about her. After confirming the facts of her life and accomplishments, the reporter made arrangements for a photographer to come and take pictures.

Nellie was thrilled! But the photographer who took the pictures could not tell them when the program would be broadcast. Emily called Jim, Larry, Michael, Michelle, and Sue and asked them to watch CBS news.

Three days later, Emily turned on the TV before work, watching with half an eye as she went about getting her breakfast. She was startled when Nellie's picture appeared on the screen. Next she saw her own face. She stared in disbelief.

Caught by surprise, by the time she found Nellie and brought her to the living room, the broadcast was over.

Emily complained to Nellie. "We were on the news, but I didn't really get to hear ..."

While she was still fussing, the phone rang. It was her friend, Sue, calling from Cleveland to say that she had recorded the show on cassette tape.

"Thank goodness!" Emily exclaimed, "Now I'll be able to tell Nellie what happened."

Emily was on cloud nine all day at work. When she got home, before she had even set her purse down, the phone rang.

"How dare you! How dare you appear on national TV?"

It was Emily's mother.

"You are an embarrassment to this family! I have even had calls from all our relatives in Texas! They all saw you. You have tarnished the family name!"

Emily slammed down the phone, "Tarnished the family name? Hah!"

Emily felt as if her mother had burst a bubble. But later that evening, her spirit revived when her friend Sue appeared at the door with her driver by her side, and audiotape in her hand. Soon an impromptu gathering took place as all their friends began to drop in. They all wanted to hear the tape.

Nellie realized that it had been a long time since they had had a party. She felt as if their college days were back. She thoroughly enjoyed being at the center of everyone's attention.

Overnight, Nellie became a national celebrity. She and Emily could not go anywhere without people recognizing them. People came up to shake their hands on the sidewalk, in the grocery store, and even when they were eating their Sunday morning breakfast at McDonald's. Nellie also received fan mail from people all across America, who felt inspired by her story.

A few days later when Emily and Nellie arrived at work, Jim was almost beside himself with excitement.

"Guess what? A representative from 'Good Morning America' called. They want to invite the three of us to be guests on their show! The program will be aired next week!"

Emily lost no time getting the word out. She contacted all the reporters she knew. Headlines appeared, announcing the date and time of the program.

Three days later, an irate stranger appeared on the doorstep of the New Life Group Home.

"Are you Jim Schneck? I am Nellie Zimmerman's niece."

Jim turned white. "Nellie is not here. She is off work today."

"Well, I did not come here to see her, I came to see you!"

Jim ushered her into his office.

She barked, "All this publicity about Nellie and these stories about her activities put our family in a bad light. We are prepared to sue you if Nellie appears on the Good Morning show! Now, I want to see Nellie. Where does she live?"

Intimidated, Jim wrote down Nellie's address on a slip of paper and handed it to her.

"Thank you," she sneered, turned and stalked out of the house.

As soon as he heard the door slam, Jim snatched up the phone and called Emily who was out at Apple Creek, telling her about the unexpected visitor who had taken Nellie's address.

As Emily left the Institute, she squealed her tires across the parking lot and sped home. She could hear Nellie howling as she climbed the stairs. Bursting into the room, Emily saw Nellie, with her right arm locked around her bedpost, screeching at the top of her lungs. A short, heavy set, gray haired woman was pulling her left arm with all her might.

Livid, Emily raised her voice above Nellie's ear splitting scream and bellowed, "Who the heck do you think you are! And what do you think you are doing!"

The woman let go of Nellie's arm. Instantly, Nellie stopped screeching.

"I am Nellie's niece. I have come to take Nellie home to live with me!"

"Oh? Then where have you been all these years?" Emily snapped.

She met the woman's eyes coolly.

"You say you want to take care of Nellie now? Go ahead! It's your right. Take her! But if you are family, then you have also been legally and financially responsible for Nellie ever since she was released from the State Hospital. I have kept the receipts for every penny I have spent on her. I have a whole file cabinet full of Nellie's bills. If you take her, you can as well pay me back!"

She paused to catch her breath.

Then she said, "I keep everything in the attic. I will bring you the files so you can see the bills."

Emily stalked off and climbed into the attic. When she returned with an armful of files, the woman was gone!

When Emily told Nellie that the woman who had attacked her was her niece, Nellie simply said, "I hope she comes back to see me again!"

Emily's jaw dropped.

She spelled into Nellie's hand, "What? Aren't you angry?"

"No, I feel like the father of the Prodigal Son. I thought they were all dead. What was lost has been found! I hope they will come and visit me now."

Emily stared in astonishment, but said nothing.

Nellie never saw her niece or any other relative again.

The next day Jim did hear from the niece's attorney who threatened to sue them if Nellie appeared on "Good Morning America." Jim and Emily took the threat seriously and agreed to turn down the invitation for Nellie to appear on the show.

However, Emily's resentment against Nellie's niece and family festered within her.

She rationalized, "Even if we can not be on 'Good Morning America,' that doesn't mean that we can't appear on another television program."

A week later, without telling Jim and without an appointment, Emily took Nellie for a drive to a Christian television station in Alliance, Ohio. To their surprise, they were greeted by a former professor from Malone College. He agreed on the spot to videotape an interview.

When Nellie told the interviewer about various head games she had invented to play with herself while she was in the State Hospital, he suggested that they should come back for a second interview and demonstrate her mental faculties.

Two days later they arrived at the studio for the second interview. A man with a calculator was on hand. First, Nellie described her Bible study and word games. Then she told about her math games.

Nellie began with an apology: "I might be a little rusty. I haven't had to play my head games for three years."

With no pencil or paper, Nellie began with simple addition. Then she added long columns of numbers and demonstrated her skill in doing some complex multiplication and division problems in her head. The man with the calculator was hard pressed to keep up with the speed of Nellie's calculations. But he confirmed that all her answers were one hundred percent correct.

When they left the studio, Nellie said, "That was the most fun I have had in a long time! Do you really think that they will put all that on the air?"

The following week Nellie's story was aired by channel 17 in Alliance. It was presented in three hour-long episodes. It constituted the most complete account of Nellie's life and accomplishments and testified to her exceptional spirit and intelligence.

Since the CBS news report, Nellie had become accustomed to being greeted by people wherever she went.

The next Sunday, after her interview was aired by channel 17, several people came up to their table while they were eating at McDonald's to say, "God bless you!"

Just as they were leaving, a man approached them and asked Emily to tell Nellie, "You are such an inspiration. After I saw your program, I gave my life to Jesus!"

His comment touched Nellie's heart. Now she felt that her life had added value. She had helped to save a man's soul.

She wondered, "How many more souls were saved as people watched my program?"

As a direct result of their appearance on the national news and on Christian television, once again, Emily's phone began to ring with invitations for Nellie to speak to various groups.

She also received an invitation to a second recognition banquet to be held in Cuyahoga Falls, on May 26.

Nellie was honored as one of four outstanding employees of the year at the Title IX Annual Regional Recognition Dinner, sponsored by the Ohio Commission on Aging. She was honored not only for getting a job in spite of her handicaps, but for starting a new career as a Federal employee and life skills instructor at the age of seventy three.

When UPI reporter Rosemary Armao, heard that Nellie had received this recognition from the Commission on Aging, she decided to do an investigative report on how Nellie was able to achieve so much at such an advanced age. She interviewed a well-known psychiatrist from Columbus, Ohio. He explained that Nellie's blindness probably contributed to her ability to achieve so much in spite of her age. He stated that Nellie didn't know that she was supposed to feel old, or act old because she could not see herself in a mirror. Likewise she could not see how other senior citizens looked and acted. By not being able to see these things, she did not have available to her the aging "cues" and other "points of reference" of normal people.

He went on to assert, "Normal people who do have access to aging points of reference behave more in accordance with societal norms. When normal people are old, and know it, they usually act accordingly."

When Emily read this article she laughed so hard that she almost fell off her chair. When she recovered her composure, she spelled out the story for Nellie.

"Hah!" Nellie snorted. "So, I guess that being blind is a blessing. Maybe it's a blessing that I can't hear. That way I don't know what old people sound like. You see, there are certain benefits to being abnormal."

At this both women laughed uncontrollably.

Nellie spluttered, "Look! I am differently able!"

They laughed until their sides ached.

A few days later, another reporter interviewed Nellie, with Emily interpreting.

She began by stating, "I understand that you just had a birthday. You are now seventy-four. You have accomplished more in less than four years than most people do in a lifetime! What do you think about the psychiatrist's theory?"

An impish grin spread across her face as Nellie said, "Being old just means it's harder to eat pizza."

Inspired by Nellie's TV interview, the women of Faith Lutheran Church in Massillon held a dinner to honor Nellie as "Christian Woman of the Year" on June 5th. Nellie was not only asked to share her life story and to talk about her work as a life skills instructor, but was asked to demonstrate her head games and talk about her faith.

At the close of the program, the president turned to Nellie and said, "Yours is truly a soul-winning faith."

She then presented Nellie with a framed certificate written in Braille. Nellie was touched when she discovered that the glass had been removed from the frame so that she could read it for herself.

But the award that touched Nellie the most was given to her at the Annual Awards Banquet of the Optimist Club International of Canton.

With Emily interpreting, the chairman said, "Nellie, even though you are not a member of our club, you have been selected as the 'Optimist of the Year.' I am going to present you with this plaque. It is inscribed with the Optimist Creed."

Promise Yourself---
To be so strong that nothing can disturb your peace of mind.
To talk health, happiness and prosperity to every person you meet.
To make all your friends feel that there is something in them.
To look at the sunny side of everything and make your optimism come true.
To think only of the best, to work only for the best, and expect only the best.
To be just as enthusiastic about the success of others as you are about your own.
To forget the mistakes of the past and press on to the greater achievements of the future.
To wear a cheerful countenance at all times and give every living creature that you meet a smile.
To give so much time to the improvement of yourself that you have no time to criticize others.
To be too large for worry, too noble for anger, too strong for fear, and too happy to permit the presence of trouble.

As Emily spelled out the last word, the engraved plaque was presented to Nellie.

The chairman added: "We believe that more than anyone else we know, you exemplify this spirit. Your eternal optimism in the face of the most difficult circumstances is an encouragement to us all."

As Nellie's fingers caressed the plaque, she dissolved into tears.

As the Fourth of July weekend approached, Jim gave Nellie and Emily a well-deserved day off. First, Emily slept in and awoke to a delicious breakfast of scrambled eggs, bacon and pancakes.

Then Emily took Nellie to the Canton Parade. As the beautiful floats passed by, she barely had time to describe them to Nellie because of constant interruptions by people who were coming up to greet them.

Some organizations tossed out candy as they passed by. At the prompting of their parents, several children gave Nellie some of the candy they had collected. As politicians passed by, they too, greeted Nellie by name.

Later that evening Emily took Nellie to see the fireworks in Massillon. It was almost dark when they arrived. They had to walk some distance to find a good spot. All along the way people recognized them and came up to greet them. Nellie greatly enjoyed the event as she felt the thunderous vibrations in her body while Emily described the visual effects of the fireworks.

Exhilarated when it was over, Nellie turned to Emily and said, "Let's go celebrate at the Pickle Barrel. We haven't been there for so long!"

Although they had not been there for more than half a year, it was like a homecoming. Suddenly they were surrounded by students, acquaintances, and well wishers. Nellie felt like a true celebrity as one young man after another asked her, with Emily's help, for a dance.

On the way home Nellie was silent for a long time.

Then she spelled onto Emily's hand, "I have everything I could ask for. I have you. I have Jim. I got a college education. I have a job. I've got my own money. And, I am famous! Even without ears and eyes, who could ever ask for more?"

=   =   =

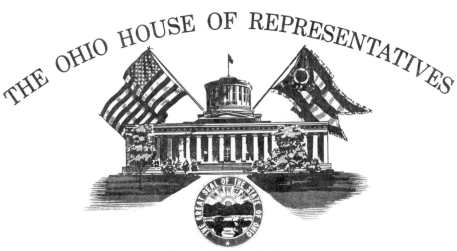

THE OHIO HOUSE OF REPRESENTATIVES

UNDER THE SPONSORSHIP OF

REPRESENTATIVE DAVID JOHNSON
HOUSE DISTRICT #70

On behalf of the members of the House of Representatives of the 113th
General Assembly of Ohio, we extend recognition to

NELLIE ZIMMERMAN

for her remarkable accomplishments as an advocate for the needs of
Ohio's handicapped, on the occasion of your being honored as the
1979 Handicapped Professional Woman of the Year by the Pilot Club
of Canton.

Profoundly deaf since the age of seven, and legally blind since
young adulthood, you have surmounted unusual barriers to become
an important and productive member of your community.

With Emily Street's companionship and help you have become a
public speaker of renown in Northeastern Ohio, demonstrating
through your own gifts and attainments, that handicapped
Ohioans are important for their skills and achievements.
Your willingness at the age of seventy-three to undertake
teaching responsibilities at the New Life Home, and your
success in teaching the deaf and mentally retarded boys
at this home attest to the strength of your character,
your knowledge and intelligence and skills.

Thus, with a great deal of pride, we congratulate
you on being chosen as the 1979 Handicapped Professional Woman of the Year and recognize you
as an outstanding Ohioan.

David Johnson

VERN RIFFE
SPEAKER OF THE OHIO
HOUSE OF REPRESENTATIVES

Chapter Fifteen

LOVE AND DISASTER

Meanwhile, Jim had caught spring fever. A few days after Easter, Emily and Nellie accompanied him to one of his fund-raising dinners. Emily noticed that Jim seemed distracted. As they sat at the table, there was very little conversation between them.

After dinner the program chairman introduced Jim to the audience. He quickly jumped into his usual talk about the New Life Group Home and their work with the boys. But when it came time to introduce Nellie and Emily, he only introduced Nellie.

With a long questioning look at Jim, Emily approached the microphone, introduced herself, and conducted her finger spelling interview with Nellie. When their part of the program was over, Emily paid closer attention to what Jim was doing. After he closed his presentation, a crowd gathered around him. She noticed one particular young woman, wearing a small white cap, who never left his side. Obviously, she was "with" him. Jim didn't hang around. Emily watched as he left with the young lady. Emily and Nellie stayed a while longer to answer questions about their work at the group home.

The next morning at work, Emily teased Jim shamelessly.

"What was going on last night? Why were you so distracted? You even forgot to introduce me to the audience when you introduced Nellie."

Jim raised his eyebrows in surprise, "I didn't forget to introduce you - did I?"

"By the way, who was the young woman you were with? The one you left with? You didn't introduce her to me, either."

Jim blushed, "Oh, that was Rosalee. Rosalee comes from near Lancaster, Pennsylvania and is now working in Orrville."

Jim paused uncomfortably, avoiding her eyes. "We are getting married in September."

Then he looked up. "You haven't met her yet?"

Emily grinned. She had never seen him so red. He was acting like a kid caught with his hand in the cookie jar. He was displaying an unusual inability to think or talk.

She teased him some more, "When were you planning to tell us about Rosalee?"

Jim brushed off Emily's question. "You and Nellie are invited to the wedding, of course. We will be married in Lancaster, Pennsylvania, her hometown."

In spite of the way that she had teased Jim, Emily was delighted that he had found a partner. Yet somehow his surprise announcement made her more aware of the lack of romance in her own life.

One day in early August, Emily and Nellie took the boys to the Canton Centre Mall to help them buy their clothes and school supplies. They agreed to meet in the center court, by the water fountain, in half an hour. As the boys scattered, Emily and Nellie sat down on a bench to wait for their return. Emily watched as the boys wandered, window-shopping through the main corridor of the mall.

Suddenly a tall, broad shouldered man with dark hair and twinkling eyes came and sat down next to Emily. Instantly feeling intimidated by this stranger and his closeness, she glared at him, and scooted over tight against Nellie. There wasn't much room on the bench, and this man was sitting mostly "on his imagination". Emily wanted the man to leave.

He brazenly turned toward her, locked her eyes with his, and grinned, "Hi, are all of these boys yours?"

Emily thought, "The audacity of this man!"

Looking daggers, she retorted, "I don't talk to strange men, especially to strange men in malls."

She tried to turn her back on him. Nellie felt Emily move closer.

Realizing that someone had joined them on the bench, she spoke up, "Emily, what's going on?"

Emily simultaneously spelled into Nellie's hands and spoke in a loud voice, "There is a strange man sitting next to us."

"Who is he? What does he want?"

"I don't know."

Undaunted, and with a twinkle in his eyes the man said, "Well, if I tell you my name and you tell me yours, we won't be strangers anymore, now will we?"

He grinned, "Oh, by the way, I'm Lloyd Hensel, and you are?"

Emily had to smile, in spite of herself, "I'm Emily Street. This lady with me is Miss Nellie Zimmerman. She is both deaf and blind."

Lloyd nodded solemnly.

"Who are the young fellows you are having so much trouble keeping up with? I see that you are talking to them in sign language. Are all of them deaf?"

With these words, the ice was broken. Emily found herself talking about where she and Nellie worked, and who the four young men were. She explained why they were at the Mall. To her surprise, she went into much more detail than was necessary.

Emily learned that Lloyd had been in the Army for six years, was now working for the railroad in Brewster, and lived with his parents in Navarre.

They talked on for about twenty minutes. Emily tried to pass along to Nellie what Lloyd was saying, but soon she was so absorbed in talking with him that she forgot to spell out their conversation. Nellie was left out of most of it.

When the boys returned, Emily and Lloyd quickly exchanged addresses and phone numbers. As they parted company, Lloyd promised to call. Emily felt as excited as a moon-struck teenager.

Before going to sleep that night she smiled to herself, "I must have been attracted to him, because for someone who doesn't talk to strange men in malls, I certainly gave away a lot of personal information."

She remembered how Lloyd had said, "If I tell you my name and you tell me yours, we won't be strangers any more."

She thought to herself, "No. We're not strangers any more."

Emily wondered if Lloyd was attracted to her.

Lloyd wasted no time getting back in touch with her. He offered to take her out for dinner. After he picked her up, on the way to the restaurant, he took her home to meet his parents. Emily was impressed that he wanted to present her to them.

When they arrived she found the whole family gathered in the living room. She was warmly received. She enjoyed the relaxed atmosphere and the good-natured bantering between Lloyd and his sisters. From their comments, she gathered that with Lloyd there was no waiting around. Obviously, he was a man of action. As she left the house, she had a premonition that they were going to get married. It was just a question of when, where, and how.

The next Friday Lloyd came over to visit Emily after work. He also showed up on Saturday and again came to call on Sunday. Emily was enthralled and totally preoccupied with him.

However, Nellie was not happy about Lloyd's intrusion into their lives. He wasn't like their other friends. His interest was exclusively in Emily. He paid almost no attention to her. In fact, he didn't even trouble himself to greet her when he came to visit. More than once, Nellie was startled when she came out of the kitchen into the living room and found him already there, seated on the couch talking with Emily.

To add to her resentment, Lloyd did not know how to finger spell. So even if he had wanted to, he couldn't talk to her. Emily explained that she was trying to teach him. But Nellie had seen other people learn how to finger spell in less than twenty minutes. It certainly seemed to her as if he wasn't trying very hard to learn. By the end of the weekend, she had made up her mind that she did not like him. And that he was not *her* friend.

Before Nellie knew what was happening, the two lovebirds were spending every free moment of their time together. Lloyd would come over immediately after work. He would stay for dinner and long into the evening. The next day he would be back! Nellie became jealous of the time Emily spent with him.

Nellie thought, "I have many friends, like Jim, who used to come to visit. They all talked with me by finger spelling. Our parties often lasted well into the night, and sometimes they even stayed over. But since Lloyd began hanging out in my apartment with Emily, my friends have stopped coming."

One hot, steamy morning in late August, Nellie decided that she was not going to go to work.

After Emily left, she found herself pacing around the apartment thinking, "I have lived long enough to know when something bad is about to happen. I think Lloyd is going to take Emily away. But then what will happen to me?"

A feeling of total helplessness overwhelmed her. She recalled that she had had those same feelings the day she was carried out of the nursing home, dragging her feet, kicking, and screaming, and was abandoned at the Massillon State Hospital. Once again, she felt powerless to stop what was happening to her.

Then Nellie thought of the one bright, happy thing on the horizon: Jim's wedding. She had looked forward to the trip, the wedding, and the big party. She thought, "Most of all, I look forward to being alone with Emily during the long drive to Lancaster."

To Nellie's chagrin, the following weekend, Emily asked Lloyd to drive them to Lancaster. But she was pleased that Emily had also invited her blind friend Sue, and her deaf and blind friend Clyde to ride along in the car.

When the big day finally arrived, and they loaded up the car, Emily rode in the front seat with Lloyd, and Nellie sat between Sue and Clyde in the back.

She thought to herself, "The wedding and the party afterwards will be fun. I'll wear my new powder-blue dress. From the way Emily described the color to me, I know it is lovely. I'll wear a pretty corsage, and be a member of the wedding party. I love going to parties."

Sitting between Susan and Clyde proved to be fun. They kept up a lively three way finger spelling conversation about Jim, Rosalee, and the wedding. When the conversation finally began to slow down, Sue and Clyde fell asleep. Soon Nellie was lulled into day dreaming by the comforting vibrations of the car. She knew they were going to be traveling near her home town of Braddock on their way to Eastern Pennsylvania. This brought back many pleasant childhood memories, especially memories of life with her father.

When Nellie awoke, she realized that the car had stopped.

Emily was spelling into her hand, "Lloyd is getting sleepy from driving. He wants to trade places with you so he can take a nap. Would you like to sit in the front seat with me, while I take over the driving?"

Nellie was delighted. Now at last she could be alone with Emily. Steering the car with her left hand, Emily used her right hand to talk. First, they discussed Jim's wedding, but soon they were talking about "Love".

Emily explained, "Falling in love is wonderful! It's like Christmas, Easter, and the Fourth of July, all wrapped into one!"

But to the seventy-four year old Nellie, who had been cut off from all boy-girl relationships after she left public school at the age of eight, these words made no sense.

Nellie raised her right eyebrow. "I know about unwrapping Christmas presents. And I know about going to church and celebrating Easter. And I know about the Fourth of July and going to see the fireworks. I know that they make a lot of noise, because I can feel the vibrations. But what does that have to do with sitting on the sofa and talking with a man?"

Emily was at a loss to explain. "It's like what happened in the Bible to Isaac and Rebekah, Jacob and Rachel, and Boaz and Ruth."

Still not fully understanding, Nellie said, "All the Bible says is that they 'knew' each other. Why is getting to know a man so different from getting to know a woman? What makes it so wonderful and exciting?"

Emily sighed, "It is hard to explain. But the minister will talk about it and I will tell you everything that he says."

With these words, the topic of conversation again returned to the wedding and all the festivities that would take place at the reception afterwards.

Time passed quickly and pleasantly as they spelled back and forth. However, when Lloyd woke up, Emily again put Nellie in the back seat so that she and Lloyd could sit together.

Soon they arrived at their destination. The wedding was a grand affair in the Mennonite tradition. Emily sat between Nellie and Clyde during the ceremony, spelling out all that took place. Emily also made sure to include Nellie, Susan, and Clyde in all of the festivities surrounding the reception. They all had a wonderful time.

But with more than a six hour drive ahead of him, Lloyd was anxious to get back on the road. Almost before Nellie knew what was happening, she found herself back in the car. Again, Nellie rode in the back seat with Susan and Clyde. Unknown to Nellie, Emily and Lloyd were busy talking about their own wedding.

It had been a long day. As Sue and Clyde snoozed, Nellie had time to think about her situation with Jim and Emily. Nellie wasn't sure how she felt about Jim's getting married to Rosalee. Jim had been her rescuer, and her hero. He was her dear friend, and her boss. It had not occurred to her that he would ever "fall in love" with someone. Obviously, now that he had tied the knot, things would change. He would no longer be living at the Group Home. He would be busy setting up his household with his bride.

Sadly, she realized, "Clearly, Jim will not be stopping by the apartment after work like he used to."

Nellie continued to ponder her situation in silence. What if Emily and Lloyd were making similar plans?

"No one seems to realize that whatever Jim and Emily do with their personal life, affects me, too."

Nellie wiped a tear from her eye. She could not help feeling sorry for herself.

On the three month anniversary of the day they met, Lloyd formally proposed to Emily. No date or definite wedding plans had yet been made. However, they announced their engagement in the newspaper on October 16, 1979.

The following day, Lloyd received an invitation from the chair of his CB club to join a club sponsored bus tour to Branson, Missouri. It sounded to him like the perfect get-away, so he invited Emily to go with him.

Emily was thrilled. Eagerly she requested the time off and made arrangements for friends to stay with Nellie while she was on vacation.

Then she explained to Nellie, "Lloyd and I are going South for a few days on a bus trip. Jim and Susan will take turns staying with you while I am gone."

Nellie sat very still, looking straight ahead, then she turned toward Emily with a smile: "Why can't I go with you down South?"

Without thinking, Emily answered, "Lloyd and I want to have some time alone together."

Nellie was horrified. She raised her voice.

"It's not fitting for a single lady to go off with a man! You are going to get in bad trouble if you do this! It's not decent. You know it's wrong!"

By this time, Nellie was screeching, something she had not done in a very long time.

Shaking all over with a nervous chill, she yelled, "I didn't like that Lloyd the first day we met him. He is going to get you in trouble."

Now Emily was angry. Nellie was waving her hands in the air. When Emily tried to grasp them to spell out what was on her mind, Nellie put her hands behind her back.

Emily shouted into her blind face and deaf ears, "Why can't you understand? Why can't you be happy for me? I have been here for you every day for the past three years. All I want is three days with Lloyd. How can you be so selfish?"

Nellie, of course, had no idea what Emily had said. With great effort, Emily finally calmed her down.

Emily decided not to tell Lloyd about Nellie's outburst. But since

Jim was going to be staying with Nellie while she was gone, she felt that she should warn him.

She confessed to Jim, "I don't know how to explain to Nellie how I feel about Lloyd. On the way to your wedding I tried to explain what it is like to be 'in love'. But Nellie just doesn't understand about love between a man and a woman."

Jim laughed, "Well, who would dare explain it to her?"

"That's not funny. I realize that she is jealous of Lloyd. How am I going to explain that we are engaged to be married?"

With tears in her eyes, she added, "I don't intend to leave Nellie for Lloyd. She will be welcome to live with us. But we're all going to have to get along."

Jim was relieved to hear Emily's last words. With professional insight, he understood that Nellie felt that she was in grave danger of losing her home. No wonder she was so resentful. But he also could see that Nellie was going to have to make room in her heart for Lloyd if she wished to continue to live with Emily as her companion. Not knowing what to suggest, he bit his lip.

"Just give her time. Maybe when you get back, she will be all right again."

The following week, Emily and Lloyd joined about sixty people before dawn and climbed aboard a bus. They journeyed through the prairies of Indiana and Illinois and the Ozarks in Missouri, and pulled into Branson just before dark. They each checked into their own rooms. Then Lloyd took Emily "out on the town".

After a wonderfully romantic evening, as Lloyd kissed Emily outside her hotel room door, he said, "Why don't we go ahead and get married tomorrow, right here in Silver Dollar City."

"Are you serious?"

"I'm serious!"

Emily's breathless kiss gave him the answer he was looking for.

The next morning, after breakfast, they made their way to the amusement park and found the lovely little wedding chapel.

The clergyman asked, "Do you have two witnesses?"

Lloyd held up one finger, as he headed out the door. "Wait here, I'll be right back. Don't go anywhere!"

Ten minutes later, he came back with two Native Americans, in full Indian dress. The younger one smiled and explained to Emily.

"We have to perform in just a few minutes. We are part of the cast for the "Wild West" show for the tourists. Both of us get killed by the guys in the white hats."

Extremely excited and nervous, Emily looked up and smiled at the tall Indian.

"We thank both of you. After we get married, we will be happy to come and watch you die."

Even the minister had to chuckle at Emily's blush of embarrassment.

"Oh! I didn't mean that the way it sounded."

The Indians laughed. Then, standing straight and tall, they made fine witnesses.

Emily and Lloyd were so nervous that they could hardly speak as they took their vows. Then they and their two witnesses ceremoniously signed the marriage license.

Lloyd shook the hand of the minister, secretly passing him a twenty dollar bill.

"Thanks man! You did all right!"

When he turned around the two Indians were gone.

"Well, Mrs. Hensel," he said, "We'd better get to that show, as we promised."

As they made their way to the Wild West show, Lloyd was strutting like a peacock. Emily felt as if she was floating on air. Dutifully they climbed aboard the miniature train that toured the Wild West show and waved and cheered for their Indian friends.

They spent the rest of the morning riding roller coasters and getting splashed on the water rides. Emily couldn't stop screaming and laughing. She was beside herself with joy.

Every time they finished a ride she turned to Lloyd, saying, "We did it! We did it! I can't believe we actually did it!"

Each time Lloyd grinned back, "Yeah, Honey, we actually did it. Hello, Mrs. Hensel!"

They spent the afternoon walking hand in hand around Silver Dollar City, listening to live music and visiting the craft shops.

When they returned to the hotel, Lloyd said, "Well, I guess we can check in as husband and wife!"

Emily threw her arms around him, and said, "What a wonderful place for a honeymoon!"

The next day Emily felt as if she was living in paradise.

Meanwhile for Nellie, the time without Emily passed slowly. She grew increasingly unhappy. No matter how hard she tried to concentrate on pleasant things, she could not stop worrying about Emily and her reputation. She could not sleep and she would not eat. She lapsed into a deep depression. Jim was unable to cheer her up.

On their way back home, Emily and Lloyd began to worry about what their parents would say. Lloyd admitted that his folks would not be pleased when they found that he had said his wedding vows without the benefit of a priest. Emily pointed out that her mother would be furious at the thought that she had left her family and Newman Baptist Church out of the picture.

She sighed, "And then there is Nellie!"

They decided to keep their wedding a secret from everyone, until they could figure out what to do. However, in order to stay together as husband and wife, Lloyd began coming to Emily's house at eleven each night and leaving at three in the morning. Of course, Nellie could not see or hear him come and go. But his parents could. After about two weeks of sneaking around, Lloyd's father confronted him. That night they decided that the secrecy idea was a mistake.

"After all," Lloyd said, "We are legally married. People will have to accept that. The only question is who to tell first. If you're not ready to tell your mother, let's get it over with and tell my parents this Sunday."

Jim stayed with Nellie while they went together to talk to Lloyd's family in Navarre. As was expected, his parents were upset. They refused to accept their marriage as legal and insisted that they had to get married again, the right way - in a church and by a priest. To smooth the ruffled feathers, they agreed to have a public church ceremony by Christmas.

As they drove away from Lloyd's house, Emily turned to him and said, "My mother will have even more of a fit if we tell her about our Silver Dollar City wedding. We have already announced our engagement in the paper. Why tell her, if we are going to have a church wedding anyway?"

"Yeah," Lloyd agreed, "We've got trouble enough as it is."

The next morning they approached the priest at St. Clement's Catholic Church in Navarre. But he refused to marry them if Emily was not ready to become Catholic. Next, they went to see the pastor at the

Newman Baptist Church. Likewise, he refused to marry them because Lloyd was not ready to become a Baptist.

When they were back in the car they both looked at each other and simultaneously said, "Let's go home."

That evening, when the two women were home from work, Emily explained to Nellie her dilemma without mentioning the Silver Dollar City wedding.

Relieved that Emily was not going to be taking any more trips with Lloyd as an unmarried woman, Nellie cheerfully suggested, "Why don't you get married at my church?"

A few days later, a pre-wedding announcement appeared in the *Massillon Independent*, stating that the wedding was set for December 6, 1979, at the Fellowship of Christian Deaf Church in Canton. The ceremony was to be jointly conducted by the Pastor, an ordained United Methodist minister, and a Catholic Priest.

Emily asked Nellie to join with her mother in walking her down the aisle to give her away.

Emily went on to explain: "After the wedding, there will be a reception. A big party. After the reception, Lloyd will come back here to live with us."

But the only thing that really registered in Nellie's mind was the word "party." She loved parties, and she enjoyed thinking about going to a big celebration.

Over the next few weeks, Nellie was oblivious to everything but her own preparations for the big event. Emily and Jim took her shopping for a new dress, and found a fancy pale blue gown. Nellie was very pleased to learn that she would sit at the head table during the reception.

The wedding ceremony was conducted in sign language. Jim translated the signs for Lloyd and all their hearing guests. Throughout the ceremony and the reception, many people greeted Nellie, telling her how beautiful she looked and making her feel as if she were an important part of the proceedings.

All at once, it seemed to Nellie that the wedding party had come to an end. Tired but happy, Emily, Lloyd and Nellie went home.

Nellie knew that Lloyd was going to come home with them after the wedding, but she didn't yet understand that he was not just visiting. She went to her room a few minutes after their return. It wasn't long after Nellie had retired that Lloyd and Emily also went off to bed.

Nellie got up first the next morning. She made breakfast for herself and Emily. She "felt" for Lloyd on the couch. He wasn't there. Then she searched for folded bed covers on the couch and didn't find any. She was relieved that she hadn't found him and decided that he had gone home after the party the night before.

Ten minutes later, Lloyd and Emily came out of their bedroom. Emily began to make some coffee and breakfast for Lloyd . When Nellie smelled the aroma and discovered that Lloyd was still there, she was mortified.

She screeched, "Where were you? I thought you had gone home."

In order to avoid a scene in front of Lloyd, and to calm Nellie down, Emily decided to lie, saying, "Oh. Lloyd must have been in the bathroom."

Lloyd was astonished. Nellie might have been satisfied with this answer, but he was not!

He asked, "What kind of lie are we going to tell Nellie tonight when we go to bed?"

Emily asked him to go along with her story until he left for work the next morning. The day passed without further incident. When evening came, Nellie went to bed first. Then Lloyd and Emily retired to their bedroom. Lloyd went to work at his regular time the next day. He was gone before Nellie got out of bed.

Oh!" she exclaimed. "I am so glad he is gone! I wish Emily had never met this man."

When they came home from work, they sat down on the couch and Emily began to spell into her hands. "You know that you and my mother gave me away at our wedding party? You gave me away to Lloyd and now he is my husband. When two people get married, they live together until death parts them. When Lloyd is home with us, he will eat with us. He will also do lots of other things with us, such as shopping, going to church, or driving us wherever we want to go. From now on my bedroom will be Lloyd's bedroom, too."

Nellie had been sitting perfectly still, nodding her head in understanding. But when the last sentence was spelled into her hands, suddenly, she was enraged. She jerked her hands away from Emily and immediately sat on them. Screeching at the top of her lungs, her body shook with anger.

"You can't mean you are going to sleep in the same bed with

him?"

Her delicate features hardened into a deep scowl. "So, that's where he's been the last two nights. So that's why I couldn't find any bed covers on the sofa."

She stood up so fast that she lost her balance, partially falling backward onto the couch. Recovering, she got to her feet and began pacing in a small oval pattern around the living room, muttering.

"You know that if you sleep with a man, you can have a baby. Do you want people to talk bad about you? Do you want people to think you are not a nice girl?"

Emily tried to lead her to the couch. But Nellie jerked her arm away from her, beside herself with rage.

"Don't touch me!" she screeched, "Get away from me!"

Emily was disconcerted, to say the least. For the first time since she had known Nellie, she was unable to communicate with her. Nellie simply kept turning away from her, refusing to let Emily talk into her hands.

Emily knew that, for the moment, she was defeated. She waited about four hours before trying to talk with her again. This time, Nellie was accepting of Emily's finger spelling, as long as she did not talk about Lloyd. Any mention of him, or anything about him, caused her to scowl and rudely jerk her hands away.

Lloyd fully expected Nellie to continue to live with them. He willingly included Nellie in everything they did. He went along on shopping trips, to church, and to other social functions. He even made a more serious effort to learn finger spelling. But Nellie always jerked her hands away each time he attempted to talk to her.

Lloyd was uncomfortable with any kind of conflict. Nellie's dislike of him defied his understanding. In his way of thinking, if something wasn't right, you fixed it; you made it right. Then you just forgot about it. It wasn't in his nature to put up with anyone being disagreeable. He became impatient with Nellie.

Emily could only watch as a battle line was drawn between Lloyd and Nellie. She was caught squarely in the middle between the two people she loved the most.

=   =   =

The tension rises...

Chapter Sixteen

A BATTLE ROYALE

Just as Nellie had put forth a one hundred per cent effort in pursuing her college studies, and in fulfilling her duties as a life skills instructor at the New Life Group Home, she now committed herself to a "declaration of war" against Lloyd. With intense deliberation, Nellie the manipulator refused to act as if Lloyd was a legitimate member of the household. When she cooked, she only prepared enough food for two people. For breakfast, she made just two servings of hot cereal, or prepared just four scrambled eggs, and made just two slices of toast. When she set the table for supper, she only arranged the place settings for two people and served up all the food so that there was nothing left for Lloyd.

Knowing that Nellie could not see or hear what she was doing, Emily went behind her back and prepared Lloyd's food. She set his place at the far end of the table and served him separately. With Nellie sitting at the table, Emily kept up a lively conversation with Lloyd.

Nellie also refused to clean up after Lloyd in any way. To keep the peace, Emily went to great lengths to clean and straighten up after Lloyd in the bathroom, living room, and kitchen.

However, there was no peace. Just as she had done with Nancy, Nellie kept up a constant tirade, reciting a litany of all Lloyd's "wrongs" to Emily. Enough time had passed for Lloyd to become accustomed to her speech. He overheard and understood almost everything Nellie said.

Emily tried to make light of the situation by laughing and joking about Nellie's jealousy of him, but her humor was lost on Lloyd. Within a week of the wedding, even Jim could no longer ignore the growing tension. Finally, he told Emily that he would like to talk to Nellie.

When he arrived on Saturday morning, Emily and Lloyd went Christmas shopping to give him time alone with Nellie. As soon as they left, he sat down beside her on the sofa, took her hands in his and began to spell. Nellie sensed that something "heavy" was going to be discussed. Jim felt her tenseness, but he didn't hesitate.

He pointedly asked her, "Nellie, what do you think happens when a man loves a woman? When they get married? When they have a baby?"

Nellie steeled herself and allowed Jim to talk freely until he spelled out the word "baby." Embarrassed, she lost her composure and turned toward him, her face stiff and stony.

Nevertheless, Jim plunged on, "Emily and Lloyd are now man and wife. There is nothing sinful, or disgraceful, about their sleeping together. God intended it to be that way. Are you upset because you are jealous of Lloyd, and you don't want to share Emily with anyone else?"

For the first time, Nellie screeched at Jim, howling, "You are talking dirty to me! You don't know what they are doing. You should be ashamed for talking to me like this!"

Tears were flowing down her cheeks: "If you are going to talk like that, you can leave!"

Jim was dumbfounded. He reached for her hands to talk to her again, but she jerked them away, and quickly sat on them. Shaking his head in disbelief, he decided to walk away and leave her alone.

For a long time, Nellie sat on the sofa, scowling. Finally, she got up and went to her room. Emily and Lloyd returned home and found her there. She didn't come out again until late in the evening, and then only to go to the bathroom to get ready for bed.

Emily and Lloyd found Jim at a loss about what to do. It was his opinion that Nellie's bizarre behavior was rooted in her fear of being pushed aside from the only security she had known since her father's death.

"I agree," Emily groaned, "But what is the remedy? I tried to talk to her. You've tried to talk to her. What can we do that we haven't already done?"

Jim sighed, "She withdrew to the bedroom because she was angry, but maybe if she thinks it over long enough, she will come out feeling better about everything. Let's see if time will solve the problem."

Jim and Emily both looked at Lloyd.

"You're the one who's going to have to 'give' the most." Jim said.

"I don't have anything against Nellie," Lloyd conceded. "She can stay here as long as she needs to, but she will have to be reasonable. We all know she can be impossible. I'll try to give her time to come around."

Nellie did not come around. Nellie consistently ignored Lloyd, still refused to prepare his food, or set a place for him at the table. However, the tension eased because their work schedules helped to keep them apart. Lloyd worked an early shift and had to leave the apartment at 6:30am. This gave both Emily and Nellie two hours of peace in the mornings, before they had to go to work. Lloyd then came home from work at 3:00pm. This allowed him a few hours of peaceful solitude before Emily and Nellie came home.

During the following week, Emily began to experience the discomfort of morning sickness. A trip to the doctor confirmed her suspicions. She was pregnant. Emily was exultant!

Dazed with excitement, she walked around in a fog for the rest of the day. She took turns, exclaiming aloud and silently praying, to herself.

"Thank you, Lord! Oh, glory! Oh glory to Jesus!"

Could she even wait for Lloyd to come home? Finally, he walked through the door. It took only one look at Emily's radiant face for him to know that he was going to be a father. He was positively delighted. Neither of them could contain their excitement. They told both sides of their families right away. Even Emily's mother was openly showing her approval and pleasure.

However, the future parents deliberately did not tell Nellie. They decided that the news could wait.

In making preparations for the Holidays, Nellie enjoyed making paper chains, and garlands of strung popcorn and cranberries for use both at the New Life Home and at their own apartment. By following simple stencils she cut out of construction paper many pretty and colorful bells, trees, and Santas.

The three kept themselves so occupied with Christmas preparations, putting up the tree, baking cookies, making pies, shopping, and wrapping gifts, that none of them had time to worry about the uneasy truce and bitter animosity that still existed between Nellie and Lloyd.

Christmas gifts for all three of them were coming daily, either by messenger, or by mail, and were being placed under the tree. Several of the young couple's friends brought Wedding/Christmas gifts. Without thinking of how Nellie now viewed their wedding, Emily made the mistake of telling her about the "combination" gifts that were under the tree.

Nellie was nosy, as usual, and wanted to know who had given each gift and to whom it had been given. One morning she sat on the floor and, child like, fingered each package and speculated about what each one contained. She laughed and talked about the time when Emily had wrapped Jim up as a Christmas present for her.

Emily couldn't help noting that since Jim and Rosalee had gotten married, Nellie didn't refer to him as *her* Jim any more. Neither was she as thrilled when Jim came to visit. She saw him every day at work and that seemed to satisfy her now. Emily silently wished that Nellie could be as accepting of her marriage as she was of Jim's. With tears brimming in her eyes, Emily breathed heavily as she talked to herself.

"I believe our situation here is hopeless. Nellie will never accept Lloyd, and I don't know what to do about it."

Emily was rudely disturbed from her sad thoughts by Nellie, making a statement about the gifts under the tree.

"What did you say?"

"We can't have those wedding party gifts under the Christmas tree. It's not right to mix them in with the holy celebration of Christ's birthday."

Emily was appalled at the thought. Somehow, in Nellie's mind, she had decided that the wedding gifts represented something sinful.

Emily went to work with her feelings hurt all over again, and seething with anger, but tried to dismiss the whole thing from her mind.

When they came home from work, Lloyd was already there, and hungry. Emily and Nellie went immediately into the kitchen to prepare dinner. Nothing more was said about the gifts under the tree, and the evening passed without incident.

Unfortunately, Nellie had not forgotten about the Wedding-Christmas gifts under the tree. Nellie knew every gift by heart. She knew which ones were hers and which were Emily's alone, and which were combination gifts to both Lloyd and Emily. She considered all of those tagged to both of them as the suspect Wedding-Christmas gifts. Sometime during the night she got out of bed and systematically lined up the offending gifts on the floor. Then she carefully carried them, one at a time, and put them in her room under her bed. Nellie brushed her hands together briskly, while a satisfied smile played over her lips.

"There, now," she muttered as she settled snugly into her bed, "That will keep those gifts out from under the Lord's Christmas tree."

Lloyd went to work at his usual time the next day. He didn't notice that some gifts were missing from under the tree. Emily busied herself with getting ready for work and picking up the kitchen. She, too, didn't notice anything amiss. However, Lloyd noticed when he came home from work.

As soon as he saw Emily, he asked, "Honey, where are all the gifts we got for our wedding and for Christmas? Did you go ahead and open them? I thought we were going to wait until Christmas."

Emily looked at the tree in astonishment.

"No, I didn't do anything with them. Aren't they under the tree?"

They both looked expectantly at Nellie, who was settling down on the couch with some Christmas craftwork. She was still making ornaments for the group home tree.

Walking softly, so Nellie wouldn't feel her footsteps, Emily went into Nellie's bedroom and right away saw the gifts tucked under the bed.

"Lloyd, they are in here under her bed. What do you want to do?"

"You take her into the kitchen for a few minutes and I'll put them back under the tree. No, I'll put them behind the tree and maybe she won't notice them there."

Emily did as Lloyd suggested. As quickly as he could, Lloyd moved the tree out from the wall about eighteen inches. He then quickly grabbed the gifts from under Nellie's bed and began to stack them behind the tree. It took him three trips to get them all.

Then he pushed the tree back as far as he could against the tall stack of gifts and called out, "Honey, I'm done. Is supper ready?"

After Lloyd had righted the situation, as far as he was concerned, it was settled. He didn't give the gifts another thought. They had supper together. Nellie worked quite a while on her paper decorations while Lloyd and Emily watched television, and then they all went to bed.

Sometime during the night, Nellie suddenly remembered the gifts under her bed. She swiftly got up and bent down to feel around for them, and discovered that they were gone.

Silent as a ghost, she glided over to Emily's bedroom and felt for the door.

"Good, they have it closed."

She went to the Christmas tree and sat down on the floor. Feeling around, she discovered that the tree had been moved out into the room.

She reasoned, "If the tree has been moved, they have stacked those "dirty" gifts against the wall behind it. That is where they are."

Quickly getting up from the floor, she felt behind the tree. With a slightly evil grin, she found all of them. Still as quiet as any ghost, she began to carry them, one at a time, back to her room and again placed them under her bed. When she had taken the last of them to her bedroom, she pushed some of the other gifts behind the tree to take up the empty space left by the ones she had removed. With all of this work done, she happily went back to bed and was soon sound asleep.

In the hustle and bustle of getting ready for work the next day, neither Emily nor Lloyd noticed the gifts had been moved again. All three went to work. When Lloyd got home, he sat down to relax and watch television. Then he looked at the tree.

"What the...?!"

His jaw literally dropped open.

"When did she have time to do that? I'll bet they are under her bed again!"

He got up out of his chair, walked into Nellie's room, and saw the gifts without even raising the bedspread. Chuckling to himself, he could only shake his head. He thought the whole thing was funny. Unfortunately, he had no clue about how serious and determined Nellie was to ensure that those wedding/Christmas gifts were not under the Christmas tree.

Quickly gathering up the gifts, he placed them back against the wall and replaced the others around the front of the tree where they had been before. He got all of this done long before Nellie and Emily were due to return home. Then, again, he sat down to relax and watch his favorite shows on television.

Nellie and Emily came home at their expected time. Lloyd had forgotten about the gifts and, therefore, did not tell Emily anything about how they had been moved again. Emily headed to the kitchen. Nellie went to her bedroom to put away her coat and purse. She didn't think about the gifts either, but went on into the kitchen to help Emily.

Lloyd turned off the TV. Then he remembered Nellie's latest prank and went to the kitchen. He stood in the doorway, explaining to Emily how he had again found the gifts under Nellie's bed, and that he had put them back behind the tree.

For about a minute Emily, too, thought that this was funny. Then doubt crossed her mind.

"Lloyd, maybe we should let her have her way on this. She will be real upset when she finds them gone from under her bed again."

Lloyd gave the situation some thought. He walked over to Emily.

"No," he exclaimed, adamantly, "We live here, too. It's Christmas and those are our gifts. They are going to stay under the Christmas tree."

About that time, they heard a muffled screech coming from Nellie's bedroom. Neither of them had noticed that she had left the kitchen while they were talking.

"Oh, oh," Emily began, but stopped when she didn't hear any more. She looked at Lloyd and saw that he had a silly grin on his face. She could see that he was feeling both guilty and mischievous, like a naughty kid.

No one said a word about "gifts" all during supper. While Emily put the food away and washed the dishes, Lloyd stayed with her in the kitchen so they could talk. When they finally came out to the living room, Lloyd looked at the tree. He couldn't believe his eyes. The Wedding-Christmas gifts were gone once more!

Nellie was innocently sitting on the couch, her eyes closed, and hands folded in her lap. If Lloyd had looked closely, he would have seen the devilish smile playing on her lips. Now it had become a game. A dangerous game, nevertheless!

Lloyd, determinedly, went into her bedroom, laid the gifts on top of the bed and stacked them, so he could carry three or four at a time. He gathered up the first stack of gifts. Then walking as softly as he could, he put them back under the tree. Then he returned for another load. While he was gathering the parcels in his arms, Nellie got up from the couch. and went to the doorway of her bedroom, waiting. When Lloyd turned around with the gifts in his arms, he saw her standing in the way, with her head cocked sideways. He was trapped. Feeling a little foolish, he called to Emily for help.

"Honey, come and get Nellie. I can't get past her. She's in my way."

Emily dutifully came to lead Nellie away, but Nellie stiffened her body and refused to move. Concerned, Emily ducked under her arm and stood in front of her like a shield. This maneuver allowed Lloyd to squeeze past her and escape from the bedroom, but he had been forced to put down the gifts. Then Nellie turned and retreated back to the couch. Emily gave a sigh of relief, and returned to the kitchen. Lloyd, however, saw his chance to finish the task and went back into Nellie's bedroom.

"If I hurry," he said to himself, "I'll have them all moved back to the tree before Nellie knows about it."

He quickly picked up an armload of the remaining gifts, and turned around. When he reached the doorway, suddenly Nellie was standing right in front of him. He stopped, taking a step back, as she reached toward him and felt the gifts in his arms.

Nellie startled him, screeching like a wild banshee. Reaching out with her left hand, she grabbed Lloyd's shirt. With a good hold on his sleeve, she hung on tight to the material so that he couldn't get away. Balling her right hand into a fist, she swung.

She hit him!

Her blow landed where she intended, connecting squarely with his jaw. Caught entirely by surprise he staggered backwards and fell down hard on the floor. The gifts skittered across the floor. The momentum of his fall broke Nellie's grip on his shirt. He had the presence of mind to roll sideways, beyond her reach. Frantically, Nellie began to grope around in the air, and then on the floor, to find him. She wasn't done with him!

By this time, Lloyd had moved about ten feet away from her. With one hand held tightly to his jaw, he stared, wide eyed, at Nellie's flailing arms, and bawled for Emily.

The Wedding-Christmas gifts did not return to the tree. Emily told Nellie she would keep them in their bedroom until Christmas. This solution was all right with her. From that day forward, Lloyd stayed strictly away from Nellie. However, the incident had been the last straw. He insisted that Emily and Jim had to find another home for Nellie.

Emily was heartsick. But at least Lloyd didn't insist that Nellie had to leave immediately. He knew that they would need time to locate a proper place for her. He didn't want to appear as the villain, when the truth was that he felt *he* was the victim.

Christmas came and went. Then the welcoming in of the New Year was celebrated. The Holiday Season, supposed to be a happy time, was not enjoyable.

Lloyd continued to stay out of Nellie's way, but he was not happy that she was still in the apartment. Emily was miserable. However, Nellie was oblivious to anything being amiss. For her, it was as if the battle royal had never happened.

Emily knew she would soon have to tell Nellie that she was going to have a baby. There was no way to predict how she would react to the news. This uncertainty kept Emily in a state of "nerves" and she put off telling Nellie from one day to the next, postponing the inevitable.

Finally, Lloyd insisted, "Honey, you know we have to tell her soon. If she touches your tummy, she is going to know. That will just make matters worse. How are you going to tell her?"

Emily turned her worried eyes full force on Lloyd.

"This should be such a happy time for us. Instead, we are both feeling guilty and scared of Nellie, and worrying about how she will react when she knows about the baby. Maybe we are making too much out of this. She may be very happy about my having a baby. I'll tell her today. See you tonight!"

It was a Saturday, but a workday for Lloyd. Emily would have the whole day at home alone with Nellie. She rehearsed over and over in her mind how she would break the news to her. There was nothing to do now but to just get on with it.

After she and Nellie had an early lunch, she walked with her to the couch and they sat down close together. She reached for Nellie's hands and instantly felt her body stiffen as she turned to partially face Emily. Nellie always could tell the difference between when Emily was preparing to make casual conversation, or when something "heavy" was going to be discussed. Everything Emily had rehearsed beforehand left her mind when she felt Nellie's body stiffen. Emily took a deep breath and began.

"Lloyd and I have a surprise for you."

The instant she had used Lloyd's name, she knew that had been a blunder. Nellie's body stiffened even more and her face turned "stony."

"What is it?"

Nellie did not raise her voice.

Emily knew that she had made a bad beginning but, nevertheless, she plunged on. She placed Nellie's left hand on her tummy, and started spelling into her right hand.

"I am going to have a ba..."

That was as far as she got. Nellie jerked her hands back. She slowly, deliberately, got to her feet. Her face contorted into a mask of rage. Emily was speechless. She looked at Nellie in absolute amazement, and expressed her thoughts aloud.

"How in heaven's name can anyone look so sweet and innocent one minute, and then look so evil in the next?"

Emily knew there was no point in trying to talk to her now. Nellie began to pace, using a defined oval pattern in the living room, with the coffee table in the center. She varied between a screech, a howl, and her fast mutter, talking mostly to herself, but addressing some of her remarks directly to Emily.

"I warned you this would happen. I told you that if you were shameless and slept with a man, you could get a baby. Now, you've done it. You had to do it, didn't you? It's that man's fault. You did the dirty stuff, now you have to pay for it. You will have to have this baby."

Over and over, as she paced, she continued her outraged tirade, with little variation. Emily left her strictly alone. Nellie continued to pace, rage, and ramble for almost an hour. Finally, she wore herself out, went to her room, got into bed, and turned her back to the door. She was so angry her tense body remained rigid, but her mind was in turmoil.

Nellie thought, "This is a terrible trouble that we are in. What are we going to do?"

Emily's mind was also in turmoil, and she, too, knew their lives would never again be the same.

When Lloyd came home, he took one look at Emily, and said, "Oh, no, you told her, didn't you?"

Emily did her best to laugh at the situation.

"She said it's all your fault."

Lloyd couldn't help laughing, too. Emily just stared at him and then tears really started.

"I don't know what to do. She cannot, or will not, accept the fact that we have made these changes in our life, and that she must accept some changes in her life, too."

Lloyd was becoming upset himself. Angry now, because Emily was so upset, he suggested, "Honey, just leave her be for now. Whatever we have to do, we will deal with it. Why don't you call Jim and ask him to come tonight? We are going to need his help on this."

Emily dried her tears. It made her furious to have to call Jim over something she knew he would think was trivial. She was right. When she called him on the phone, he did think they had blown the situation out of proportion. He said he was sure that once there was a baby around for Nellie to fuss over, she would again become completely agreeable and a pleasure to be around. Emily felt sure that he couldn't be more wrong.

Jim did come over that night and tried to talk to Nellie, but she wouldn't allow him to come into her room. Lloyd wouldn't discuss the matter anymore. Emily and Jim again decided to give Nellie more time to get used to the idea of a baby in the house. Maybe she would finally come around.

After staying in her room for more than eighteen hours, and when she knew that Lloyd had gone to work, she came out looking for Emily. Now that she had time to think about it she was sure she had the perfect solution for this new "trouble" that Emily had brought on herself.

She found Emily busy in the kitchen. Nellie sat down at the table and beamed a lovely smile toward her.

She spoke in an authoritative manner, talking to Emily like she was a wayward child, "This is what we will have to do. You will have the baby; there isn't anything we can do about that."

At the first sight of Nellie, Emily had unconsciously inhaled deeply and was holding her breath. She exhaled loudly, and began to breathe normally again.

"Maybe," she said to herself, "Nellie is going to come around, after all!"

Nellie smiled and continued, confident that she had solved all of their problems.

"Together, we can raise a baby, but that man, he will have to leave. We can't have him here with us any more. He got you in this trouble and he will keep on getting you in trouble. He can't stay here another night. You will tell him tonight that he has to go!"

Frantic, Emily grabbed Nellie's hands and began to spell, "No, Lloyd lives here. He is the baby's father. He is my husband. We will all live together. O.K.?"

Nellie allowed Emily to continue until she finished what she had to say. Then she shrank away from Emily, her hands were claw-like, and her face was almost unrecognizable as it became frozen into a deep scowl. She screeched her displeasure.

"Then I will have to leave. Call Jim and tell him I will have to leave here. Tell him you are forcing me to leave. You are siding with that man against me. This is my home, too! It is your fault that I am being forced to leave my own home. After all we have been through together, how can you do this to me?"

She continued to screech and howl at the top of her lungs with rage and grief. Nellie was crying, the tears were rolling down her cheeks, and her nose was running. She was a mess. Emily, too, was feeling miserable because Nellie was so upset. She had never seen her like this. There was nothing Emily could do to console her. She wouldn't allow Emily to touch her.

Finally, after several heartbreaking, great, gulping sobs, Nellie hushed all sounds of her distress and forcibly composed her face. Then, while Emily watched helplessly, Nellie assumed an air of dignity and a sad finality about her. It was almost as if someone had died.

Without speaking another word, she walked in a straight line, with shoulders squared, and her head held high, into her bedroom and softly closed the door.

=   =   =

Nellie savors a happy moment at the Columbus Colony for the Deaf
Courtesy of Akron Beacon Journal

Chapter Seventeen

FREEDOM, INDEPENDENCE AND LOVE

It was a frigid day in mid January. Snow began to fall as Lloyd walked to his car after work. By the time he reached Massillon, the snow shower had turned into a full blown blizzard. Lloyd could barely see the road ten feet in front of him.

Turning into his usual parking spot in front of their house, he almost slammed into a twelve foot U-Haul trailer. He skidded away and pulled in two doors down the street. When he reached the front steps, he almost collided with the middle aged bachelor who lived in the upper floor of their duplex.

"What's that U-Haul all about?" Lloyd asked.

"I'm moving out. You people are too noisy! I'm all packed up. Here are my keys: Would you give them to the landlord?"

When Emily arrived, Lloyd was grinning like a Cheshire cat.

"Guess what! The apartment upstairs is vacant. I've got the keys. Why don't we take a look. If you like it, you and I could move upstairs and let Nellie live by herself down here!"

Since the night she had decided that she would have to move out, Nellie had been throwing tantrums, screeching about anything she found to be wrong. Emily soon learned that when she went into one of her tirades, the best thing to do was to just walk away and leave her alone. Usually, Nellie would wear herself out, retreat to her bedroom, close the door, and isolate herself from them for several hours while she sulked in her room. Then, in order to disturb them when they were sleeping, Nellie came out of her room in the wee hours of the morning, making as much noise as possible as she compulsively did the housework.

Exhausted by the emotional trauma and lack of sleep, Emily agreed to look at the upstairs apartment. Upon inspection, it appeared to be in very poor condition. Plaster was falling down from the ceiling where the roof leaked, and it was in sore need of a coat of fresh paint. But it had two bedrooms, a spacious living room and a small kitchen.

"It's not the Ritz," Lloyd said as he gave Emily a hug, "But I think it would solve our problem. We can have our own space and Nellie can have her space, too. If she has a problem, all she has to do is call for you. We will be able to hear her from here. And you can check on her as often as you like."

Emily looked for a way out of making this radical decision.

"How can we afford it?

"I will pay the rent for both apartments. I will fix them up and paint them both."

In spite of herself, Emily smiled. The intensity of his passion and his willingness to make such a costly sacrifice touched her heart. It was an offer too good to refuse.

Emily decided not to tell Nellie about their plan until everything was prepared. Lloyd made good on his word. He spent the next two weekends sprucing up their new apartment. Then he brought his own furniture, leaving everything in its place for Nellie in the lower apartment. Finally, the two love birds moved Emily's bedroom furniture and personal belongings upstairs. She especially enjoyed finding places for all their wedding gifts.

Unable to see or hear, Nellie was oblivious to what was going on. Finally, when everything was prepared, Emily led her to the sofa and disclosed their new living arrangement.

"Good!" Nellie said without her usual smile.

Then dusting off her hands, she added, "If that's what it takes to get rid of that man, it's fine by me."

With tears in her eyes, Emily spelled out, "Nellie, everything in the kitchen is the same except, for your safety, I turned off the gas to the stove. I can turn it back on if someone else is going to be here when you are cooking."

Scowling, Nellie jerked her hands away, sat on them and remained motionless. With no way to communicate any further, Emily caressed her hair and tearfully walked out, closing the door behind her.

After Emily left, Nellie walked around her apartment, checking to see what furniture was gone. She was surprised to find everything in its place. Only when she found Emily's bedroom empty did she realize the true meaning of what had taken place. A gnawing sense of loneliness began to grow in the pit of her stomach.

However, when morning came, Nellie's spirit revived. She felt as if she had won a victory. She was dressed and waiting when Emily came downstairs after breakfast to go to work with her. She enjoyed telling the boys that Emily had moved upstairs and that she was now living independently. Immediately, Mickie and Ken wanted to see her apartment. When Ted and Ron arrived home from school they all were eager to walk her across the street to check out "Nellie's pad".

Ron spelled into her hands, "You are free! You are living all by yourself. Do you think I will ever be able to live on my own?"

Nellie grinned, "Just don't wait until you are seventy four years old!"

The boys thought that it was "awesome" for her to have her own space. This affirmation helped Nellie to see her whole situation in a better light. Throughout the month of February, Nellie worked every day at the group home. She easily managed to get herself ready for work and take care of her apartment. She had an active social life. Emily came to look in on her two or three times a day. Almost every evening one or two of the boys came over to hang out. Jim and some of Nellie's church and college friends also came to call.

But a shadow remained in Emily's mind. Moving into separate quarters resolved the immediate crisis. But it was clear that Lloyd could not afford to pay the rent for both apartments indefinitely. Nellie still refused to be reconciled to Lloyd. With Jim's support, Emily began to search for a permanent placement for Nellie. Finding a new companion or an appropriate place for Nellie to live proved to be more complicated than she had anticipated. She quickly exhausted the most logical channels, including their church contacts, friends in the deaf community, and the Nellie volunteers.

When the novelty of having her own apartment began to wear off, Nellie slipped into a profound depression. Knowing that Emily was actively trying to find alternative living arrangements for her, Nellie could not help feeling like a "throw away" person once again. Swallowed up by grief and anxiety over the future, she became reclusive. Every morning Emily tried to coax her to go to work. But only once or twice a week was she successful in walking her across the street to the New Life Group Home. And then Nellie would only stay for a few hours, before asking to be walked back home.

To make matters worse, in addition to morning sickness, Emily began to develop symptoms of Toxemia. Her blood pressure rose to dangerous levels. She began to gain excessive weight and her ankles and feet swelled to the point where she could barely put on regular shoes.

With Nellie cutting back on her hours, Emily became compulsive about going to work and staying as many hours as possible. In spite of her tiredness and discomfort, Emily went to church on Easter. But having swelled up from a hundred and thirty pounds to a hundred and sixty pounds, she had a hard time finding comfortable clothes to wear.

The next day she passed out while working at the group home. When she awoke the housekeeper was slapping her face.

"Girl, you're going home!"

Two of the boys walked her outside to sit on the porch and catch some fresh air. When Jim returned from running errands, his response was swift and final.

"I am placing you on sick leave until after you have your baby. You are going home!"

Still protesting, Emily was practically carried across the street, and deposited in her bed.

That evening, Jim called on Nellie in her apartment.

After telling her, with his fingers, about what had happened to Emily, he asked, "Why didn't you come to work today?"

"Because I didn't feel good."

"Most people who are almost seventy-five years old don't feel good enough to work." Jim responded. "That's why they retire."

"Jim, are you firing me?" Nellie spelled back.

"No, Nellie. Emily is being laid off, but I'm retiring you. I will call on you for special projects, and as long as you live here the boys will certainly come over to visit you. But from now on, you are strictly a volunteer. You don't have to do anything if you don't feel like it."

Nellie did not put up a fight.

But after Jim left, her spirit took a nosedive as she berated herself, "The award winning handicapped professional of the year is too old and tired. Jim doesn't want me anymore. The boys don't need me. I'm not useful to anyone, anymore."

Tears of misery ran down her checks, but she did not even have the energy to wipe them away.

Her thoughts went back to the hot and humid night last July when she had been recognized by the Optimist Club. Optimist of the Year! She had felt so strong and vital. Life had seemed so wonderful! Her own words came back to haunt her:

"I have everything I could ask for. I have you, Emily. I have Jim. I have a job. I have my own money. And, I am famous! Even without ears and eyes, who could ever ask for more."

Sobbing, she told herself, "Everything I thought I had, has all slipped away. It all has slipped away!"

However, Nellie's spirit revived when she discovered that she did not lack for companionship. Almost every day, the boys from the group home came across the street to visit. Ever the teacher, she continued to instruct them, while they helped her with cooking or baking. They worked with her on various crafts. They also enjoyed just "hanging out" in her apartment and talking to her with their fingers. Knowing that they truly liked her was good medicine for Nellie's soul.

Now under strict doctor's orders to stay in bed as much as possible, and with nothing else to do, Emily turned her full attention to searching for new housing for Nellie. Having been unsuccessful in finding a permanent placement, she now put out word that she was looking for someone to adopt Nellie temporarily, until she had her baby. She decided to enlist the power of the media in her search.

Feeling housebound, after contacting her list of reporters, Emily wanted to go shopping for some new maternity clothes.

"Just in case a reporter wants to take my photo," she told herself.

She called her blind friend Sue Franklin and invited her to come along for an outing.

The two long time friends had a wonderful afternoon. But on the way home, just as she stopped at the traffic light in front of her house and was preparing to turn left on Lincoln Way, a man motioned for her, mouthing the words, "go ahead". As she pulled into the intersection, a driver behind him stepped on the gas and, passing around him, struck Emily broadside with such force that the car almost rolled over.

Sue was sent flying into the windshield but her injuries were limited to some cuts and bruises. Saved by her seat belt, Emily did not lose the baby. But she was badly shaken up and sustained an injury to her already swollen right leg.

Waiting for the police, Emily surveyed the damage. She saw that her car was totaled.

As she hobbled around on her injured leg, a sobering thought crossed her mind, "How am I ever going to get up and down the stairs to look after Nellie?"

Three days after the accident, on April 24,1980, an article appeared in the *Akron Beacon Journal*, written by staff reporter Pat Norman. When Lloyd arrived home after work, he found Emily lying on the sofa, with her leg propped up, grinning from ear to ear.

"I've got something to read to you from the *Journal*!"

Speaking with a dramatic voice she began reading.

BLIND, DEAF AND 74, WOMAN NEEDS A HOME

Nellie Zimmerman, who is blind and deaf and will be 74 years old Wednesday, is up for 'temporary adoption'.

Emily Street Hensel, her companion and interpreter, said she has been calling various social service organizations throughout Stark County for three months to try to make arrangements for someone to care for Miss Zimmerman when Mrs. Hensel goes into the hospital in three months to have her first baby.

"Nobody could help. They just kept telling me to talk to somebody else," Mrs. Hensel said...

Now Mrs. Hensel must find another guardian for Miss Zimmerman even sooner than she had expected. The problem became critical Tuesday when Mrs. Hensel had an auto accident, demolished her car, and developed a blood clot in her leg

"I'm supposed to lie down and prop my leg up and put ice on it to try to dissolve the clot without surgery," she said.

"But with Nellie living downstairs and my living upstairs, I haven't had time to get off my leg. My leg is so swollen I can't put on shoes, so I put on an old pair of boots and went grocery shopping and did my washing at a coin laundry Wednesday."

"It's just come to a point that I've got to put Nellie up for adoption for about six months. I don't like to leave her alone. She needs a nice family to take her in for a while."

Anyone who can provide help is asked to call Joanne Stogran at the Massillon Advocacy Program at 837-9110.

Emily went on, "The article goes on to describe in great detail Nellie's story. It even has quotes from Jim and tells about how Nellie refused to accept a store bought birthday cake last year because she wanted to bake her own. And, listen to this:"

She communicates with others who spell letters of the manual alphabet in her hand. She can speak, and she also reads Braille books, particularly the Bible, and likes to sing hymns...

"What do you think? Do you think that we will get any offers?"

Tired of paying double rent and for the first time seeing a glimpse of light at the end of the tunnel, Lloyd sighed, "Let's pray for a miracle!"

The story of Emily's search for an adoptive home for Nellie was also front page news in the *Massillon Independent* and went over the wire service, where it was picked up by numerous newspapers throughout Northeast Ohio. Joanne Stogran reported a phenomenal response. Emily followed up on all the strong leads. But after she had interviewed dozens of good, willing people by phone, she felt that the ideal situation had not yet presented itself.

Having read about Nellie's story in the *Columbus Dispatch*, the administrator of the Colony for the Deaf located in Columbus, Ohio called Emily. She suggested that their colony might offer Nellie exactly what she needed. Knowing that Jim's friend Clyde, who was deaf and blind, was already living there, Emily talked Lloyd into driving her to Columbus to look over the facilities on the following weekend.

She met briefly with the administrator who explained, "For the deaf, feelings of isolation can be the result of communication barriers between them and the hearing world. It can be overcome by contact with others who speak their own language. It's a barrier shattered by the Columbus Colony Housing and Elderly Care."

"Nearly a century ago," she went on, "Members of the Ohio School for the Deaf Alumni Association recognized the need to provide care and housing for the elderly deaf. Founded in 1896, we now provide two life style options. The Columbus Colony Housing, located in the building next door, now offers independent living with more than 100 private one-and two-bedroom apartments. The Columbus Colony Elderly Care, located in this building, is a licensed skilled nursing home facility. Both are owned and operated by the deaf for the deaf. Both are geared towards improving the quality of deaf resident's lives. Every member of the staff is required to learn sign language and interpreters are available 24 hours a day."

"We provide subsidized housing for low-income residents, two meals a day, and medical doctors and nurses are on call twenty four hours a day. We also provide classes, organized social activities, regular shopping trips and weekly excursions by bus. We even provide church services and have a large signing choir."

Emily interrupted, "Yes, but how many deaf\blind residents do you have?"

"At least ten. We have Braille on all our directional signs and Braille numbers on the elevators. We keep Braille books in our library and have staff on call to read mail and assist all our vision impaired residents with their correspondence."

After their interview with the administrator, they talked with a man who was visiting his relatives in the lobby.

Smiling, he said, "I looked at many different nursing homes throughout the country before deciding on Columbus Colony as the best suited place for my aunt and uncle. The reason we chose the Columbus Colony is that the staff really bends over backwards to take care of the people here, as well as the fact that many of the folks that work here have been working here for more than 10 years. That means that they really get to know the residents. They know their little idiosyncrasies and what they really like."

Then they went to visit Clyde. They found him sitting alone in his room, slouched down in his chair. His face lit up immediately when Emily touched him on the shoulder.

"What a nice surprise," he laughed.

Never one to beat around the bush, Emily spelled into his hands, "How do you like it here?"

"It's boring!" he spelled back.

That was all Emily needed to hear. She disliked the idea of putting Nellie in a nursing home, even if it was only independent living. Also, the Colony was over a hundred miles away from Massillon. She hated to think of placing Nellie so far away.

After discussing the matter with Lloyd, she decided to try again and take her case to the media. On May 3, a beautifully written article by Amy Shriver appeared in the *Massillon Evening Independent*.

Once more, with an air of importance and with great expression, Emily read the article to Lloyd when he got home from work.

PEOPLE MORE GENEROUS THAN GIVEN CREDIT
MANY OFFER A HOME FOR NELLIE

There are times when everyone thinks that mankind as a whole has become hardened to human problems, that no one really cares any more.

Well, Emily Street Hensel has had the opportunity to learn that some people really do care.

Emily made a public appeal almost two weeks ago to locate a temporary residence for Nellie Zimmerman, the 74 year old blind and deaf woman with whom she has shared a residence for three years.....

The response to a front page story in the Independent and subsequent articles in other newspapers has been great, according to Emily. The story was picked up by the Associated Press, prompting calls from as far away as Lima and Mansfield.

"A lot of people have really responded and shown concern. I was thinking that people are a lot more generous than they are given credit," she said.

Some 30 people have contacted Joanne Stogran or the Massillon Branch of the Citizens Advocacy Program to offer assistance.

"A lot of people said they were unable to take Nellie in, but they offered money. About 30 really nice people called and I am in the process of contacting them," she said.

Emily said she hoped to be able to place Nellie with a family, because she has become used to that type of independent living.

Among the people who called offering help was a deaf lady who offered to take Nellie into her home, a deaf couple who made a similar offer, and a woman from Akron who lives with two epileptics and offered Nellie her own room.

"One very nice gentleman from Canton called to say he lived alone in a four bedroom house and he would be glad to give Nellie her own room in his house," she said.

A representative from the Downtowner, a residential facility for senior citizens in Canton, called to see if perhaps Nellie could come live there. A woman from the Columbus Colony also called to see if perhaps Nellie wouldn't like to move there. ...

"I will try to place Nellie with a family, but if that doesn't work out, we may send her to the Columbus Colony."...

Nellie has a gentleman friend who resides at the Columbus Colony, Emily added. He is likewise deaf and blind."

"He sometimes comes up to Massillon to visit Nellie and they go on 'dates' together, usually for pizza."...

Emily turned the page and continued, "The article goes on to say,

Emily said Nellie's social life had been pretty active lately. The Pilot Club of Canton had a birthday party for her last week, complete with chocolate cake and chocolate ice cream.

"Nellie likes chocolate cake and she dearly loves chocolate ice cream," Emily said.

The women from the club which named Nellie "Handicapped Professional Woman of the Year" last year also brought a big bottle of perfume and Braille magazines for Nellie.

"Nellie had a wonderful time. She sang in sign language and showed off her cat's tricks," Emily added.

"She is very attached to her feline pet."

"What do you think?

"You make Nellie sound positively adorable!" Lloyd quipped, "It sounds as if you are saying to all the people who called, "Thanks, but no thanks."

All I can say is, we need a miracle, and fast!"

Out of his personal frustration with the situation, Lloyd called to ask Emily's mother's advice about what to do with Nellie.

With no hesitation she answered, "Put her away."

Hearing what he wanted to hear, Lloyd agreed with her. Emily's mother invited the couple over for Sunday dinner. Then the two of them double-teamed Emily, trying to pressure her to make the decision to place Nellie in the Deaf Colony.

But Emily remained obstinate.

"I haven't checked out all the people who offered to take Nellie in. Besides, it's not just up to me. It's up to Nellie. And, it's also up to Jim!"

However, after careful consideration, Emily was forced to admit that none of the people who responded to her articles could provide appropriate care for Nellie, especially considering her agitated state of mind. The Deaf Colony appeared to be the only feasible possibility.

Early in June, Emily took Nellie to visit the facility in Columbus. Nellie had to admit that the model apartment they were shown was very attractive and more spacious than expected. After making conversation with half a dozen residents, she realized that she would be able to socialize with everyone. She was told that her quarters would be close to Clyde's apartment.

This time, Emily was satisfied that, under the circumstances, this was the best move that Nellie could make. She had to admit that living at the Columbus Deaf Colony would give her a solid support system, the opportunity to make new friends, and enjoy an active life.

Before they left, the administrator assured them that there would be an apartment available for Nellie whenever she was ready to move.

Upon their return to Massillon, Emily's toxemia continued to escalate. When she went for her July check up, the doctor concluded that her symptoms had become potentially life threatening to her and to the baby. He told her in no uncertain terms that she was ordered to strict bed rest. She was not to lift anything, climb any stairs, to drive, or even to ride in the car. He concluded, shaking his finger at her:

"You could go into premature labor at any time! If you do, it is imperative that you get to the hospital immediately. It is a matter of life or death!"

That evening, Lloyd reinforced the doctor's decree. He packed her suitcase for the hospital and forbade her to get out of bed to provide any kind of personal care for Nellie. He was adamant:

"I'm serious! Get your priorities straight. It's not just your life, but the baby's at stake!"

Realizing that she had no choice, the next morning Emily called the Columbus Deaf Colony and made the necessary arrangements for Nellie to be admitted.

Knowing she was not allowed to help Nellie pack up her things or to drive her to Columbus, she waited until Lloyd came home from work. But he flatly refused to take her, saying,

"Listen! That woman hates me! Even if I wanted to take her, which I don't, and even if I could get off work tomorrow, which I can't, Nellie would never accept my help."

Trapped between a rock and a hard place, Emily was forced to call Jim the next morning. But Jim also refused to drive Nellie to Columbus, saying he was too busy.

Now it was Emily's turn to have a temper tantrum. Fuming, the pregnant and now hundred and ninety three pound woman stomped across the street, blasted through the door and cornered Jim in his office.

"You ...! You got Nellie out of the State Hospital. You are responsible for her. And I don't care if you are busy or not, You are going to take Nellie to the Columbus Colony for the deaf, today!"

His own adrenaline rising, Jim yelled back, "Who are you to come in here and tell me what to do? You agreed to be Nellie's companion. You shouldn't have gotten married, and you certainly shouldn't have gotten pregnant! It's your fault Nellie is in this mess!"

With that Emily lost her head. She called him every name in the book, interspersing her words with colorful metaphors.

"You... You are married. You ..., you are expecting a son! How dare you judge me! You got her out of Massillon State. You are the one who is legally responsible for Nellie, not me! You ..., you take her home, 'Married Man'! See how Rosalee likes that. If the shoe fits, wear it!"

With that, Emily turned on her heels and stormed out yelling, "Take her to the Colony or take her home, and I mean today!"

Jim was incensed by Emily's rudeness and profanity, but her words found their mark. This made him even angrier.

Later that morning, Jim came to Nellie's apartment, hurriedly packed up her belongings, and quickly hustled her into his car. Then Jim drove away. They did not even come upstairs so Nellie could say goodbye.

Jim stayed with Nellie at the Colony until she was settled into her new apartment, and observed as she was introduced to the staff who would be responsible for assisting her. In tears, Nellie clung to him as he tried to say good bye. Then, with a short prayer, he was gone.

That night the finality of her separation from Jim and Emily fell on Nellie like a rock. But she was a survivor.

Shaking herself free from sad feelings, she comforted herself with the thought, "The problems that Emily is suffering because of her pregnancy will pass when the baby is born. Then, soon she will be better. After the baby is born Emily will come to see me, and she might even be able to take me home again."

For the moment, she made herself believe in this possibility.

With that in mind, she thought, "My good friend, Clyde, lives here. Ever since I have known him, he has had good things to say about the Columbus Deaf Colony, and the people who work here and those who live here."

Taking a deep breath, she made up her mind that it was time for her to learn all she could about the place where she was now living.

Then she remembered putting away her "In Pieces" Braille Bible Carrie had given her when she was still in the State Hospital. She realized that in her distress over Emily's affair with Lloyd, she had fallen away from her fellowship with Jesus and from her daily Bible study. With tears of remorse, she opened the sacred book to Psalm 31 and traced the raised dots with her finger:

In Thee, O Lord, do I put my trust; let me never be ashamed: deliver me in thy righteousness. Bow down thine ear to me; deliver me speedily; be thou my strong rock, for an house of defence to save me. For Thou art my rock and my fortress; therefore for thy name's sake lead me, and guide me. Pull me out of the net that they have laid privily for me: for thou art my strength. Into thine hand I commit my spirit; thou hast redeemed me, O Lord God of truth.

More tears flowed as she recalled how Jesus had been with her in the State Hospital, and how Carrie had broken the silence and saved her from the abyss while she was spelling out the Lord's Prayer.

A complete sense of peace fell over her as she repeated: *"Into thine hand I commit my spirit; thou hast redeemed me, O Lord God of truth."*

The next morning, Nellie was ready to learn how to get around in her new surroundings. With the help of a sighted neighbor, she counted her steps down the hall, across the court yard and to another building where the meals were served. She counted steps to the lobby, the laundry room, the chapel, the sitting rooms, and walkways to the outdoor grounds.

Nellie was also shown the Colony newsletter in Braille. With delight, she spent the rest of the morning studying the daily, weekly, and monthly schedules. She also enjoyed reading about all the planned activities and special events. She discovered that there would be always something to look forward to.

Knowing that Clyde lived on the second floor, after lunch she asked someone on the staff to show her how to get to the elevator, and how to find the Braille controls and the Braille directional signs.

Then she knocked on Clyde's door and invited him to come outside and sit in the fresh air to talk. To the amazement of the staff, Nellie appeared to already know her way around and confidently led the way as they walked to the courtyard.

Meanwhile, when Lloyd came home from work and realized that Nellie had been moved out, he bounded up the stairs and, pointing to the plaster damage from the leak in the roof, exclaimed, "Let's blow this dump. This is no place for my beautiful bride to live!"

He went on, "Besides, I worry about you staying here alone while I am at work. If you have an emergency, there is nobody here to help you, or take you to the hospital. Why don't we move to your mother's house? Then, after you have the baby, we can get our own home in Brewster, close to my workplace."

Seeing the logic in his argument, Emily reluctantly agreed. Two days later, as she closed the door to their apartment for the last time and left her own keys as well as Nellie's in the mailbox. She knew in the pit of her stomach that she was also closing the door on her life as Nellie's companion.

Fearing for the safety of Emily and her baby, the doctor finally decided that it would be best to induce labor. On August 1, Lloyd took the day off from work and drove his wife to Doctors Hospital in Canton.

With great difficulty, Emily gave birth to an almost eleven pound baby boy. Lloyd named him William, but gave him the nickname "Billy" after a good friend who passed away on the same day.

Emily's recovery from the delivery was slow. After a week at the hospital, the toxemic swelling had not yet gone down. Still in need of support, Emily returned to her mother's house for convalescence.

When Emily finally wrote Nellie to tell her that she had given birth, Nellie responded saying that she was terribly homesick. "I promise to be good and to try to get along with Lloyd. Please come and get me, or send Jim to pick me up."

Under pressure from her mother and from Lloyd, Emily felt that she had no choice but to write back and tell Nellie that what she was asking for was impossible. However, she promised to come down to visit and bring the baby as soon as the doctor gave his permission for her to travel.

To Emily's surprise, she immediately received an answer.

"I am sorry I was such a 'wet blanket'. I just had a terribly bad day, but now I am fine."

It was clear from the rest of the letter that she had settled in and was enjoying an extremely active life at the Colony for the Deaf.

When Billy was about a month old, Lloyd bought a house in Brewster. It was small, but Emily was thrilled to have her own nest where she could raise her son. Still too weak to go back to work, Emily became a dedicated, busy, full-time, stay-at-home mom.

Three months passed before Emily had the opportunity to drive to Columbus. One cool, crisp, blue-sky morning in early November, Billy woke up at dawn. After Lloyd went to work at 6:30, Emily seized the opportunity to show off her baby. She hurriedly packed Billy's diaper bag and left by 7:00. She decided to take Route 62 to Columbus just in case she needed to stop along the way to feed or change Billy.

As she drove through the rolling hills of Amish country, she worried, "What if Nellie still wants to come home with me?"

When she arrived at the Colony two hours later, Emily found Nellie sitting in the lobby after breakfast. She was absorbed in a deep, flying-finger conversation with Clyde and another deaf friend. Nellie looked radiant.

She was delighted to see Emily and Billy. Almost mesmerized, she cooed over the baby, stroked his little furry head, felt his face, his little ears, and counted his fingers and toes.

As she stroked his body, she grinned, and said out loud, "I can't believe how tiny he is!"

Then a look of concern crossed her face, "Is he healthy? Can he hear? Can he see?"

Emily playfully spelled on her forehead, "Yes!"

For the rest of the morning, Nellie gave Emily the grand tour. She proudly showed off her apartment and the new crafts she had made. She excitedly told her about the new friends she had made and the excursions they had been on.

After sharing lunch with Nellie in the dining room, Emily packed Billy back up in his car seat and took her leave. As she drove away, she had to admit that she was surprised. Nellie had not said one word about wanting to come back home to live with her! At the same time, she realized that while she had taken to Billy as any grandmother would do, she had not asked after Lloyd in any way, nor said one word about him the whole time.

Pleased with her visit, Emily pulled into the driveway before Lloyd arrived home. After this, Emily again took Billy along to visit Nellie once before Christmas and, again, in February.

In April, Emily received a letter from Nellie inviting her to come for a visit.

She hinted, "There is someone I want you to meet."

To Emily's great surprise, this time Lloyd was invited to come along.

When they arrived, they found Nellie walking down the corridor, flanked by two men. Both seemed to be deaf and blind. To Emily's astonishment, she could tell from Nellie's finger spelling that she seemed to be having two completely different conversations!

To the man on her right, Nellie apparently was talking about going out for pizza when the Hensel family arrived. At the same time, she seemed to be making a date with the man on the left to join her for an excursion the following Tuesday.

Emily poked Lloyd in the ribs with her elbow.

"Look at that! Nellie has two deaf and blind gentlemen friends, but I don't think that either one of them knows that the other one is there!"

Lloyd laughed back, "Now that woman knows how to play the field!"

When Emily touched Nellie on the shoulder to greet her, Nellie spoke out loud, "You both know my good friend Clyde, but I would like to introduce you to my boyfriend. This is Richard."

Lloyd exclaimed, "Honey, Nellie is in love!"

"Why would you say that?" Emily asked.

"Just look at her! We are the ones who are always saying that Clyde is her boyfriend. But she just introduced Richard as her boyfriend."

Lloyd immediately took Billy in his arms so that Emily's hands would be free to talk to Nellie, and went for a walk around the lovely grounds of the Deaf Colony, leaving Emily alone with Nellie and the two men. Once seated, Nellie and her three friends embarked on a lively four-way conversation.

When Lloyd came back an hour later, he suggested that he take all four of them out for pizza. Nellie was delighted and both men accepted the invitation with relish.

Lloyd drove them to the Pizza Hut, which was only a short distance away from the Deaf Colony. Nellie sat between the two men at the table. After they had finished eating, it was apparent that even when there wasn't a conversation going on between Nellie and Richard, they were holding hands. Clyde appeared to be oblivious to the budding romance that was going on between his two companions.

Confined to a high chair, Billy eventually became fussy.

Emily told Nellie, "We have to go, now."

To her surprise, Nellie replied, "You don't have to drive us back. We can walk to the Colony from here."

As they said goodbye in the parking lot, Nellie spelled silently into Emily's hand. "I'm sorry I gave you such a hard time about Lloyd. But I didn't know the difference between having a friend, like you and Clyde, and being in love. Richard has taught me that!"

As Nellie turned and walked away, with her two deaf and blind friends leading the way with their blind canes, tap tapping down the side walk, tears of joy came to Emily's eyes.

"Now Nellie is truly walking free. She has found her own friends. She has found love.

THE END

EPILOGUE

Nellie continued to live a full and rewarding life at the Colony for the Deaf in Columbus, Ohio. Richard remained the love of her life until his death. Several months later, Nellie passed away on October 18, 1995 at the age of 89. Clyde continued to reside at the Columbus Colony until his death in 1999.

Emily visited Nellie periodically over the next fourteen years. She and Lloyd still live in Navarre, Ohio. Their son William is attending Walsh College in North Canton, Ohio. Emily eventually went back to school to become a Licensed Practical Nurse. She has devoted her life to providing private nursing care and advocacy services to the disabled.

Jim Schneck concluded his studies at Akron University and left the group home to teach children with disabilities at Weaver School in Akron, Ohio. He also served as an elementary school principal in Akron, Ohio. Currently, he is the Executive Director of the Deaf and Hard of Hearing Services of Lancaster County, Pennsylvania. Rosalee was Director of Deaf Ministries in Orrville, Ohio prior to moving to Lancaster County. In 1998, Jim co-authored the book, *The Complete Idiot's Guide to Learning Sign Language*.

Nancy matured as a result of her experiences while living with Nellie. She now lives independently. For many years, she and Emily worked together to raise consciousness about the needs and abilities of the handicapped throughout Northeast Ohio.

Ron graduated from Timken High School and has been living independently in Massillon, Ohio. Ted, Ken, and Mickie continued to live in a variety of group home settings.